'…a brilliant book.'
Georgia Holmes, Holmes Editorial

'…inspiring, moving, and vivid.'
Jennifer Barclay, Editor, Reedsy

'Your story is certainly inspirational,
and the 'happy ending' is very touching.'
Natalie Wilson, Health Journalist

'Factual, suitably humorous and a little self-deprecating
– all good.'
Zena Knight, Director ABC Training

'Absolutely mesmerising.'
Henrietta Hawkins, Author

PHIL APPLETON

is a former British Airways pilot
and VIP Handling Officer. As Philip Delancy,
he is a film, tv, and business actor, having appeared in
Star Wars, *Grace of Monaco*, and *London Has Fallen*.

He began writing in 1981 following the loss of his health, career,
and marriage through illness. During the course of his recovery,
he was sent to Rome in 2014 on behalf of The Foundation for
European Initiatives to deliver a workshop to international
psychiatrists under the banner: *Maximising Patient Outcomes
Long Term.*

He divides his time between England and France as a writer,
actor, and communications skills coach.

BLUE SKY RED CARPET

In memory of John Appleton, 1955 - 2017

This book is based on actual events, but the names of certain individuals have been changed in the interests of privacy and security.

For once you have tasted flight, you will walk the earth
with your eyes turned skywards, for there you have been
and there you will long to return.

Leonardo da Vinci (apparently)

'If I wasn't an actor, I think I'd have gone mad. You have to have extra voltage, some extra temperament to reach certain heights.'

Laurence Olivier

Contents

Prologue

Short, frail, and bald, Air Vice-Marshal Dr Paddy O'Connor welcomed me into his office, which looked more like a Victorian drawing room than a consulting room. Books on shelves ranged in subjects from black magic to neurological dysfunction; there was a discreet portrait of the Virgin Mary and Child in view. On Dr O'Connor's antique desk sat a small pot of clotted cream. With the fading carpet and the quiet ticking of the wall clock, the atmosphere was both calming and intimidating.

Responsible for drafting the international legislation on the psychiatric aspects of aircrew licensing, Dr O'Connor was the Supreme Being as far as I was concerned. Old, wise, and kindly, he was also the perfect man to deliver bad news. As I listened to his softly-delivered words about stringent medical regulations, I felt the cold shock of reality. I was living a nightmare and didn't understand why. Patiently, Dr O'Connor listened to my reasons for claiming I was well, then tore them to shreds. I had to accept I would never fly again.

1

Blue Sky

I was born Philip Idson Appleton on 7 August 1954 in Wellington, Shropshire, of a French mother and English father. To my knowledge, there was no history of insanity in the family up to then. 'Philip' was supposed to work in English and French, whereas no-one knew where Idson came from, except that my father and grandfather were the only other people on the planet who had it as a middle name.

My English Grandpa Harry Appleton worked in a factory for 40 years, making metal office furniture and parts for Spitfires. He lived with his wife Jennie in a small house in Oakengates with an outside toilet until they qualified for a council house.

From there, Jennie served large portions of food from immaculately starched tablecloths with instructions to visitors not to pull the curtains too far back so the neighbours could see they had some. Despite their poor backgrounds, Harry and Jennie voted Conservative all their lives on the basis that Conservatives were educated, well dressed, and spoke properly.

Having been in domestic service, Jennie wanted her two sons to do better and made her eldest Ronald - my father - practice the piano every day. If he missed an hour, it was double time the next. Ronald persevered and went on to study Music and French in Winchester. It was there while playing in a concert that Simone noticed him, a dark-haired French *assistante* from the Sorbonne in Paris, and for her, it was *le coup de foudre* (lightning strike), i.e. 'love at first sight.'

In a less fortunate alignment of their respective languages was 'Salop,' the older, Norman-derived name for Shropshire, which meant 'slut' in French (*salope*.) Which was more or less what Jennie thought of Simone. She wanted Ronald to marry a local lass, while Harry thought Simone was *splendide*. Ronald was even more smitten with Simone, and despite his mother's prejudice, their cross-Channel romance blossomed over the two years leading up to their wedding in Oakengates in 1953.

Looking more favourably towards the match, Simone's parents, Edouard and Yvonne Gauttier of St Lunaire, Brittany brought a bottle of champagne with them for the celebrations, an item which the Appletons had never seen before. For her part, Jennie offered Edouard and Yvonne the best room in her house and a cup of tea in bed in the morning, something which the Gauttiers had never seen before either.

Neither future in-laws spoke a word of the other's language, including at the follow-up meal in France, a full-family affair running from one to six o'clock. The bottle of champagne that Edouard had brought to England mysteriously reappeared on the dinner table in France.

Having entered into this bi-cultural bubble a year later, I was sent to live with my French grandparents for the first two years of my life, my parents having taken separate teaching jobs in other parts of France. Pépé and Mémé Gauttier were more about kindness and forgiveness than Granny Appleton, and I grew up fit and strong on Mémé's traditional French cooking and Pépé's vegetables. Calves' brains were occasionally on the menu, which may have given me the ability to practise speaking French words in my cot at the age of one. Three I strung together early on were *moi tout seul* (me by myself.)

Being self-reliant didn't stop me being told by my parents that they were to be referred to as 'Maman' and 'Papa,' rather than 'Mum' and 'Dad,' to please my mother.

This was awkward on our return to live in England, then accompanied by a younger brother, John. At primary school, the other kids called me frog's legs and told me the French were cowards, cheats, and pushed in at queues. To avoid the embarrassment of saying 'Maman' and 'Papa' in public, I would grunt 'Mmnngh' and 'Ppphh' with my hand in front of my mouth. So began the story of my life, being different.

Being in the top three for everything at school helped me survive, even if my peers told me it was 'just because your father is a teacher.' My mother was a teacher too, travelling an hour each way five days a week on the underground to the French Lycée in South Kensington. Careful with money, they both worked hard but were unmotivated by it, per se.

My parents preferred music, ballet, and romance, with perfection in everything their ultimate goal. Together they sought excellence; my mother would pass judgment on the shape of a dancer's legs, while my father would pick out the one note a pianist played wrongly. This drive for faultlessness led to them try to change John from left-handed to right-handed for a while. He did more to satisfy our parents love of the arts than me by starting ballet classes at the age of five.

As an educated French woman, culture, intellect, and elitism were fundamentally important to my mother. Loving my father was the only explanation for her decision to live in England all her married life, only visiting France for the summer holidays. It must have been difficult for her, as she complained about pasty-skinned, crisp-eating, ill-mannered English children and dry, tasteless, undercooked English food. For her, these fell into the same cultural abyss as greeting cards entitled *What is a Nana?* over a pink teddy bear. While she may have had a point, there were days when I wished for a proper English mum, who would say 'there, there,' and make tea all the time.

Coming from a country where she asserted there wasn't a class system, my mother felt that its influence on the British way of life was major. She admired beautiful, intelligent people, preferably in vocational professions such as teachers, scientists, and surgeons. She would concede that the English were good at inventing things, such as the engines on Concorde, while the French were better at designing the fabrics for the aircraft interior. More narrow-mindedly, she would also assert that all Americans had white teeth, all Russians liked singing, and all black people had rhythm and played bongo drums.

A legacy from his working-class parents, my father lived in a class-conscious world where builders were cheery, decent chaps who would say 'Right you are, sir,' and rescue law-abiding folk from thieves and vagabonds, while lawyers and doctors were to be worshipped in an almost fawning way, mainly if they were the 'Big Boss,' i.e. a senior consultant or partner. My father never took me to a pub or football game; my abiding memory of his family's social activity was being told to keep quiet by Granny when the football pools results were being checked on Saturday afternoon television, after the wrestling.

Other than my mother, my father didn't seem to be close to anyone or have the easy, friendly conversations that most people had; they were more competition to get the last word in and be proved right. For him, there was always a reason not to do something, mainly if it involved social situations where he might be put down, e.g. the embassy parties and functions he was invited to through my mother's contacts at her work in London.

A committed Francophile with the courage to have stood up to his domineering mother in favour of the woman he loved, my father was honest, hard-working, and obsessively intelligent, constantly seeking answers about life and the universe from anyone who would listen to his relentless questioning.

While I inherited obstinacy, attention to detail, and good English from him, I failed to follow his habits of making sure each finger tapped the same number of times when he was drumming the table, constantly lining up books, papers, knives, and forks, and rolling small pieces of bread or strips of torn off paper between his fingers.

I loved my parents in a grudging sort of way; it wasn't their fault I felt embarrassed about them at school; they were the product of their circumstances too. These led us to move to an unremarkable, semi-detached house in Natal Road, Bounds Green when I was eight.

As I grew up, I saw my mother making most of the day-to-day decisions while my father pontificated, generalised, and explained, expounding his thoughts about the wider world. The television would occasionally stimulate the abstract conversations he seemed to enjoy.

Papa 'Yes, one wonders why one would want to play golf.'

Me 'There's a spider by the television.'

Papa 'This par golf thing, there must be a lowest possible score anyone can get?'

Me 'The average for the hole for a professional player is called par. They're on a par four now.'

Papa 'No, I mean if the biggest, strongest man alive hit perfect shots as hard as he could round the whole course, he would get 18?'

Me 'It's moved.'

Papa 'It's about man's relationship with nature.'

Me 'The spider is going into the kitchen.'

Papa 'How will the cosmos survive without one spider?'

Me 'Probably okay.'

Papa 'There was a programme about Brazil. They have these HUGE spiders.'

Me 'It's gone into the kitchen.'

Living 50 yards from the North Circular Road, the primary neighbourhood attractions were the *Cornucopia*

Natural Food and Wine, a *Mini Mart*, a chicken and burger bar, a couple of hair salons, and a *Jehovah's Witness* temple. My bedroom window was my chosen route to escape - I yearned for the patch of blue sky beyond it, to push upwards into the light that promised freedom and adventure.

I wanted to be like Biggles - the fictional pilot, policeman, and hero created by Captain W E Johns – travelling across the world with his friends Algy and Ginger, tracking down villains and taking them out. We were the good guys: brave, honest, and upright, while the bad guys were treacherous, murderous, and greedy. When the baddies got their comeuppance, it was uncomplicated and morally satisfying. I never understood the boys at school who pulled the wings off flies or were naughty in class, preferring to be on the side of authority.

Poring over maps and atlases, while reading and re-reading most of Johns' 104 Biggles books, I imagined flying to parched wastelands and insect-infested jungles in Africa, Mexico, and the Far East killing 'crooks' and 'savages.' This briefly made me consider a career as a professional assassin – on the good side of course - practising by lining up my air rifle from an upstairs window at anyone I thought had an unkind face. Until I visualised my target lying on the ground in a pool of blood and went off the idea.

At about the same time, I was cast as the 'First Soldier' in the primary school play – my first acting role – which was especially exciting for the wardrobe: a military uniform in line with my developing interest in both the Army and the Air Force. With my father a classical pianist, my parents would have preferred me to have had a career in music, but as my musical tastes were more attuned to Elvis than Elgar, they soon gave up on that prospect.

My sister arrived when I was 15. She had two effects: with me having no friends nearby, she was someone small to care about, and she displaced me to downstairs. This gave me a room of my own and the facility to watch black and white television almost constantly, interrupted only by a bang on the wall to signal mealtimes. I knew every detail of all the programmes on the main BBC and ITV channels, with *The Dambusters*, *633 Squadron*, and *Reach for the Skies* introducing the growl of Merlin aircraft engines to my ears, and the curves of the female dancers of *Pan's People* to my approving eyes.

Other than pilots, my heroes were the guys with big pecs who looked like real men: Sean Connery as *James Bond*, James Drury as *The Virginian* - a clean-cut cowboy with scruples but no name - or any Tarzan. In uniform, I admired the leadership qualities of Rock Hudson as an air force colonel knocking a B-52 squadron into shape.

Ursula Andress, Raquel Welch, and Sophia Loren were my ideal women because they were curvy, beautiful, and exotic, while I also had a soft spot for Liesl in *The Sound of Music*. At the cinema, Stanley Kubrick's *2001* made me gape at space appearing before my eyes to the music of *The Blue Danube* waltz.

With my brother boarding at the Royal Ballet School and no friends to play with locally, I made model aeroplane kits on an industrial scale. My pocket money and birthday presents led to an assortment of *Airfix* and *Revell* boxes littering my desk. Their plastic contents looked dull and lifeless when I opened them until - following the assembly instructions faithfully and lovingly - fighters, bombers, and transport planes came to life.

I would sandpaper off the tabs of extraneous plastic where I had snapped the parts from their protective frames and open the glue with its pleasant, heady smell, then line up the *Humbrol* paints in their tiny pots and carefully bring colour to the black, white, or grey curves of wings and fuselage, eager for the paint to dry.

The final addition was to apply squadron transfers; then, I was ready to push the replica through my bedroom air.

This became the wind in my face as I manoeuvred a First World War Sopwith Camel biplane into a winning position over Manfred von Richtofen's red triplane above the French countryside (actually the bedroom carpet.) Making throaty engine noises, I felt the thrill of victory as I shot the German down. Then the bigger, faster, more advanced aircraft of the Second World War began to fill my shelves: the Spitfire, Lancaster, and Mosquito.

As the planes took shape, the idea of actually flying in a real one began to grow. Placing the pilots in their seats and encasing them in their protective Perspex canopy, it was always as them that I identified myself. I felt I would be of more use to a crew, and to support soldiers on the ground by flying and leading from the front.

Many of the fast and noisy jets I made were in active service, making their toy look-alikes even more appealing. While I would never fly a Spitfire, it was realistic to see myself in a single-crew Mirage or Lightning, even a Phantom. The tough and mean-looking twin-jet McDonnell Douglas F-4 Phantom fighter-bomber was my favourite aircraft. My place was in the front seat while the second crew member had his head down behind me, taking care of the weapons systems.

I made up checklists for the start-up sequence and imagined myself in the cockpit, flicking the switches then roaring off into the grey with afterburners glowing, the master of so much power and noise. The US-built Phantom represented brute force, while the Gnat of the Royal Air Force Red Arrows was quieter and better suited to formation aerobatic displays. I made all nine Arrows, hanging them from the ceiling in their diamond formation with white cotton thread, cut painstakingly to length.

Alone at home, the model aeroplanes inspired me to dream of exploring the wider world. Otherwise, the routine was school, mealtimes, and the family entertainment on a

Sunday afternoon of either card games, *Monopoly*, or settling arguments between my brother and me. For the rest of the week, my parents were too busy to talk to us about anything important, such as relationships, sex, and feelings. The six-week summer holiday at my French grandparents' house in the seaside town of St Lunaire was the highlight of the year for all of us to look forward to.

I don't remember why we went to Paris by plane one year rather than the usual journey by car ferry to Brittany, but I do remember the scream of the Air France Caravelle's engines on my first flight in an aeroplane, and the big four-bladed propellers of the BEA Vanguard on the return to Heathrow. Inside the cabin, I felt warm and secure, with pretty girls to look after me and a window from which I could survey the scene.

It was somewhere peaceful I could contemplate growing up, surrounded by reliable machinery and other people doing their jobs well. With only a tantalising glimpse of the flight deck and the patch of light at its front, I saw the pilots as gods. I wanted to be in a cockpit, flying a plane to wherever I was asked, enjoying the thrill of travel, and seeing unfamiliar places. The only question I had to answer was whether to become an airline pilot or a fighter pilot.

2

Différent

Magali, Mémé and Pépé's townhouse in St Lunaire was white-painted, green-shuttered, and wooden-floored, with a freshwater pump in the garden and a septic tank under it. Two hundred yards from a vast, clean beach, the nearby boulangerie, épicerie, poissonnerie, La Poste, La Mairie and La Librairie could have come out of a French school textbook, while men with real berets sat inside or outside the cafés reading copies of *Ouest-France.*

I didn't like the charcuteries so much because they had tongues, pigs' heads, and brains in the windows. Walking to the market with the sound of church bells ringing on hot, bright, cloudless days, I saw good-looking French people all around, their smooth brown skins glowing with life and energy.

Generally a well-behaved boy, I could be persistent and manipulative, especially with *Parrain,* my French godfather. He was a retired teacher, well-read and therefore my parents' choice to be technically responsible for my religious upbringing. However, that also meant he was sensationally boring. He played the cello, with the kind of music I associated with dying and misery in general.

With his neurotic wife Denise, Parrain and my parents had plans for me to be a cultured, literary genius, while I was more interested in Dinky Toys' model of a military bridge-laying lorry. I pestered Parrain and Denise to buy it for my collection, but they refused, either for pacifist reasons or because they didn't want to spoil me. Watching their angst as they debated the decision with my parents was fun. I didn't care, they could afford it, and I got the toy.

My godmother was another Denise, my mother's sister, an arty and attractive painter who had married René, a practical and pragmatic Gauloises-smoking Aéronavale officer. He would keep me up past my bedtime with dramatic stories of shooting up the insurgents in Algeria from some worn-out Breguet Atlantique Alizé, of guys sweating their way through thunderstorms with an engine on fire with so much drama that my buttons were being pushed for flying as a seriously cool thing to do, while Mémé worried that my brain would explode. When I saw René in his uniform whites, I wanted to look like him.

St Lunaire was a holiday destination for the well-brought-up, rich kids with whom my mother aspired for me to socialise. When I saw the seemingly endless stream of fit, olive-skinned, dark-haired girls, and athletic lads in the town, I saw how my mother wished people, and therefore me, to be. She had memories of the resort as a mecca for the sophisticated dinner-jacketed crowd in the 1920s and 1930s, with rich Parisians coming to *Le Grand Hotel* for the summer season.

Ours was the posh, sheltered end of *La Grande Plage* (main beach,) where staff from the big houses overlooking the sea bonged gongs to announce lunch and dinner and where there were tiny, individual cabins for changing and storing beach chairs and inflatable boats. Ironically, the downmarket end of the beach was nearest to the yacht club where they would put up a small circus every year, which was always disappointing because the tigers never escaped, and the clowns weren't very funny.

While enjoying the hot July sun, I would feel sorry for the man in long trousers, straw hat, white shirt, and bow tie pushing the ice cream cart that didn't seem to go forward because his feet kept sinking into the soft sand. For years I had a recurring nightmare about standing next to an ice cream stand and being eaten by a tiger, superseded only by a fear of death itself, fortunately short-lived.

Mémé and Pépé owned a second home away from the bustle of St Lunaire, a country house two kilometres inland. Surrounded by trees, it was a darker property with a 200-foot garden complete with its own freshwater spring and apple trees from which Mémé made jam and Pépé made cider. From my upstairs bedroom window, I could just see the sea and hear its glass rattle from the sonic boom of French Air Force Mirages screaming overhead. I'd leap up to catch a sight of their silver profiles, thinking how cool it would be to blast over St Lunaire in one of them.

In the garden, when no-one was around, I'd lay a towel on the grass to sunbathe naked and daydream about flying and girls. I'd hope that a girl would pass by, and we'd both go 'Ooh!' and pretend to be embarrassed and then spend the whole afternoon in the hot sun. It never happened.

I would tease Mémé because she was afraid of biting her tongue off when she tried to pronounce an English *th*, then I would frighten her by grabbing the pins of unplugged plugs and pretend I might get electrocuted. She wasn't scared of spiders, though and would corner the big fat garden ones and squash them with her finger until they burst. I was in awe of my grandmother as a killing machine after that.

At the tennis club, I had rarity value in being an English lad who could speak French yet didn't quite fit in with the local teenage culture. I was more comfortable pretending to fly the aircraft arriving and departing to Dinard airport by waggling my racquet between my legs as if it were a joystick. On the beach, I longed to be a French hunk, with a tight arse, straight legs, and able to play beach volleyball to impress the girls.

Failing on all these counts, I contented myself with pretending not to ogle the skimpy bikinis showing off acres of smoothly tanned, female flesh while lying on my front to hide my excitement. Never quite feeling I belonged in either

France or England, I expected to be rejected in either country, a self-fulfilling prophecy. As a result, when I eventually found the courage to talk to girls, I could produce a combination of arrogance, lack of confidence and rudeness all at once, giving me more chance of having a relationship with a giant panda than any of them.

Both my father and mother would have been chuffed if I'd have paired up with the daughter of the hardware shop owners - the lovely Dominique - especially as she was dark-haired, demure, *and* wanted to be a teacher. With her Catholic upbringing, she would be my ideal wife, and in a replay of my parents' life, we would live in England for the 46 weeks of the year outside the summer holiday. Dominique decided to go for that plan, but with an English banker instead.

According to my parents, the children who dropped their t's and were heading for a life of crime went to Southgate County School, so to be with the 'in' crowd, that was where I wanted to go. But my parents overruled me, deciding I was going to sit two scholarship exams instead. Having done the decent thing and passed them both, I was sent to the Haberdashers' Aske's Boys' School at Elstree, an hour away by bus.

An apostropher's nightmare, the school had 11 rugby pitches, an indoor swimming pool, a fives[1] court, tennis courts, a 25-yard indoor shooting range, and an assault course. My parents were planning for their little boy to go from there to Cambridge, but I was more interested in its proximity to Elstree Aerodrome.

Of the three boys from my primary school who went to Haberdashers', I was the only one to get a free place, which may have led to Jonathan Gershfield teasing me for having chubby legs and David Clapham teaching me to smoke. My parents rewarded me by phoning the school on my first day

---

[1] A sport similar to squash, except with a smaller court, and using a gloved hand to strike a hard ball.

to ask that I be moved from my first German lesson to the Latin class. Singled out in front of all my new schoolmates to do a subject that I considered a complete waste of time was more embarrassing than if I'd been asked to take my clothes off in Assembly.

However, there was one significant benefit to the Latin class: the back seat by the window. It enabled me to watch Piper's Indian nation spluttering down onto Elstree's runway. Cherokees, Comanches, Aztecs and Navajos droned their way past my window, their oil-smeared underbellies considerably more exciting than *amo*, *amas*, *amat*.

Not liking any of the music everyone else seemed to, being half-French and having my school blazer pockets sewn up by my mother to stop me from filling them with conkers and other essential schoolboy junk made me a nerd and subject to mild bullying. I was one of only two boys in my class who didn't go on a Geography weekend trip to the South Coast because my mother thought I would fall off a cliff.

The other boy was universally recognised as a prat, so I assumed I was also included in that category, compounded by my tendency to follow my mother's example in speaking my mind without much regard for the consequences. While the numbers said my IQ was high, I didn't always engage my brain before opening my mouth. The result was that sometimes my thoughts were so far ahead of everyone else's that I came across as stupid.

For an English teacher, Mike Tabbard was the coolest. He had lived in South America and would sit cross-legged on his desk, reading us extracts from *Catcher in the Rye*. I would cry with laughter and wonder why English couldn't always be that much fun. 'Mike' went around the room early on, asking each of us what we wanted to do with our lives.

I felt sorry for those who didn't know because there was no doubt in my mind I wanted a flying career. During breaktimes, I compared notes with other spotters of the aircraft registrations I'd seen and logged neatly in a notebook.

Other boys saw this pastime as slightly weird but acceptable in the context of my firm desire to be a pilot.

Occasional visits to air shows were the ultimate day out for me, but a joyless duty for my parents, although preferable to having a rebellious, long-haired teenager in the house playing pop music and taking drugs. Other than using deviousness and deception to do as few chores as possible, my vices were smoking Piccadilly cigarettes and thumbing through my mother's thick mail-order catalogues to pore over the models in the ladies' underwear section.

At school, *Forum* was the most sought-after soft porn magazine, in its easily hidden A5 format and with stories of schoolboys being seduced by older women. I thought this fantasy might become a reality in the real-life curves of Madame Tissot, one of the French assistantes, who I fancied had taken a shine to me only to realise it was because I was best at French.

Even though I spent more time looking at her voluptuous figure under a one-piece woollen dress than the blackboard, I took the French O-Level a year early, then scored 8% in the Latin O-Level, which was a fair reflection of my disinterest over the five years I'd studied it.

The only useful Latin phrase I remembered was *reductio ad absurdum*,[2] which my father had taught me anyway. To make a point to my parents, I got the German 'O' level one year later, giving me a total of ten O-Levels. If there'd been an O-Level in aircraft recognition, I'd have scored 100%.

With Madame Tissot unavailable, my formal sex education took place at locally run classes in the Catholic faith and with Lyndsey for the practical work. Introduced to me by our old landlady, Lyndsey was a girl of my age with white skin and spots which contrasted unfavourably with the smooth complexions of the French girls I lusted after. In

---

[2] A method of proving the falsity of a premise by showing that its logical consequence is absurd or contradictory.

compensation, she was willing to display her fulsome figure in my bedroom during the weekends my parents were conveniently away.

On our journey from sofa to bed, Lyndsey would wait in vain for romantic statements from me while I wondered how many of her ample curves I could explore without getting her pregnant. I had no idea what to say, especially as her large breasts constantly distracted me. While instinctively feeling it was my responsibility to take the initiative, I respected Lyndsey's reticence. The final wave of my handkerchief signalled our mutual surrender from our teenage impulses and relief at their conclusion.

To be a pilot, I had to be physically fit in other ways, which meant avoiding severe injury. The toughest boys played First and Second Team rugby, so I settled for a regular place in the Thirds, which was more fun than cross-country running. I was meticulous about protecting my eyes. Knowing this, Simon Gelber once tried to grind his thick, wiry red hair into them in the front row of the scrum.

I punched Gelber so hard in the ribs he was out of the game for a while, to the amusement of the master refereeing as Gelber was at least four inches taller than I was. After showing more aggression during another game, I was briefly moved up to play with the Firsts and Seconds, then decided that pretending to be Bruce Lee with Harold would be more beneficial to my training if I had to hit anyone again.

With a German mother and also wanting to be a pilot, Harold Bailey was my best friend at school. We dreamt of being international globetrotters sitting with Ray-Bans on a terrace, looking bored as women flocked to our feet. Away from school, we would play boogie-woogie and Elvis Presley songs and deliver blood-curdling screams during kung-fu practice.

Once, and only once in my entire time at school, I had Harold and a few other friends round to the house in Natal Road to play poker. Never having been shown how to socialise, entertain or host parties at home, I felt like one of the gang. I even sold my French army Dinky Toy models for stake money, which was foolish because they were probably worth a fortune, especially the bridge-laying lorry prized from my godfather's wallet.

Selected by the school with two other boys to be on BBC's *Crackerjack* quiz show, I made my first TV appearance facing three bright and pretty girls at Shepherd's Bush Studios. Leslie Crowther and Peter Glaze were the hosts, and the guest group were *The Fortunes*, the wheel of fortune hanging up in the rafters as part of the set design.

We boys were supposed to put balloons into a box fastened to our backs, and as I was the only one of the three of us who worked out that bending over to pick up balloons tipped the others out, was the one to go head to head with the winning girl from the other team in the quiz part of the show. Despite not knowing what a padi field or a plectrum was, I won three prizes: a Merit microscope set, an iconic Crackerjack pencil, and a few minutes to chat up the girl. The winning was satisfying, but I surprised myself by feeling comfortable in the spotlight too.

This may have led to me being appointed a School Prefect and House Captain, where the roles seemed to be those of figurehead for the younger boys and appearing confident while reading the lesson in morning Assembly. As well as having a passionate interest in aeroplanes, it seemed I was also sensible and responsible, so joining the Royal Air Force (RAF) Section of the School Combined Cadet Force (CCF) was an obvious choice. The alternative was 'Social Services,' for the boys with long hair, less enamoured by the concept of discipline.

On the basis that I could shoot straight at paper targets, rather than at a teacher or another schoolboy, I was also asked to become the school armourer. Unmindful of any considerations of the trust bestowed on me for overseeing racks of .303 calibre rifles, I was more interested in the

17

opportunity for a quiet smoke in a lockable room. Unexpectedly and in line with my military aspirations, my mother bought me a French paratrooper combat jacket for competition shooting at Bisley, which my fellow shooters acknowledged as the coolest.

Feeling secure in the structure of military routine, I blancoed my belt, polished the buckles, and shined my shoes enthusiastically for the Friday afternoon CCF sessions. Taking parade ground drill, I enjoyed the satisfaction of taking charge of a squad of lads to work coherently and willingly towards a common aim.

In my final year, I was appointed the Cadet Warrant Officer of the RAF Section, the senior cadet of the entire CCF. My fiefdom included having the use of a room near the junior playground with some old armchairs, a kettle, and a darts board. The usually fearsome master in charge would remind us to keep the windows closed when we smoked.

Camps to St Mawgan, Culdrose and RAF Brüggen in Germany, with air experience flights in a Hercules transport, Chipmunk aerobatic trainer, and Wessex and Puma helicopters were much more fulfilling than academic work. Shooting machine guns, a gliding course at RAF Henlow, and running the flying controls simulator during the school fête gave me the idea that a life in the services might suit me.

Studying for 'A' levels was becoming tedious, but I knew I had to pass them to be a pilot, my only motivation. I came close to failing two out of three. In the Physics exam, we were supposed to measure the time taken for metal objects to reach the bottom of an oil-filled tube at different temperatures, but I uncorked the tube and got oil all over the place. Fortunately, the invigilator felt sorry for me and gave me another tube, resulting in a generous 'E' grade.

In the Maths exam, I spent most of the time trying to work out a formula, which had already been provided at the back of the paper and was lucky to get an 'O' grade. With a 'D' in Chemistry, I certainly wasn't going to go to

Cambridge, but that had never been my plan anyway - I wanted to fly.

A career in the RAF flying fast jets looked attractive, so I applied for a Flying Scholarship where the RAF gave keen air cadets 30 hours flying in the expectation that they would eventually join. The selection tests were carried out at Biggin Hill, where I was passed as A1 medically fit and underwent an interview, during which I was asked: 'Why do you want to join the RAF?'

While my father had helped me with my written application, his two years National Service in the Royal Army Service Corps hadn't helped me prepare an answer to this crucial question, so I was only able to mumble something about comradeship, which wasn't particularly true. I thought I'd blown it, but the RAF gave me the Flying Scholarship anyway, which I thought was jolly decent of them.

With school out of the way, I arrived at White Waltham airfield near Maidenhead in the heat of summer 1972, all set to learn how to fly before I could drive. At 17, I lived on-site with rows of light aircraft that sat on the grass just outside in front of the Flying Club, similar to when it was the Air Transport Auxiliary Headquarters during the Second World War. Except I would be flying four-seat American-built Piper Cherokees with a 140-horsepower engine, the type I used to watch flying overhead in the Latin class. They looked basic and functional, and I couldn't wait to get inside one. Nothing could stop me now except for Maurice Loudon.

He was the Chief Flying Instructor, an ex-Shackleton pilot with a handlebar moustache and all the interpersonal skills of a buffalo with a poker up its backside. He made the whole learning process as much fun as three weeks in an Iraqi jail; shouting, criticising, constantly yelling at me to do something different. As he took me through engine starting, radio and emergency procedures, then circuits and landings, and engine failure after take-off drills, I wondered where the romance of flying had gone. My flying was safe and accurate, but I wanted to push Maurice through a rotating propeller.

Then on one sweltering day, he told me to do a circuit on my own. My heart raced as I followed the checklist carefully and methodically before taxying to the holding point. Everything was happening as it had done when Maurice was sitting next to me, except that he wasn't there shouting at me.

As I lined up on the runway and pushed the throttle fully forward, I remembered that the aeroplane was lighter with only me on board, and therefore the take-off run would be shorter. It was only when I was airborne and had checked my speed, rate of climb, and heading that I allowed myself a moment of subdued but unabashed glee. I was flying, away from the constraints of the ground, free and elated.

There was still plenty to do: turn crosswind at 500 feet, maintain speed, level off at 1,000 feet, constantly lookout for other aircraft and listen to radio transmissions. Then the downwind checks, checking attitude and power settings, preparing for landing. Finding the runway, turning in, lowering the flaps, and keeping the speed to around 85 mph in the turbulence. The landing was uneventful; I cleared the runway, looking out for other taxying aircraft, raised the flaps and prepared to face Maurice.

I was sure he would find something to find fault about. As I walked to the clubhouse, I pretended to be calm, but I was heady with excitement. I felt proud that I could bring an aeroplane to life with my own hands and take it aloft. Even my backside - too big for my liking - was perfect for sitting in a cockpit for hours at a time. Maurice said nothing when he saw me, so I kept my joy to myself, assuming that was the cool thing to do. Yet inside, I was bursting with satisfaction and fulfilment - flying solo for the first time had made it the best day of my life.

A sheltered upbringing had left me short in awareness of some aspects of growing up, so when Ken, the ex-marine barman at the Flying Club, offered me five pounds a night to put his 'prick in my ear,' I thought it a little unusual. I was more interested in the women who came to the bar in the evening. However, spotty seventeen-year-old student pilots weren't even close to the action, so I busied myself by avoiding Ken's approaches and making fun of his lack of height, which was reputed to be on a par with the rest of his body. Until two of Ken's old Royal Marine mates turned up, and I said something half funny about Ken. I only did it once because the two six-foot-three marines gave me a look that could have melted tarmac at fifty yards.

With my 30 hours completed and paid for by the RAF, I had to decide to continue flying either with them or in a civilian career. Without encouragement or guidance from anyone, I had to make the decision by myself without really knowing why. My mother was afraid of me getting hurt, while my father's involvement in fighting skills only went as far as watching the occasional boxing match on TV.

They were both more interested in the arts than anything military; the only book they had given me to read about war was Russell Braddon's *The Naked Island,* which was more about dealing with suffering than fighting. I could fight if I had to, but would I choose to?

While I had felt different to the other boys at school for being half French, I had always felt at home in my RAF uniform. Yet, that also made me different from civilians. I dithered for weeks, not helped by my father's frequently asked question: 'Why does anyone do anything?'

Eventually, seduced by the advertisements with pretty girls and long-haul travel, I applied to British European Airways (BEA) for sponsorship for airline pilot training. Twenty-five thousand hopefuls applied for 500 places a year at the civilian College of Air Training based at Hamble, with its small grass airfield. Instead of fighter jets, there were shiny red and white Cherokee 180s.

After passing the BEA and Civil Aviation Authority (CAA) medicals, I was interviewed by real BEA pilots who would decide if they wanted me in their cockpits. For the stress test, I had to join up circles on two sheets of paper with pencil lines, holding a pencil in each hand and alternating my hand movements to the sound of a tape-recorded beat. The tempo was increased until nobody could keep up. Some candidates would throw the pencils across the room and fail. I just sat there looking smug, so I passed.

While waiting for the result of the selection process, I took a job as a temporary clerk for the Eastern Gas Board in Wood Green, checking in the meter readers as they returned to the office after their rounds. It was my first experience in a grown-up working environment and doing a job solely for the money.

The day's highlights were the scrambles for the 11 o'clock and three o'clock tea trolleys and a glimpse of Agneta's long and well-shaped legs. Agneta was a Swedish secretary in her early twenties who could type at eye-blurring speed and almost always wore a noticeably short skirt.

We would eat our lunchtime sandwiches together in the pub next door, where she would tell me about her boyfriend, and I would talk to her about wanting to be a pilot. I took her to see *Last Tango in Paris,* which she thought was about dancing and wasn't entirely as liberated as Swedes were supposed to be when Marlon Brando was bringing out the St Ivel unsalted.

Then the letter from the College of Air Training arrived telling me I had been accepted onto Course 732, the second intake of 1973. When it arrived, I was thrilled, yet also felt it was only part of the plan, Plan A. Plan B was a vague idea to be a policeman, but at 18, there had never been any real doubt in my mind I would be a pilot; for me, it was as obvious as night following day.

3

College of Air Training

After the Eastern Gas Board, the College of Air Training at Hamble was like a holiday camp with the best toys in the world to play with: real aeroplanes. We were cadets, not students, and wore blazers, white shirts, and ties, which, having come straight from school, I thought was fine, but which the university graduate entrants thought puerile. There were 16 in my all-male class out of an intake of 48, brought together for 21 months of full-time training, with five weeks holiday a year. I felt a mixture of excitement, apprehension, and focus.

We were housed in modern blocks around an outdoor swimming pool and a tennis court. Marvena, the giant Australian cleaning lady, would look after our interests and hers by trying to enter our rooms when we were as naked as possible, or if that failed, going for the keyhole option.

Away from Marvena, we studied Aerodynamics, Propulsion, Electrics, Systems, Radio, Navigation, Meteorology, Instruments and Air Law. Sitting right at the back of a classroom with desks laid out in neat rows, I was able to observe my fellow cadets and hide my occasional inability to put on a pair of matching shoes before breakfast.

Compared to some of the graduates with Engineering degrees, I found some of the work stretching. Still, I discovered I had some talent for putting on accents when we practised our radiotelephony procedures. The tutor would play the air traffic controllers (ATC) part while I would take every opportunity to play the foreign pilots.

Pan Am	'Ah, Clipper 45, we're outta three seven zero for One Hundred Echo.'
ATC	'Er, Clipper 45, we don't have a reporting point One Hundred Echo. Say your position, sir.'
Pan Am	'Dude, ah got it right here on mah chart, one zero zero echo.'
ATC	'I see. That would be Looe, on the English coast, sir. Call coasting in. Speedbird 4582, are you a Viscount?'
BEA	'Negative old chap. Just plain Mister.'
ATC	'Roger Speedbird 4582. Air France 316, climb to flight level one eight zero.'
Air France	'One ett zéro? Pff, I ask for two ett zéro. I spit on your flight level.'

Performing in this way was fun and helped turn me from an overly serious young man into one who could make others laugh, but I couldn't see myself making a career out of it. After 16 weeks of ground school, we were desperate to get into an aeroplane, in this case, the slightly more powerful version of the White Waltham Cherokees. In 1973, private pilots had to pay £80 an hour for flying lessons, and we were getting them for free.

One of the youngest on the course, excitable and immature, I was paired up with Trevor, one of the oldest; married, calm, and who took everything in his stride. Our instructor was a kindly, white-haired gentleman called Ron Street. Ron was the complete opposite of Maurice Loudon. An ex-commander of a low-level bomber squadron, he knew how to get the best out of me through patience and understanding, without compromising the unforgiving standards of British Airways flight operations (BEA became British Airways in 1974.)

I failed my first flying test twice on practice forced landings, with the final attempt more a test of my nerve than my flying ability. If I failed a third time, I was for the 'chop,' expulsion from the course. Knowing that my entire flying career depended on a one-hour flight, I walked around in the depths of despondency for the week before the final check ride. My mates were supportive, but I knew it was down to me.

For the test, I needed to complete a simulated engine failure from about 2,000 feet, judging the glide down to a few feet above a farmer's field with no margin for error. On the day, the air was as still as space, and the examiner was kind. To my intense relief, I passed and was a trainee pilot once more, 'one of the lads,' and my confidence level was pretty much back to normal.

When this became over-confidence, the threat of the 'chop' would reappear, bringing me to my senses, sometimes literally by fractions of an inch. On one of my cockier days, I was taxying too fast at the Royal Navy's Lee-on-Solent airfield in between solo circuits and swung my port wingtip so close to the control office that it virtually touched its reflection in the window. The man behind it stood up with an expression as if he'd just seen Elvis trotting by on a white horse. I spent the rest of the day worrying about whether the man would report me, but he didn't - I think he was glad to be alive.

Bristol, Manchester, and Swansea may not have been the most glamorous destinations in the world, but planning routes to their airports gave me the same sense of anticipation and adventure I'd had studying an atlas at home. They were for routine cross-country navigation exercises but exhilarating nonetheless - I felt like an intrepid aviator going somewhere, like Biggles.

As I unfolded my aeronautical chart and filled out the navigation log, I measured tracks and distances with precision, then calculated headings and times as if I were on a mission to conquer empires. There were danger areas and military airfields to avoid, high ground to allow for, and radio frequencies to note. On a route to Manchester, I made a point of flying past Wellington in Shropshire, where I was born and over Oakengates, where my Granny and Grandpa lived.

As well as the cross-countries, there were aircraft handling and instrument flying tests to pass, which I did the first time. Then it was playtime. The CAA required us to complete 155 hours on the Cherokee as part of the licensing requirements, and I'd a few to make up. Ron Street had taught me how to fly safely at low level, so I considered a circuit of the Isle of Wight at ten feet above the waves but discarded that option as too risky with only one engine. Low-level flying over land could get me chopped, and the aeroplane wasn't designed for aerobatics, so I decided to go for the altitude record, taking Pete, a fellow cadet, with me for company.

We headed off to our local flying area over the Isle of Wight, and I began the slow climb upwards. It was routine up to 10,000 feet, but the Cherokee struggled in the thinning air from then on. We were fine-tuning the engine fuel/air mixture as best we could, and I was nursing her up on the flaps at sometimes no more than a pedestrian 50 feet per minute rate of climb. After 45 minutes, we were bored and had only reached 14,000 feet. We didn't know what the official record was and didn't have oxygen on board, so I thought a spin would be the quickest way down.

The Cherokee was technically safe for spinning, providing the centre of gravity was forward enough, which it should have been with two of us in the front, but the College didn't allow it. We did incipient spins[3] with the instructors and on tests, but we weren't supposed to do them for real, and certainly not as a lark. But Pete thought it would be fine, and as he was a better pilot than me, I believed him. The aeroplane was practically hanging on the stall anyway, so it only needed a firm boot of left rudder to flip us over and into the spin.

---

[3] The transition phase from an aerodynamic stall to just before a developed spin.

Flick, flick, flick, a gentle rotation with lots of soft green scenery below - no problem. While the airspeed was low, the rate of descent was high, so it didn't take long to reach 8,000 feet - time to go home. Standard spin recovery action: full opposite rudder, pause, control column forward, level the wings and pull out of the dive, done it dozens of times before. But this time, it didn't work. I tried again. It didn't work the second time either; we were still spinning. This wasn't the plan. I tried engine power, but the engine had stalled, probably because the mixture had gone awry in the descent.

'What do you reckon, Pete?' I asked.

'Try the flaps.'

I tried dropping a couple of notches of flap, but apart from a slight pitch change, nothing else happened.

'What about the door?' I said.

'Yes, you could try that.'

Opening the door was just another way of upsetting the airflow around the Cherokee, which by now was approaching 5,000 feet and showing no signs of cooperating with our intention to visit the pub that evening unless it was straight through the roof. I was looking down to see where we were going to crash. Neither Pete nor I panicked; we were just resigned to the situation, which was more credit to Pete as he wasn't in control. He just sat there as calm as a clam as I wondered what we were supposed to do next.

In the event, neither of us had to do anything. Either through good training or because I couldn't think of anything else, I'd held the flying controls in the correct position for spin recovery, so the aircraft flipped out by itself, and the engine restarted. I eased us back to straight and level as we sat in silence, privately contemplating our relief to be alive.

Cherokees weren't designed to fly much above 10,000 feet, and there hadn't been enough airflow at the higher altitude for the flying controls to work correctly. But we hadn't known that at the time. As it was, there was now a good chance we would enter the pub through the front door rather than down the chimney. Pete must have had more faith in my ability than I did because the first thing he said was:

'How about doing a barrel roll?'

There are old pilots and bold pilots, but there are no old, bold pilots said an aeronautical genius once, so I bottled out and took us back to base.

I wasn't the best pilot on the course, but I passed all the technical exams with just one re-sit and prepared for the Advanced Flight in Bournemouth. There, it was serious pilot stuff: night flying, single-engine circuits, airways flying in controlled airspace, all leading to a Commercial Pilot's Licence with Instrument Rating. The aircraft we flew was the Beechcraft Baron, a twin that could fly in the same skies as commercial airliners to exotic destinations like Jersey and Dinard in France.

Dinard's Pleurtuit Airport was just down the road from my grandparents' house in St Lunaire, and on my first trip there, my instructor let me stretch the circuit slightly so I could see Magali and the beach. The French controllers transmitted a shrug over the radio and told us to get on with our circuits while they went off for their lunch. The sun shone, and I felt like the dog's bollocks, Monsieur super-cool pilot driving over 500 horsepower of turbocharged machinery with minimal payload over the beautiful emerald coast of northern Brittany.

We lived in digs for three months where there was a race to see who could find out where Maria, the student girl housekeeper at our lodgings, bought her underwear. I don't remember the name of the underwear, but I do remember being the first to see it. I liked her, and we went out for a while. She was smart, attractive, had long, straight legs, and pilot-hunting was her game. She wasn't afraid to kiss, although anything more was complicated because my mates were always around, so we went for walks and talked about our dreams.

She switched to another one of the cadets who had more money and a sports car, and I got my first lesson in being dumped. Once I'd got over my disappointment, I harboured no hard feelings towards Maria; there were plenty of Saturday nights on the calendar.

The local dancing emporium was a magnet for local girls looking for trainee airline pilots with prospects, even when the latter had the more limited desires of an alley full of tomcats. Arrogant as ever, I would head straight for the best-looking female on the premises, blind to the reality that attractive girls on their own were more likely to be waiting for someone in a white suit than looking to be propositioned by a nineteen-year-old on a local authority grant.

One evening, a stunning girl in her early twenties gave me a millisecond's worth of eye contact, which I took as a signal that she condescended to be amused, especially with the rest of the boys egging me on. With a glowing, bottled tan perfectly spread around a firm, micro-skirted body and legs longer than mine; she watched me cruise over with my cigarettes in hand, trying to look nonchalant. I was disconcerted to find that she was two inches taller than me.

'Smoke?' I said, as she looked me up and down and nodded imperceptibly. In an attempt to meet her gaze, I managed to drop the cigarettes all over the floor, then smiled weakly as I picked them up and offered her one, putting one in my mouth at the same time. The vision of loveliness was not impressed when I dropped the matches too.

She continued to chew her gum and examine the ceiling lights as I picked the matches up, took one, and put the rest in my pocket - time to impress. I had a trick where I could light a non-safety match by holding it in my right hand and by quickly drawing my thumbnail across the matchhead, set it on fire.

It worked the first time, regaining me a semblance of dignity; however, it also caused a substantial chunk of the flaming material to lodge itself under my nail and burn enthusiastically and painfully. This got the girl's rapt attention as well as drawing thigh-slapping, raucous laughter from the boys lurking in the shadows nearby.

Once I'd got over the agony and noted that the object of my desire was showing interest in me, I lit her cigarette the old-fashioned way with another match from the box and did the same with my own. Which was when I discovered that I'd put my own cigarette into my mouth the wrong way and had lit the filter. I was sure there was a faint glimmer of a smile in the corner of the girl's face, but by then, we had both decided not to pursue a long-term relationship.

The final flying tests of the syllabus were a General Flying Test, the Baron type rating test to get it stamped on my licence, and the Instrument Rating test with a CAA examiner from Stansted. I passed all these without drama and prepared to join the remaining three-quarters of our initial intake that had made it through to graduation.

Other than those who'd got chopped because they didn't meet the standards, some had left midway for reasons including: to become a stockbroker, to re-join the family shipping business, giving in to a 'flying or me' ultimatum from a girlfriend, and to commit suicide by pulling a trigger on a shotgun.

My parents turned up at the graduation in March 1975, leaving me with the feeling they would have preferred me to be collecting a music prize, but I didn't care. I was a pilot - my certificate said so -, and I was quietly enormously proud of myself. Later, someone found the files that had been kept on us, with mine reading:

'Bright in Technical Studies but started his flying with some unwarranted overconfidence. His early performances robbed him of this, and thereafter he settled to a steady and

*unspectacular progress. Has adequate ability and personality
to become an average airline officer, but not – as yet – much
more.' Principal, College of Air Training.*

In 1975 there was a surplus of pilots, so British Airways
gave us £600 each and told us to go away until they had an
airliner type conversion course for us. Some of the guys were
offered office jobs in the airline, and others worked as
stewards on scheduled flights. I signed up for unemployment
benefit, passed my driving test, and phoned a modelling
agency to try and get on their books.

When they told me I would have to pay to get some
photos done, I tried the Savoy Hotel for a porter's job,
expecting a bonus for speaking French and hoping to pocket
a fortune in tips from the bored, rich women I thought were
waiting for me everywhere. The head porter wasn't
impressed, especially as he didn't get any extra for speaking
five languages, so my career as a gigolo model ground to a
halt. Fortunately, something much better turned up.

The College of Air Training were offering four-week
Assistant Flying Instructor's courses for £500, so I booked
myself on the first one and used the remaining £100 from my
pay-off to buy a car, a Hillman Minx complete with starting
handle and drove it down to Hamble for the training.

Learning how to teach flying was quite different to
doing it. Above-average flying was taken for granted, and
there were patter and observation skills to learn. Not being a
'natural' pilot initially, I found it easy to put myself in the
position of a trainee pilot, having been one myself not so long
ago.

With the Instructor's test passed, one of the instructors
told us about a job at the Liverpool Flying School, which
three of us were interested in taking. It paid £18 per week and
80 pence per flying hour. I pulled the long straw for the job
and couldn't get to Speke quickly enough to meet Mr Keen,
the owner.

4

Love in Liverpool

A short, balding man, Jim Keen had learnt to fly while selling insurance to dockers and bought the Flying School business with a win on the horses. After that, he set about undercutting every other flying school in the country. That I'd been British Airways-trained was good enough for Mr Keen, so five days after a short interview, and lodging with my college friend John Corcoran's family on the Wirral, I prepared to start work at Liverpool Airport. With low prices and in a convenient location, there was plenty of it. Mrs Keen would book clients on the hour, every hour while charging for complete hour lessons, unworkable with turnaround time.

My first student was Mr Bouqdib, a Moroccan almost impossible to understand either in English or French. A succession of other clients followed ranging from the diminutive Miss Little (her real name) who spent so much of her hard-earned money on flying lessons that she had to come to the airport by bus, to Dave Siwoku, a six-foot-four ex-Liverpool heavyweight boxing champion and second-hand car dealer, who would arrive in a pink Jaguar. Dave was the better pilot and easier to teach, so I made sure it was Miss Little who got her full hour, even if it meant the day ran late.

Dave Lonsdale, the other full-time instructor and I would help refuel the aircraft by handpump in the morning with a keen eye on the weather, as if it was bad that would mean no work and less pay. Ours was always the final decision to fly, whatever Mr Keen said. However, working six days a week, we were becoming hoarse with the amount of flying we were doing, as Mr Keen wasn't ready to spend money on headsets.

We were just cheap labour, but not as cheap as Mr Aboud, the Jordanian engineer, who once managed to connect the flying controls of a Cherokee the wrong way around, which fortunately was picked up by my student on the pre-flight check. This standard of maintenance caused me some concern during the compulsory practice engine failure after take-off exercises, gliding down to five feet above the muddy waters of the River Mersey and hoping the engine would open up again.

Most clients showed me respect, including a gentleman ex-Spitfire pilot called Brian Bird with more hours in his logbook than I had; an exception being Ron Pimlett, a disc jockey, who bent a propeller on a solo landing after ignoring my instructions to come in.

Mr Keen asked me what I was going to say to Pimlett about the incident. I'd been trained at one of the best flying schools in the world but was still only 20 years old with no real-life experience, so I didn't have an answer. But no one had been hurt, and I assumed Pimlett hadn't done it on purpose. The aircraft would get repaired, and life would go on.

My first lesson was understanding that my work wasn't just about aeroplanes; there were human factors involved with behaviours and emotions in other people to learn about. When my more affluent students invited me to their parties and found out what the person they had been entrusting their lives with was being paid, they were horrified.

Others attended the advanced ground school lectures I set up, with a meet-up in the airport bar afterwards. Telling myself I hadn't done it just to get attention from the lady pilots, our little group flourished. I felt appreciated and grown-up, even if I didn't think the lady pilots were too impressed with my Hillman Minx and its starting handle.

The vintage (old) car and moving to a £4.50 a week bedsit was helping to establish the persona I was creating for myself as a devil-may-care flying instructor, poor but with prospects. British Airways had mapped out my career path, so my only real cares were accumulating flying experience, getting laid, and looking cool.

A second-hand flying jacket with a sheepskin collar fulfilled the latter requirement in my eyes, prompting Dave Lonsdale to voice his concern for my moral welfare and my lack of a relationship with the Lord. He was persistent, and it passed the time if we were waiting for the weather to clear, but I was looking for better things than God.

These took the shape of two six-seat, twin-engine Piper Aztecs operated by Keenair Services, Mr Keen's air charter company. The Aztec could fly 1,000 miles, enough to get well into Europe, which was where my ambitions lay. Brian, the Keenair Chief Pilot, taught me to fly the Aztec without the benefit of the airline-standard training I'd received, including flying without contingency fuel so that we could fill up at airfields with cheaper fuel[4].

Then came a request from the Liverpool Echo for a picture for the front page of their 24 March 1976 edition. I was to fly their photographer around a giant drilling platform being towed to the Isle of Bute. As the tug company doing the job owned the Aztec I would be flying, I decided to stretch the low-flying rules to give the photographer the best view from the seat behind me. We removed the window, and I gave him his shot, looking *up* at a tug, from only two or three feet above the Irish Sea.

It was dangerous, but I remembered what Ron Street had taught me about flying safely over calm water without reference points. Trimming slightly nose up and judging height by the distance to the aeroplane's shadow, I kept the speed up to around 250 mph, which gave me more control and time to react if I lost an engine from a bird strike. I also

---

[4] Brian was killed on 21 May 1982 near Paris when he ran out of fuel.

remembered to climb a few feet before turning to prevent the wingtip from touching the water. It was fun too.

The photographer asked me if I'd flown with the Red Arrows, which was a supreme compliment, so I celebrated my 1,000 hours with some aerobatics in a Cessna 150 Aerobat accompanied by my new French housemate Jean-Marie as a passenger. I enjoyed his child-like enthusiasm - which I missed in English people generally - and his aplomb when he threw up, managing to put it all in the sick bag which I'd thoughtfully provided, given that aerobatics wasn't my strong point.

He and I also went to see my first professional football match, Liverpool vs Barcelona at Anfield. Attending a school where football was a minor sport, I admired the occasional displays of skill by the best players but never understood the hate and tribalism of some supporters. I loved the notion of the game bringing people closer together but felt that the generally low scores made it a frustrating game, potentially explaining the violence amongst fans. I looked forward to the day when an overpaid prima donna star missed a penalty, and the linesmen and referee crowded around him and shouted at him for making a mistake.

Soon after I arrived in Liverpool, I met my first proper girlfriend. Gail Elizabeth Darbyshire was a nurse, full of life with long, thick, soft brown hair, blue eyes, flawless skin, and a wholesomeness that made me feel like a serial killer. She was the kindest, sweetest, most beautiful human being I'd ever met, who made me feel good about myself as a person, not just a clever son or a pilot.

She lived in a detached house on the Wirral, her father an estate agent and her mother a homely and welcoming English housewife. Gail was always immaculate, not just in her neatly pressed clothes but in the purity of her mind and heart. She never preached but believed, never swore but always spoke her mind, never acted tarty but wasn't afraid to take me to a secluded spot on the Wirral to demonstrate her interest in matters physical.

One such day, I asked Gail if she wanted to go for a swim.

'I can't,' she said.

'Why?'

'I just can't.'

'Can you swim?'

'Yes.'

'Then why can't we go?'

'I just can't.'

'What's the problem?'

'No problem, I just can't. Another time.'

Irritated, I didn't understand. This wasn't like Gail; I'd never seen her stubborn or contrary before. But then, no one had explained to me about periods or much else useful relating to women. My Catholic education had given me the belief that sex was for making babies after marriage; the fear of unwanted pregnancies or catching sexually transmitted diseases frightened me.

In any case, while I wanted to see Gail in a swimsuit, she was too perfect just for sex. I wanted to make love to her in line with my purest ideals after we were married, and I was sure she felt the same way. When I first stuttered out the words 'I love you,' she checked I knew exactly what I was saying and meant it.

I was as sure as I could be, but British Airways were always going to call me back to London, and Gail wouldn't leave Liverpool and her family. I did contemplate giving up an airline career and working for Mr Keen for the rest of my life to be with her, but I knew it wasn't realistic for either of us. I would have to move on, and she would find some great guy to love as she loved everyone else.

On my 21st birthday, she cooked for us in her parents' house - they went out, bless them - and it was just the two of us. The evening passed in an intimate closeness where time stopped, and we knew we had everything we wanted in the world but that it would all have to end, sooner rather than later.

The end came in the shape of a short, smiling Irishman named John Ward, one of my old college mates who occasionally passed through Liverpool in a relatively new sharp-nosed Aztec E. With Japanese symbols on the tail meaning 'Summer Swirl,' it looked a lot faster than Mr Keen's Aztec D's, which looked as if they'd been around since Pontius was a pilot. From Belfast, John was the pilot for Airde Ltd based in Newtownards, Northern Ireland, operating the one aeroplane.

He'd got himself a job in Norwich flying F27s for Air Anglia. When he asked if I was interested in taking over from him, I couldn't say 'Yes' quickly enough. The pay was £2,500 a year; there was a caravan on the airfield to live in, lots of twin-engine flying, and a uniform with three stripes. Heaven!

John's instructions were: 'Pick up the aeroplane in Manchester after its C of A (Certificate of Airworthiness,) don't let the boss push you around, and don't walk down the Falls Road[5] in your uniform. Don't talk politics, and don't forget to ask for a new gas cylinder for your caravan. You'll pick up the rest as you go along.'

If I'd been a little wiser, I might have asked for more information about Airde, but as John and I had been trained to the same standard, I assumed I would slot in easily to the job. For me, it was a straightforward decision; 'Summer Swirl' had to be better than Mr Keen. I'd been in Liverpool a year when I telephoned my parents to give them my new address, a caravan on an airfield in Ulster. My mother responded in French, a bad sign.

'*Why*? But why do you have to go there? No, Philip, bombs are going off all the time; you've only got to watch the news. Every day something happens; somebody gets killed by a terrorist. Why, Philip - why do you have to go there?'

---

[5] Catholic-controlled road in Belfast.

I did my best to communicate a Gallic shrug over the phone and tried some reasoning: 'There was a murder 500 yards away from where I live in Liverpool a month ago.'

When I gave Mr Keen my notice, he also tried to convince me that I would be better off staying in Liverpool, but a new and exciting life was beckoning from across the Irish Sea. I had enjoyed my time in 'The Pool,' but I was ready to move on, confident I had enough experience to run an air-taxi operation. I would sort everything else out when I arrived in Newtownards.

My next call was to one of my students to ask him to sell my Hillman Minx, primarily the number plate 123 EWC, worth more than the car. Then I went to see Gail knowing it would be for the last time. She cried, and I did too. I would never forget her hugs, her soft words, and the aura of a saint around her.

The plan was to take my few belongings to Manchester Airport where Airde's Aztec was on maintenance, get the Certificate of Airworthiness test flight done, then fly the aeroplane over to Newtownards. The point of the C of A was to see if the engineers had put the plane together again properly after having taken it apart to check it wasn't rusting away. If the wings stayed on, then it was happiness all around. I decided to be particularly pleasant to anybody with oil on their hands.

There was a problem, but it wasn't technical. Mike Abbott, the regular pilot, approved by the CAA to do test flights was ill, but he managed to convince them that I was competent to do the test with him sitting in the right-hand seat guiding me through it. He looked the colour of plasterboard throughout the flight, so I flew as if my life depended on it, with airspeeds and altitudes nailed to zero tolerance, even during the single-engine work. In return, the aeroplane behaved flawlessly, Mike Abbott was impressed, and Summer Swirl got its C of A.

5

Northern Ireland

Flying West from Liverpool, finding Ireland wasn't too demanding, and I was able to enjoy my first view of the approaching coastline on a bright and sunny afternoon in May 1976. The view from 2,000 feet was stunning: rich green fields and dark hedgerows; old castles and solid farmhouses; narrow lanes and the swell of the hills hiding smoke-covered Belfast. Located at the northern end of Strangford Lough, County Down, Newtownards airfield was also easy to find.

Keeping a good lookout, I remembered the basics: fly overhead, look at the landing 'T' to determine the runway in use, and check the windsock. I tried the VHF radio frequency to request an altimeter setting. There was no licensed air traffic controller on-site, but there might have been someone passing who would pick up the microphone and give out some local knowledge. I descended dead side – the opposite side to the traffic pattern – for a left-hand circuit giving way to landing aircraft. With a short runway, I told myself I'd need to land on its designator numbers every time to avoid an early arrival at the cemetery a mile from touchdown on final approach.

Putting the Aztec down firmly rather than trying for a smooth landing, I noted the position of the potholes on the runway for future reference. In case there was another aircraft waiting to land, I swung round and cleared the runway as quickly as I dared, not wanting anyone to test my nerves by landing next to me. As I did so, I raised the flaps; there was a tradition amongst pilots that anyone who taxied in with flaps down had to buy a round of drinks.

A small crowd provided a reception committee - watching other pilots park aeroplanes in small spaces was an entertaining sport. Crunching gravel and a cloud of dust saw the Aztec stopped adequately enough for some willing hands to push me back to a safe position out of the way for the night. With the parking brake set, I gratefully removed my hot headset, unbuckled my straps, and swung the door open.

Revelling in the light breeze that was ungluing the perspiration from my shirt, I stepped out onto the ground, enjoying a long stretch of my stiffened muscles. The sweat was running down my wrists, but I tried to look cool. I needed a cold drink. People stood around and stared. A dog scurried, and a door creaked. Everybody was waiting for something to happen.

A big man in his thirties emerged from a battered Nissen hut a few yards away and approached me. He looked friendly, his red *Aero Club* t-shirt and baseball cap telling me he liked being around aeroplanes and airfields, as I did when I was 15.

'Waddabiteye, then?' he said.

'Hi,' I responded as I tried to work what he had said from his Ulster accent, 'Can I get a beer somewhere?'

'Aye, com with me.'

Martin McDonagh formed Airde Ltd once he had made a large amount of money as a second-hand car dealer. A competent private pilot, he had bought a 15-year-old, six-seat, single-engine Beechcraft Bonanza to take himself and his friends on local sightseeing flights, with the occasional trip further afield.

From Newtownards, this usually meant the Isle of Man. 'The Island' was easy to find, had cheap beer, and was almost foreign. During the Isle of Man motorcycle TT week, Martin quickly found he had many friends, some of whom were even prepared to pay money to 'help pay for the petrol.'

Soon, even the mole-eyed CAA inspectors suspected there was something illegal going on. Private pilots weren't allowed to fly for 'hire and reward,' and taking fare-paying passengers over water in a single-engine aeroplane was prohibited. The inspectors would watch for any activity on the tarmac at Ronaldsway, the Isle of Man airport.

Eventually, the CAA suggested Martin might like to buy a twin-engine aeroplane and hire a professional pilot if he wouldn't mind. This softly-softly approach was in line with the government's policy of avoiding exacerbating the tensions prevalent in Northern Ireland at the time.

John, my predecessor, had obtained an Air Operator's Certificate from the CAA, which in reality meant a badge stuck on the side of the aeroplane to impress the clients. As the chief and only pilot, I was responsible for not only the flying but updating the operations manual, keeping the flight time limitations records, customs and police regulations, the maintenance, the operational expenditure, the cleaning and refuelling of the aeroplane, filing the flight plans, and taking bookings.

With Martin's primary interest being to make as much 'dough' as possible, he left the running of the office to me and an older man, Alec. Alec answered the phone and reported everything I did back to Martin when he wasn't playing golf, snooker or drinking. Martin and Alec's friends obtained most of the business through word of mouth. With low costs such as my salary and undercutting both British Airways and Woodgate's at Belfast, there was plenty of work. Soon enough, it became clear that the actual flying was going to be the easy part; otherwise, life in Northern Ireland would be a new experience.

Martin had provided a caravan for my accommodation situated five yards from the aircraft. He made me pay for the discomfort of living in it, with its leaking roof providing me with an advanced forecast of rainy conditions. I'd meet the passengers, collect their pound notes, carry their bags, clean out the ashtrays, check the engines' oil level, and finally do the part that made me get up in the morning: fly the aeroplane.

A frequent visitor to the office was Sergeant Jimmy Leyton of the Royal Ulster Constabulary Special Branch. He had won medals for saving people from burning buildings but was afraid of flying. Part of his job was to hang around Newtownards Airfield to watch for gun-running and other undesirable activity in plain clothes. He let me play with his gun to see if I was used to handling pistols, which I wasn't, and checked me out to see if I was the naïve young pilot that I claimed to be, which I was.

He often talked about taking his wife to the Isle of Man, which would be tricky if he didn't like flying, but eventually, he summoned up the courage, gripping the armrests all the way. We found mutual respect; Jimmy was someone I would want on my side - gun or no gun – and he would only fly with me on his part.

As my caravan was usually cold and damp, I would spend as much of my spare time as possible sitting at the bar in the warmth of the Flying Club, with my hotshot pilot face on, trying to look debonair by drinking whiskey which I didn't like much, and by smoking Gauloises, which made me cough. I had never been exposed to such a variety of characters making up the clientele.

There was Luke, the wild-haired homosexual flying instructor who lived in a caravan just a few yards from my own; Tubby Dash, another flying instructor who was 76 years old and only had his medical certificate renewed by renewing the local doctor's pilot's licence in return; Martin's cronies - 'businessmen' whose businesses they didn't like talking about; aeroplane owners; drunks; the occasional soldier; and Lynn.

One night the barman leaned towards me.

'There's someone who wants to meet ye,' he said, jerking his head towards a tall woman of about 50 with dyed black hair, yellow teeth, and a cigarette in her hand. I was about to give the barman my most withering glare when I noticed a young girl standing next to the woman, who I assumed was her daughter. The girl had dark, shoulder-length hair and streaks of unattractive grey makeup plastered all over her eyelids, which distracted her eyes, which were brown and warm. A quick vertical scan told me that her calves were slim, her figure was strong, and her hands were delicate, with long fingers spoilt by creamy nail varnish.

Being told that a girl wanted to meet *me* had never happened before. What was also new was having to deal with a chaperone. The mother introduced herself as Pearl and her daughter Lynn who looked at me expectantly, waiting for me to speak. I went for the drinks option: something soft for her, a Scotch for her mother, and a rum and coke for me. Lynn didn't make a great impression on me that first day, so I wondered if the hotshot pilot routine was working. I'd no idea that she was saying to herself: 'I'm going to have that little man,' an affectionate diminutive nothing to do with my five feet 11 or anything else.

Lynn worked in a boutique clothes shop in Newtownards and was training to become a dental nurse. When she eventually spoke, she made a point of telling me she wasn't stupid and that she had perfect teeth with no fillings, like a filly on show. We were frequently taken for brother and sister. It was clear everyone expected us to go out - which we did - driving around in her father's battered old Austin 1000, which kept breaking down. We'd end up in my caravan, locking the door in case her father came around looking for her.

Major Thomas Jermy had been the youngest sergeant-major in the Army, a boxer who'd once killed 16 men before breakfast. He was 73, but I wasn't going to mess with him. Pearl, his wife, was 20 years younger, smoked like a chimney and would often be in her dressing gown mid-morning. She fussed over me like an old hen while eyeing me up and down, saying: 'If I was 20 years younger…' I wasn't going to mess with her either. They didn't have much money, but some of my most contented hours were spent in their living room lying on their sofa in front of a real fire, stroking Lynn's thick, soft hair as we all ate peppered tomato and salad cream sandwiches in front of her dog, her granny, and the TV.

When the sandwiches were finished, it was the signal for Lynn and me to go into the front room and draw the curtains. The electric fire would give our bodies a healthy red glow as we stripped off and played with all the energy of dogs on heat. Lynn was certainly extremely comfortable with anything to do with sex. However, my fear of being trapped by early fatherhood ensured that I restricted our activities to 'heavy petting.'

With Lynn's family Protestant, the prospect of a mini sectarian conflict loomed, but religion wasn't discussed once established that I didn't go to Mass and was disenchanted with Catholic rituals and my mother quoting Nostradamus. I was starting to feel at home with Lynn, to the point where her parents let me sleep on their sofa, with warmth and tea brought to me in the morning providing a welcome improvement on the caravan, with its attendant risk of an approach from Luke.

Perhaps as a result of this domesticity, it wasn't an aeroplane that got me excited on the annual flying club outing to Kirkbride Airfield in Cumbria. Someone put a baby in my arms. It was quiet, dark-haired, beautiful, and didn't have any bodily fluids dripping out of it. I held it, looked into its eyes, and it looked back. All the women around cooed and went 'aah' while someone said: 'It won't be long.' Lynn and her mother were smiling, and time seemed to stop.

Sharing that private moment with the baby, I thought about life, the future, love, and fatherhood. It felt like my own child, and I wouldn't have minded if it had been. Lynn was impressed, but as she was sharing a bedroom with her mother, there was no chance of us being tempted to practise for our own that night. Yet, I still felt it was too early for introductions to my family, so I took a week off to go to St Lunaire on my own.

Back in the Flying Club snug bar on a Saturday night, somebody's wife came on to me. If it was a test of my feelings for Lynn, I failed it with honours, showing the world what a complete idiot I could be. There was too much drink, a grope, some encouragement, and lots of folk watching. The next day, word spread like wildfire, Lynn refused to speak to me, and it was moi tout seul with a vengeance. It was the worst day of my life.

What made it so bad was that it was self-inflicted. I spent most of the next few days in the caravan, bawling my eyes out. Then God came into my head to sort me out - or so I believed - because there wasn't anyone else to tell me otherwise. If a psychiatrist had been present, they might have said I was having a psychotic episode, but there wasn't – it was just me, and whatever 'god' happened to be around. I sobbed my heart out until I felt all the weight coming off my soul, shoulders, and conscience, smiling towards the roof and thanking 'The Lord' for saving me.

As my self-pity transformed into a big, beaming grin, I didn't know what was happening, just that it was a lot better than what had been going on previously. Desperately sorry for everything I had done, I was asking for forgiveness and wanting to get back into Lynn's life, so I wrote a letter; seven pages of how much I missed her, what a terrible mistake I'd made, and how I would make it up to her. It had one thing going for it; it was all true.

When she came back to me, I knew that we were going to get married. I asked her father for his permission, and he gave it with a glint in his eye that said he'd be after me if I mistreated his only daughter. Some said I was being led, some that we were too young, and some that I was lucky to have a second chance. Whatever the truth, the show was on the road, and I was being swept along. I let Lynn and her mother get on with the planning for the wedding while I went back to my comfort zone: the aeroplane and flying.

I was the ace on the base, confident I could fly a twin-engine aircraft anywhere in Europe. I'd heard of the points marking dangerous overconfidence: ten hours flying experience, just after first solo; 100 hours when pilots think they know it all; 1,000 hours when they do know it all but push the boundaries.

Returning to Newtownards from the Isle of Man one day with no passengers and just over 1200 hours in my logbook, I decided to put on a show for anybody watching from the clubhouse. Flying past at 200 mph low-level from the Lough – too fast for lowering the undercarriage – I decided to delay dropping the wheels until I had carried out a slowing turn onto final approach.

It was as I was flaring for landing, five feet above the runway, that I snatched a glance at the undercarriage lights to check three greens. No lights. Without even having time to say 'Fuck' or anything else, I applied full power, raised the flaps, and climbed away. If the aircraft had had a passenger or two on board or more weight of fuel, the momentum of the Aztec would have caused the propellers to touch the ground, and I'd have been digging for oil. Anyone who might have been able to operate a fire extinguisher was probably in the bar.

Dambustering in one early morning at full speed below the cloud base provided further excitement when I hit a seagull. Usually dopey and grounded after a night on the tiles, one had felt the urge to get airborne and make a mess of the leading edge of my wing. Had it been a bigger bird or had some of its mates with it, it might have gone for an engine, which would have been terminal for the birds and possibly for me. I was shaken but more fortunate than the seagull and only had to wipe the blood and feathers off before carrying on with my day.

On another flight, I'd taken off without the port inboard fuel filler cap being properly secured on take-off, and fuel had gushed out all over the wing. Fortunately, nothing had caught fire, but these incidents were a warning that while flying single-crew was rewarding, if I became tired or distracted, there was no one to provide a fallback.

My willingness to please and fit into the anarchic Northern Irish culture was starting to create conflicts within my character, which Lynn referred to as 'straight,' in a complimentary way. As a favour to Martin, I'd kept the private flying club trip to Kirkbride out of the maintenance log and agreed to spread the peak of flight movements during TT races week across the months before and after to make the flight time limitations records look legal.

In return, Martin bought me a beer, a *whole* one, assuring me that the CAA Flight Operations Inspector wouldn't notice when he made his next six-monthly inspection. He was right, as when Basil the Inspector arrived, Martin took him out to lunch in the roughest part of town, to ensure that Basil's whole purpose in life was to get out of Northern Ireland as quickly as possible, rubber-stamping the Airde paperwork as he left.

However, when Martin told me to put six passengers on five seats of the Aztec, I felt my standards had been compromised far enough and refused. Martin told me how 'it would be all right,' and 'he's only a child.' The 'child' turned out to be a 12-year-old boy – ostensibly an infant - who would be sitting on someone's knee. If I got caught, I would be the one in trouble, not Martin.

Decisions involving aeroplanes were easy, but I was struggling with making them about people. I could feel myself getting stressed and anxious and tried talking to Alec, but he was only interested in playing golf. I thought of confiding in Jimmy Leyton, but he was all about stopping the

IRA, and if I told him, he couldn't condone me breaking the law and might tell the CAA. I talked to Lynn instead.

'Martin's a rascal, Phil,' she said, 'Just look at the car he sold my Dad. It's given us nothing but trouble from the day we bought it. I'd string Martin up by the balls if I'd half a chance.'

She probably would have, but I dithered and procrastinated, losing sleep and confidence. I would never ask my parents - they were black and white about everything and didn't begin to understand the grey areas that lurked in real life. I checked with Nigel Crowe, my flying club instructor best mate, and just about everyone else I could find until I came to the only conclusion, it was down to me.

I called Mike Woodgate at Belfast's Aldergrove Airport to see if he had any jobs available. Mike ran a respected air charter company and flying school, but I still felt guilty about speaking to him, so I made sure I used a phone where no one could eavesdrop. Being British Airways-trained and having the Aztec on my licence was good news for Woodgate Aviation as they also operated Aztecs and would be glad to do anything that might put Airde out of business. Mike offered me a job, and I accepted. I just had to tell Martin and, more importantly, get paid any money owing to me.

'I'm not going to break the law for you, Martin.'

'Everybody breaks the law, son.'

'It's not just about the law. There's the question of safety.'

'Bollocks. The Aztec can carry five passengers easily enough. An extra kid won't make any difference. They won't have much baggage going to the Island for the weekend.'

'You don't know that.'

'Just fuckin' do it. You're supposed to be good enough.'

'Yeah, well, that's because I stick to the rules.'

'Don't be such a prick. Just get on with your job. You're lucky to have one. John would have done it.'

'I don't think so.'

'You're getting a bit cocky for your age, son.'

'Well, I'm not putting six passengers in the Aztec.'

'You'll do it or get yourself another job.'

'I have got myself another job. I'm going to Woodgate's.'

'You fucker. You're a cheating bastard.'

'I'm giving you notice, and I want my money.'

'What money?'

'What I'm owed up to now.'

'Fuck off.'

'I want it before I do the Aberdeen trip.'

'Do Aberdeen. You'll get your money.'

'Before I do the trip.'

'I told you, you'll get your money.'

'Before I do the trip.'

'Just do it, then I'll give you your dough.'

'No.'

'Well Phil, you know what you can do? You can fuck off, and if I ever see you again, God help you.'

In the context of paramilitary killings in Northern Ireland at the height of the Troubles, this focused my mind somewhat. Martin was willing to sacrifice the trip to Aberdeen to spite me to show me how ruthless he was. As for me, I had grown up a little but hadn't enjoyed the experience at all.

6

Married

After I started work for Woodgate Aviation at Aldergrove, I did some more growing up living on a farm within the airport security cordon and travelling through Belfast by bus to Lynn's house in Newtownards for weekends. Children would throw stones at the bus windows as it travelled down the Crumlin Road towards the central station where I'd change buses, walking past the Europa Hotel, supposedly the most bombed hotel in the world in the 1970s.

Night-time stimulated my paranoia - journeying through the blackness, not knowing where I was and trusting that the bus wasn't going to get hijacked. I was in admiration of the bus drivers who plied the route day in, day out.

With Christmas approaching, I was invited to the annual turkey strangle by my landlord, the farm owner. Unable to find turkey strangling in my pilot training notes, I left that to the professionals. Instead, I drove Lynn over to England for Christmas at Natal Road to subject her to my parents' interrogation, which would have made the Royal Ulster Constabulary look like a bunch of sissies.

Typically, my parents didn't tell me how they felt about her until I was back in Northern Ireland. They called her a princess, but not in a positive way. My mother reckoned she was lazy, my father said little, perhaps remembering that he had married in spite of his mother's objections. I told Lynn, who was unimpressed.

Back in my new job at Woodgate's, I pushed my flying skills to the limit. Flying an empty sector into Aldergrove,

ATC asked me to turn off the main runway as quickly as possible to make way for a scheduled aircraft. Always ready to please, I decided to land as close to the turn-off as I could. Approaching from the South down the centreline of the cross runway in a steady descent, I turned 90 degrees over the airfield at the last second, dropping the gear and flaps together. With no passengers and half fuel, I allowed the speed to drop off until it was practically zero, effectively stalling the Aztec onto the runway from a few feet with a landing distance of a few yards, maybe 20.

Looking similar to a bird landing, it was spectacular but extremely dangerous. There was no room for error. Aeroplanes didn't glide with their wings stalled; they lost their lift and crashed. My stomach was somewhere in my boots when Bob, the air traffic controller on duty, drove over from the tower in a Land-Rover and told me he had never seen anything like it in all his years in aviation. He looked at me as if I was mad.

If I was, I didn't know it at the time, but I was certainly getting better at flying. This included scrambling like a Battle of Britain fighter pilot late one night to deliver a kidney to Heathrow for a transplant. With virtually no preparation and never having flown into such a large airport before, I raced to Aldergrove, got airborne in record time, and with priority clearance, was soon shutting down the engines next to a waiting police car with blue lights flashing on a central parking stand at Heathrow.

Once the kidney had been offloaded from the Aztec into the care of the police, I turned to a tall, slim man standing nearby who introduced himself as an officer from the British Airways Executive Aircraft Handling Service (EAS.) He told me his name was David, that the fuel bowser was ready, the return flight plan had been filed, then offered me a cup of tea. I thanked him, said I wanted to get back, signed the handling form, and shook his hand. As I started the engines, David waved me off and returned to his car. I didn't give him another thought as I called the ground frequency for clearance and flew back to Aldergrove.

Flying oil workers to the Shetland Islands in the oil boom of the 1960s and 1970s was very lucrative for operators like Mike Woodgate. We would fly five hulking great Irish workers the two and a half hours to Sumburgh on a weekly basis. With the rigs being dry and four-month shifts to look forward to, the flight up was an opportunity for the men to tank up with as much liquor as possible in the time available. I was an experienced pilot with 1,000 hours on twins in my logbook, but I looked like the fresh-faced 22-year-old that I was.

I'd done a few of the Shetland flights and knew that the boys would have knocked back a few drinks before take-off. On one trip, they were particularly hulking. Take-off was long and slow with their toolboxes and baggage on board, but we staggered into the air and headed North-East towards Scotland. It wasn't long before a big, hairy Irish arm draped itself over my shoulder, and its owner enquired after my health with an 'Ar y'allroit den Phil?'

The Aztec's seating configuration was three rows of two with dual controls at the front. It was when my neighbour began eyeing the instruments and the control column that I worried. When he grabbed the control column to the raucous cheers of his mates, I worried even more. From my experience as a flying instructor and the whiteness of his knuckles, I knew that 'Hulk' wasn't a pilot, and I could tell from the glazed look in his eyes that he wasn't going to let go in a hurry.

The autopilot wasn't engaged, and even if it had been, it would have disengaged after giving up the struggle against Hulk's vice-like grip. He looked as strong as a bear, and there was no way I was going to fight him for control of the aeroplane and risk breaking something vital.

'Would you mind letting go of the controls, please?' I asked politely. No response.

'I think I'd better have control now if you don't mind.' Still no response.

So, I turned to Hulk and folded my arms.

'Okay, I tell you what: you fly the aeroplane, and I'll look out of the window.'

Hulk's mates must have heard this because four wide-eyed faces quickly appeared from behind, wondering how Hulk would make out as the next Neil Armstrong[6]. Hulk's grip tightened even further on the control column, and I could see his scan darting all over the instrument panel. Turning round in my seat, I got comfortable for a view of the water below.

Ignoring the altimeter, unreliable due to local pressure variations, I was looking down at the sea very carefully to judge the aeroplane's height, grateful for the choppy water and the clearly visible whitecaps. We had started a high-speed dive, which did have the advantage that if an engine failed, it would give me more control, provided I kicked the rudder in quickly enough.

There was gradual silence from the back of the plane as the boys realised something important was going on in front of them. After a few seconds, the aircraft banked gently left as I kept my arms firmly crossed. Six hundred hours of instructing had given me a 'chickening out' factor much higher than a group of drunken Irishmen. With the increased turbulence at lower levels, they would soon be feeling sick, which was now my main concern; whether any of them would manage to get any of their technicolour yawns into the sick bags.

Hulk wasn't coping at all well with the demands of becoming an instant aviator. He'd released his grip on the controls with his right hand and was uselessly trying to gain

---

[6] Neil Armstrong was the first man to walk on the Moon and reputed to be the best pilot in the world.

comfort from holding onto the door, which was a good start from my point of view. The rest of the lads were by now using words like 'fuck' and 'fuckin'' a lot, and I detected a vote from the floor for Hulk to 'leave the fuckin' thing alone,' and for me to '*do* something.'

But I didn't want to rush things now that I'd got the upper hand. There were still a good few hundred feet before we made a splash, and we hadn't reached 90 degrees of bank. However, with the aeroplane heavy, I didn't want to get too close to the sea and be unable to pull out. I turned around and said to Hulk:

'I tell you what, you sit still and keep quiet, and I'll fly the aeroplane, okay?'

Hulk's mates agreed enthusiastically, so once Hulk had let go, I got on with re-setting the aeroplane for straight and level flight. The guys were my passengers, and I didn't want to upset them anymore. I couldn't blame them for wanting a drink before being stuck in the middle of the North Sea for four months. Some of the oil they would be pulling out of the seabed might become the Avgas (Aviation gasoline) that would power my aeroplane on future flights.

So, I cruised along at 50 feet above the waves for a few minutes, then pulled up into as steep a climb as a fully laden Aztec could manage before levelling off gently weightless and heading for the Scottish hills. Then low enough for the sheep to notice, and a detour over Loch Ness towards Tingwall, Lerwick's airstrip on the Shetland Islands. The boys loved that, and we were all friends again. Further North than the southern tip of Greenland, Tingwall had no ATC, fuel, or facilities except a 740-metre strip of tarmac. I felt like a low-level bomber pilot going in there.

The Shetland weather could be vastly different from that on the mainland. On one return flight, having left in glorious sunshine, I encountered severe icing conditions over the Scottish Highlands. Forced to remain below 10,000 feet in the freezing cloud and turbulence because of the unpressurised cabin, ice built up on the wing leading edges within a few minutes, and I knew the same was happening on the tail.

Even with no passengers and half fuel, and almost full power set, the aeroplane was descending. The pneumatic boots that were supposed to break the ice off were useless, I was unsure of my precise position, and the rudder control was unresponsive. Really frightened, I visualised the windshield filling with a rocky mountain, and seconds later: oblivion.

Still descending, I eventually broke cloud over the sea, wondering if I could reach land or would have to put down on the water. Fortunately, at 1,000 feet, the ice began to melt, and I was finally able to maintain altitude and head for Belfast. After landing, I saw that the weight of ice had broken off the radio navigation aerial at the front of the fuselage, which had then wrapped itself around the tail. No wonder my rudder control was stiff. I made a note in my diary: 'Nearly hit Rathlin' which wasn't about a striking a stroppy Irishman, but about missing a large island just to the North of Ulster.

When Mike Woodgate offered me the job of managing his operation on the Isle of Man, I thought it was about time I left the turkey farm at Aldergrove, so I accepted. I rented a flat in Castletown, ready to start work at Ronaldsway Airport with my own office and a secretary.

With my airline training, I naturally assumed I would be a better pilot than my predecessor Mike Grace, but he appeared to have something else. He was an easy-going, nice guy, popular with everyone, and was particularly good at networking and bringing in new business. This was disconcerting, as it was revealing my shortcomings. Focused on flying the plane, I was unprepared for any work and social contact where my personality might be assessed.

On top of this new pressure was that of the impending wedding. My parents and my boss thought I was too young to get married. I was 22, Lynn was younger, and we'd known each other exactly a year. My parents thought Lynn was a gold digger and was only after me to take her out of Northern Ireland and cash in on an airline pilot's salary as soon as British Airways called me up.

They wouldn't entertain travelling to Northern Ireland for the wedding because of the bomb that was going to go off as soon as they stepped off the plane. It didn't matter that I'd lived there for a year without seeing any serious incidents. 'Why can't you get married in London?' asked my mother selfishly. For his part, Mike Woodgate didn't want me distracted from work by a teenage bride who would need a work permit for any kind of job on the Isle of Man.

Without any helpful guidance about marriage or planning for the future from my parents, I didn't know I was supposed to spend my stag night off my head with drink, running naked down Newtownards High Street with creosote and feathers up my backside. Instead, I had a quiet drink in a bar with Patrick, one of Lynn's two brothers. Both Patrick and Sean were honest and hard-working and seemed pleased that I was marrying their little sister. I was all set to live a fine, upstanding life as a married man and member of a church somewhere.

My previous Catholic credentials being no impediment, Lynn and I were married in a Presbyterian church on 21 May 1977. My parents and sister stayed away, but I had to put my address down as Natal Road, London. Nigel from the flying club agreed to be my best man. The wedding happened as planned, and Lynn and I were soon sitting on an Aviaco Caravelle at Aldergrove, waiting for someone else to do the work and fly us to Palma for our honeymoon.

Which was when Lynn showed me her passport to prove that we were married on her 17th birthday. I was utterly gobsmacked; I'd been going out with a 16-year-old without realising it. While I felt Lynn had taken advantage of me, I wasn't angry with her, and in any case, there was nothing I could do about it.

Lynn was young but seemed able to handle people with a confidence and maturity that I couldn't match. After she won the *Miss Lancaster Hotel* title at the honeymoon venue, I watched while she got chatted up by a drunken Englishman. My companion at our table wondered why I didn't take the guy on. I didn't think the drunk meant any harm, so I did nothing, which seemed reasonable, but I worried about it afterwards. Should I have made a scene or made a fool of myself by politely asking him to desist? I didn't know the answer, while Lynn was unfazed by the incident.

After the honeymoon, Lynn joined me in Castletown, one step closer to England, where I would join British Airways, feel more settled, and we'd live happily ever after. I could see Lynn wanted to have children, but I wasn't so sure. She was doing her best to make the flat a home but relied on me to take the lead, look after her and take charge.

Wanting to keep her happy, I couldn't say no to the next lampshade or bed cover, so I was putting myself under pressure, with the growing feeling that I was losing control. Away from flying, my anxiety caused me to think too much, too deeply, and too alone. Being an adult was more complicated than I had expected.

So, when Lynn was confirmed pregnant six months after we were married, again, I didn't know what to do. She told me she'd had an abortion before I met her, which shocked and upset me, and made me feel less secure about starting a family with her, especially without a call-up date from British Airways. If I approached my parents for advice, I knew my mother would criticise me for getting married and Lynn for getting pregnant.

I wanted the situation to go away, ignorant of Lynn's feelings and needs. Quietly she took herself to hospital while I carried on working, and five days later, she wasn't pregnant anymore. I was so wrapped up in my work and thoughts I didn't even visit her.

Together with my ineptitude at running the commercial side of Woodgate's business, the pressure began to affect my flying. Once, leaving Blackpool alone, I left the right-hand seat strap outside the door by mistake. It flapped and banged so much I had to try and get it back inside the cabin, in an aeroplane doing 150 mph, without autopilot. Reaching across to open the door and pull the strap in was easy but shutting the door against the airflow was impossible, even when slowing the aeroplane down until there was a real risk of stalling, a likely fatal move at only 500 feet above the waves.

Rather than head off across the Irish Sea with the door open, I returned to Blackpool, failing to talk my way out of a further landing fee, so Mike Woodgate found out. Even the flying that was supposed to be my escape from life's challenges on the ground wasn't always fulfilling that purpose.

My three-year deferment by British Airways was due to end in two months when I would have the option of working as a steward or on a ground job on full British Airways co-pilot's pay. But I wasn't going to give up flying to work in an office at Heathrow listening to aeroplanes passing overhead, whatever the money. With 1500 hours total flying experience, I had qualified for an Airline Transport Pilot's Licence (ATPL), which meant that I could captain any aircraft in theory and was therefore marketable.

The decision was made for me with the offer of a job as the Deputy Chief Pilot for BOC Aviation, flying a Cessna 401A based at Stansted. It was a private, company operation, so there were no public transport regulations to comply with. The destinations were varied, and I would be flying single-crew with four rings on my uniform. Three years after graduating from flying college, I accepted and prepared to go back to England with a new job, a new wife and what I thought was a certain future.

7

Captain Appleton

Tony Barton was the only school friend I had kept in touch with, and when he and his wife Sue offered Lynn and me a room in their house in Watford, I was surprised and grateful that anyone would be so kind. From there, I could drive to Harlow in my company car, where Josh Taylor, the BOC Aviation Chief Pilot and I had an office in the main building.

On my first day at work, two unsettling events occurred. First, a Union man on a picket line asked to see my ID. I had no idea what his dispute was about, only that he was barring my way. As I looked meekly in my briefcase for my pilot's licence, all my papers fell out onto the pavement. Fuming and embarrassed, I asked myself who the hell the guy thought he was.

Which was the problem; I asked myself, I didn't ask him. Frustrated by a situation I couldn't control, I felt like a coward for not standing up to him or at least asking him some pointed questions. As seen from a cockpit window, my comfortable view of life didn't allow for an industrial dispute in an Essex new town.

The second event was when Josh showed me the 'adverse' reference that Mike Woodgate had sent him about me. I didn't understand why Mike had sent it. I was a good pilot, and considered myself intelligent and sharp, always ready to please, a guy admired and liked by everyone. Or was I? Perhaps Woodgate had wanted to prevent me from leaving? Fortunately, Josh decided to ignore the reference, but again I was left feeling that the world outside of flying was a harsh and unforgiving place, far away from the fluffy clouds I had dreamt about as a boy.

Josh had 5,000 hours of general aviation flying experience but wasn't airline trained. Our aeroplane had seven seats, with five in the cabin, including an emergency toilet under one of them. There were no expensive and heavy fittings, making the plane go up like a fart in a bath. Josh showed me how he thought the Cessna should be flown and put me in for the CAA 1179 test, which would get it stamped on my dark green ATPL (Airline Transport Pilot's Licence,) which was better than his light blue CPL (Commercial Pilot's Licence.)

I took the test at Leavesden Airfield, starting in daylight and finishing with some night circuits, flying as Josh had taught me. The examiner prepared to fail me on the spot; wrong speeds, power, flap settings, pretty much everything - Mike Connor was not impressed.

'But that's what Josh told me to do,' I muttered feebly.

Then Mike showed me how the Cessna engineers had designed the aeroplane to fly. I was convinced he was flying on some invisible rails that were nailed to the sky. All the instrument needles seemed stuck to their dials as the beautifully synchronised engines rumbled in appreciation of a perfectly balanced machine.

Finally, I understood, Josh was a lousy pilot. I'd known instinctively that something was wrong with his technique but didn't have the guts to challenge him. Mike handed control back to me and quickly saw that British Airways hadn't spent thousands of pounds on training me for nothing. We both agreed that the Cessna was a superb aeroplane, and Mike passed me after all.

Josh would have first pick of the trips, so I would often end up on RAF bases as BOC were a supplier to the Ministry of Defence. The military efficiency was impressive, but they looked desolate, lonely places for the most part. It was only when I saw a Phantom thundering off into the sky with afterburners glowing that I felt any nostalgia for my RAF Cadet Warrant Officer's uniform. Turning my back on the Services for an airline career was probably the pivotal point in my life.

However, I was embarked on a career in civil flying, with scheduled half-past five Monday morning departures to Newcastle to pick up the BOC Medishield Managing Director. Occasionally I would get trips further afield, usually where speaking French would be an advantage. A three and a half hour flight to Nice was the highlight of my career as a professional pilot in command, taking John Corcoran with me as an unofficial co-pilot, in recognition of his friendship and kindness towards me since college.

I relished the early start, the sound of birdsong, the touch of cool, fresh air on my face, and the drive to Stansted on empty roads as the sun slowly eased into view to warm the earth and burn off the morning mist. With the build-up of light and energy, rabbits emerged to bounce away as I made the short walk to the aeroplane, stowing my bags in preparation for a new journey and chatting to John. While I'd been flying, he'd been a salmon fisherman in Canada before returning to fly for British Airways as a steward.

Even the effort of pulling two tons of metal out of the hangar failed to dampen my excitement at the anticipation of a perfect day at work. Once aboard the Cessna, I settled into the cold familiarity of the lifeless cockpit, flicking switches, turning knobs, and pushing levers with practised confidence until radios chattered and navigation equipment hummed before shattering the peace of the dawn by starting the twin engines. On the face of it, life was good.

After a month staying with Tony and Sue, Lynn and I found a house to rent in Old Harlow for what should have been the best time of our married life. We listened to *The Andrews Sisters* because they were upbeat and happy, and with Lynn on the pill and both of us young and fit, we had sex most days and nights. She seemed content being in the house reading magazines and cooking, but I was starting to feel unhappy, constantly anxious that I was doing the right thing. I was a Captain at the age of 24 with a hot twin to fly and an equally hot woman at home, yet I felt something was missing but didn't know what - perhaps it was a lack of friends.

I did sometimes wonder how anti-social I was, following my father's example. On flights where Lynn acted as stewardess, we had received invitations from BOC directors to visit them - once to South Africa - when my first reaction was to politely decline for fear of imposing, a trait I recognised in my father.

In contrast, as a friendly and emotionally intelligent person, Lynn was ready to meet anyone and go anywhere with me. If I'd appreciated her qualities instead of trying to change her into what I thought my mother wanted for me, life might have taken a different course. Lynn had a few worries about her lack of formal education but only wanted the best for us while collecting a little jewellery on the way.

Then the BOC management decided that maintaining a company aeroplane, even a small one like ours, couldn't be justified financially, so I was out of a job once more. At the same time, the owners of our house decided they wanted it back, so Lynn and I moved into a council flat. Before leaving BOC, I took Tony on a short flight from Luton to Stansted.

He had always wanted to be a pilot too, but because of his colour-blindness had embarked on a career in the Inland Revenue instead. He told me that our ten-minute trip was the best experience of his life, leaving me speechless and humbled. I was flying for a living while he spent his days in an office trying to squeeze money out of people who didn't want to pay.

I was taken on by Executive Express at Luton flying more Cessna twins, the pressurised 421 Golden Eagle and the 404 Titan workhorse. The new regime was about operations manuals, procedures, and frequently flights with two pilots. After four years of single-crew flying and the freedom of private flying with BOC, I had a feeling I wouldn't fit in with Executive Express's mentality, which didn't bode well for a career with British Airways. I was right, soon arguing with the Chief Pilot over what I considered were unsafe practices, such as reading checklists while taxying, and wrote a letter to the Senior Flight Operations Inspector of the CAA about the company.

By mutual consent, I left Executive Express a month later to freelance. At the same time, Lynn found work as a dental nurse, which helped us survive financially until I found the pilot's favourite method of birth control: night flying. I would set off from Harlow at half-past midnight to drive to Luton, where Air Continental was also based. In contrast, this smaller company treated me like an adult, hiring me on a self-employed basis to fly British newspapers from Luton to Geneva in Piper Navajos, the bigger brothers of the Aztec.

Working for myself suited me well, allowing me to set my own standards and be content in my work, but without anyone breathing down my neck. With my body telling me I should be in bed with Lynn, I entered the night world with its own eerie and claustrophobic peace.

Take-off from Luton's westerly runway was around 03.30, struggling fully-laden over the Vauxhall factory under the cloak of darkness. On fine nights, the ground would sparkle with a thousand orange lights making a vain attempt to compete with the canopy of stars. Up at cruising altitude, I would turn the cockpit lights down to enjoy the starlit sky away from the light pollution near the ground.

The bucket and spade charters would twinkle their way southward, their jet aircraft climbing to more than three times my altitude. Over France, I would chat to the French controllers in their language, exchanging a joke and picking up more of their jargon to use on the next flight. After making sure that the engines were behaving themselves, which they always did, I would watch the sunrise and look out for the Alps.

When the weather was clear, I'd cross the Jura Mountains and turn right over Lake Geneva, then fly on down to the familiar white numbers marking out Runway 23. I had to land in Geneva at 06.00 on the dot - too early, and the airport wasn't open, too late, and the papers would miss their train connection. It was a matter of pride to calculate the optimum altitude, groundspeed, and route so that the aircraft's tyres would kiss the Cointrin Airport tarmac as the second hand of the aircraft clock was sweeping past the hour.

Even bad weather brought its rewards; watching the needles on the navigation displays line up, then following them down to cloud break, and seeing the runway appear out of nowhere. Early mornings coupled with mist usually meant calm conditions, so there was no excuse for not greasing a landing for the benefit of the handling staff waiting to unload my cargo and get me out of their way before the big aeroplanes arrived.

Delayed on one occasion leaving Luton because the newspapers were delivered late, I climbed to 19,000 feet to catch the forecast 150-knot winds instead of the usual 80-knot winds at 10,000 feet. Wearing an oxygen mask in the unpressurised cabin made me feel like a Battle of Britain pilot again until the heater failed. With an outside air temperature of minus 30 degrees Centigrade, the instruments had frozen up, leaving ice on the inside of the glass.

My teeth chattered, and I sat on my hands, thinking I wouldn't be able to fly the approach and landing because of the cold in my fingers. I could only sit on one hand at a time because the autopilot didn't like working at high altitude, which also meant I couldn't go back and fetch my jacket. I then discovered that the winds weren't as strong as predicted, so I was late for the first time and had nothing to show for my efforts except balls like sultanas.

The sector back to Luton was longer due to the prevailing headwinds, and once I'd eaten my breakfast sandwiches and tried to read one of the newspapers I'd kept back, there wasn't much to do. My priority was to get home and go to bed. Flying into the sun was uncomfortable, and watching for climbing and descending aircraft, with constant chatter in French and English, was tedious. I was on my fifth trip of the week, and I'd been cleared 40 minutes direct to the Abbeville beacon when I heard the urgent call from the French sector controller:

'Golf Tango Alpha X-Ray Yankee, this is France Control, do you read? You are ten miles North of Abbeville, turn left heading two seven zero.'

It eventually got through to my porridge-like brain that I'd overshot the Abbeville beacon, which was bad but had enjoyed ten minutes refreshing sleep, which was good. It was an eye-opener, literally, and I didn't do it again, but at least I could say that I could do that route in my sleep and mean it.

Tired after another night flight, I collided with a deer on the drive home just after daybreak. I'd never hit anything of that size before and never killed anything bigger than a spider, so it was a shock. Why did the bloody thing have to choose that moment to leave the safety of its forest, walk out into the road and get hit by my hard, unforgiving front bumper? Yet again, I didn't know what to do, as the problem wasn't about flying. I wanted to walk away but didn't want to leave a twitching body lying in the middle of the A414.

Flustered, I paced up and down, trying not to look at the beautiful creature in distress and feeling like a complete waste of space. Eventually, a lorry stopped, the driver got out and took the animal away while I slunk off like a wounded hyena, ashamed to call myself a pilot, supposedly decisive and positive. I felt guilty about the whole episode for weeks, another reminder that life wasn't all happiness and joy.

Brought up by perfectionist parents, my view of life was that it was supposed to be blue skies, warm sunshine, and sparkling seas, with fit, happy, smiling people all around. The practicalities of daily existence were expected to slot into place, while professionals all did their jobs faultlessly.

There would be those who grew food, swept the streets and begged for money, but they too had their places in a perfect world. I would fly for a living, and a woman would take care of the house, my body, and our children. Good things would happen as a matter of course. Then the call-up letter from British Airways arrived.

8

Airline Pilot

The classrooms of the Heston Training Centre were far removed from the tropical palms of the recruitment posters but being able to hear and see big planes roaring overhead every few minutes and imagining flying one was compensation enough.

Signing my pilot's contract, I turned down the opportunity to take out loss of licence insurance, which would have given me about £60,000 if I had to stop flying for medical reasons. Young, fit, and indestructible at 25, I considered it a waste of money. Lynn and I moved in temporarily with John Corcoran, who was on the same training course and lived on his own near Maidenhead.

Ground school was going to be a comedown after four and a half years flying, but I didn't think learning about a 1946-designed propeller aircraft was going to be too difficult. I'd be a co-pilot on the Viscount, a British Airways airliner, yet with more hours in command than some of the captains, I would be flying with. There'd be a team of cabin crew at the back to look after the passengers, and the only decision I'd have to make other than those about flying the aircraft would be which meal to choose.

My first training captain soon put me in my place. A calm, youthful 40-year-old, Geoff Mussett was not only a good pilot, but he knew how to teach and how to handle hotshots like me who thought they knew it all. Instead of giving me a hard time and making me resentful, he quietly allowed me to make mistakes, then patiently showed me how to fly according to British Airways procedures. Then I could be plugged into the seat next to any captain, and we'd both know what to do, especially if anything went wrong.

The Viscount was a touring aircraft that meant five days away flying to exotic destinations such as Aberdeen, Sumburgh, Kirkwall, Glasgow, and Stornoway. Having walked across their rain-lashed aprons many times, I felt for the British Airways engineers getting wet and cold during refuelling. Then, as we cruised, a friendly stewardess served lunch, and I decided airline flying wasn't so bad after all.

Until my captain asked me for the Kirkwall weather, which I'd just missed from the Volmet continuous weather broadcast and would have to wait for it to play through again. He kept on at me about it, which was annoying not just because my chicken meal was getting cold but because we were flying over Kirkwall at the time, with excellent visibility all around. To his credit, the captain apologised, and mutual respect was established.

With my moi tout seul philosophy and having flown mainly single-crew, it took me some time to understand the teamwork and increased responsibility involved in operating large aircraft. I would want to get home safely in an emergency, whether I was in a Viscount or a Navajo, regardless of how many passengers were on board. However, that didn't take into account the myriad facets and frailties of human nature I was unaware of and ill-equipped to deal with.

I began to learn that being an airline captain required advanced people management skills, even from those with unusual personal habits, such as the one who would sing Elvis Presley songs for the whole flight and, on arrival, rush off to change into women's clothes before wandering into town.

Lynn seemed to view that as an airline pilot, I had an unlimited supply of money, so in between revising for my exams, we were soon chasing all over South-East England trying to get a mortgage on a terraced property in Reading. Taking her with me for support, I went to see my Flight Crew

Manager for permission to do more newspaper runs in the Navajo. He was surprised that a pilot had brought his wife with him for such a request but ultimately agreed, reminding me that if I tried to land the Viscount thinking I was in the Navajo, I would be making holes in the runway 20 feet deep.

Meanwhile, life, and death, continued. Wanting to connect with the English side of my family, I had previously taken Lynn to visit my Granny and Grandpa, where they lived in the same house they always had. Granny hadn't been well, and I had this brilliant idea to take her up in a light aircraft from the Shropshire Aero Club.

I could see the newspaper headline: *Grandmother takes first flight with grandson at the controls*. Typically, I dithered about the details, so it never happened. Now Granny had died without ever flying in an aeroplane, making me more aware of my shortcomings in behaving and floundering on, wishing that I had someone to talk to.

With no experience of talking about my feelings, I couldn't effectively confide in Lynn, and my relationship with her suffered. She looked to me for leadership, yet I questioned everything she did and must have come across to her as intense and intimidating. I found it hard to refuse her demands for what I considered non-essential items and was envious of the close relationship she had with her family, even though her only contact was a weekly telephone call.

In our new home, there were carpets to fit, furniture to be delivered, a boiler to be serviced, as well as a simulator check to complete and a day trip to Le Touquet in Air Continental's Navajo to fly. Feeling out of my depth with domestic responsibility and the pressure of my job, I was losing confidence in myself.

Yet nobody else knew, including on my type conversion course to the Trident. After ten months on the Viscount and having passed the technical exam and the simulator, British Airways sent me to Prestwick for base training on the three-engine jet. While it was said disparagingly that the Trident only got airborne because of the curvature of the earth, feeling the power of 60,000lbs of pure thrust behind me on a lightly loaded aeroplane was exhilarating. The Tridents were crewed by three pilots rather than two pilots and a flight engineer to comply with the demands of automatic landings. The third pilot (P3) looked after the systems panel, a role I was not looking forward to with 2,500 hours in command as a P1.

It was at Prestwick while waiting for some of Woodgate's passengers that I had heard the mother of a young lad say: 'He's a pilot,' before sending him over to ask for my autograph. Feeling proud, I had chatted to them about my job, reminding myself how in awe I was when I saw my first pilot up close.

Wearing my Ray-Bans and a calm and confident expression, I had pointed to the aeroplane parked outside, telling the boy: 'That's my plane.' I had loved being in charge of the little Aztec, wondering then in the back of my mind how I would feel as a British Airways co-pilot. Now I was finding out; the world of the airlines was a big, overpowering place, however well paid.

Line training with real passengers in the cabin on scheduled flights was the final stage of becoming a fully qualified airline co-pilot, a distraction too from my growing uncertainty about my relationship with Lynn. Both were unaccountably unfulfilling.

Flying into Barcelona, I made the smoothest landing I ever did on any aircraft, and the only comment the training captain made was: 'Don't call me Bert; it's Captain Bertram to you.' I didn't like him or his type, miserable and complaining about everything instead of appreciating the privilege we had of flying.

John Longley was the opposite, always up for a joke and not taking life too seriously. As I prepared my first cabin address in French, he waited patiently until I pressed the switch to deliver it, then placed a pair of wind-up chattering plastic teeth on the radio console. He and the P3 found it funny, but I thought it was silly and childish - I had started to lose my sense of humour.

Who better to turn to than the happy-clapping, singing, and smiling faces of the Airline Aviation Aerospace Christian Fellowship at Heathrow (the AAACF), where planes and the Lord met in a chapel under the control tower? There, airport staff disillusioned with hedonism knew they could find someone they could look up to: God.

Stewardesses fed up with leering males could meet good, wholesome Christian men living according to scripture and from whom they could take spiritual leadership, while the men could find partners who were more interested in charity work than room parties.

For me, I thought joining the AAACF would restore my authority and belief in something, possibly even in myself. I wanted to be in a family environment where I felt looked after, something that had been missing from my life. I spent some leave with the group in Brighton and took up Bible study.

Meanwhile, after Lynn and I had celebrated our third wedding anniversary and her twentieth birthday, she started looking for jobs and had her engagement ring valued. If that was a signal that she was becoming dissatisfied with her life, I missed it completely.

As a member of the AAACF, I went to meetings, sang songs, got baptised and generally behaved like a man on drugs, except without the drugs. Leaving Lynn at home, I attended 'love feasts,' which sounded like orgies but were all about giving food and possessions to the needy. I read heart-warming books like *The Cross and the Switchblade* and thought I'd found the answer to everything.

Lynn couldn't understand it but still loved me enough to get baptised and be 'saved.' I was hardly sleeping, often putting the radio on in the middle of the night to see if there was a sign from God that momentous events were happening in the world.

I thought Lynn and I were on the verge of a new, fulfilling future and pushed towards this to the limits of my willpower. Avid readings of the Bible were providing clear answers to my questions about how to behave, and I had found someone I could count on to satisfy my emotional needs: The Lord.

Having wedged His foot firmly in the door of the caravan on Newtownards Airfield, I believed He was always going to be with me. He would tell me what was right, what to do, even tell me what to think. If God was with me and I was with God, everything would be perfect. I wrote notes to myself as if I'd found the Holy Grail: *The only way to see God at work is to BUTT OUT of His operation!*

Garnering my heartfelt thoughts about life, the world and human nature, I wrote what I thought was a clever parable about the Bible for the British Airline Pilots Association's magazine, called *A Christmas Story*. Writing as 'Anonpilot,' it was meant to show my diversity, humility, and love for the human race. I wanted to solve all the problems in the world through God, Jesus and me, or any combination thereof.

The pilot in the story was meant to be the perfect man, showing believers *The Way*, the kind of man my mother would have approved of, and therefore who I wanted to be. When I tried to talk to other pilots about this, their eyes glazed over - the story was never published.

However, I persevered, sure that my life was about to change. How right I was, but not in the way I expected. During this time, I passed my annual CAA Class 1 medical examination; it seemed no one had an inkling of what was about to happen, least of all me. But that didn't stop me. Rather than trying to convert the non-believers in the British

Airways Flight Crew lounge, I decided to go to my pastor to get his support.

I put on my old captain's jacket and went around to Neil's house, where I donned my headset and explained how I would plug into the Lord's communication system to get my instructions. Neil said something like 'you need help,' which I thought was a decent offer on his part and prepared myself for the day when I would start the Perfect Pilot's job. God would be at the controls in the left-hand seat, and I would be His co-pilot.

My day job as an airline pilot was purely practising for the real work of showing others *The Way*. Someone had to do it. Who better to point others in the right direction for life than a pilot? It was an honour to have been chosen by God; all I had to do was stay modest and humble. According to the CAA medical examiners, I had a perfect body and was one of only a tiny proportion of people in the world with the skill and ability to fly towards heaven.

I had witnessed to others about the Lord with my Christmas story, with rejection a test of my faith and commitment. God had destined me for better than being an airline pilot anyway - I would be serving His purpose, as in 'the Services,' particularly the Air Force, confirmed as I watched an F-15 Eagle jet fighter line up ahead of us from the right-hand co-pilot's seat of a Trident cockpit on a flight home from Frankfurt.

Looking down at the little grey plane, I knew I wasn't meant to be a man's co-pilot, only God's. As the Eagle pilot slowly moved his aircraft into position and lit his afterburners, I was him, as I had been the pilot in the cockpit of the Phantom model I had made as a boy. Accelerating down the runway centreline, the F-15 jinked up, then rotated through 90 degrees to the vertical, so I could see the plan view as it climbed vertically through the cloud layer.

Staring in awe at gravity being defied so comprehensively, I was its pilot bursting through the grey into a sunlit bowl of blue sky, leaving pristine white cloud below. 'Those who hope in the Lord will renew their strength. They will soar on wings like eagles; they will run and not grow weary; they will walk and not be faint.' (Isaiah 40:31)

It was my leg (sector), so I was handling pilot (P2) for the take-off. Airborne, I followed the departure routing and climbed through the cloud, briefly glancing around in a vain attempt to see the F-15. No chance. I levelled off at 30,000 feet and engaged the autopilot, with the 400 knots wind rush noise steady in my head.

The little windows of daylight cast sharp shadows across the instrument panel as bright sunlight dazzled my eyes. I put on my sunglasses and surveyed the scene. All was peaceful. The captain watched the systems panel as the P3 ate his meal. I was holding a track between Cologne and Brussels. The instrument needles were oscillating gently about their datum points, the captain's cursory glance signalling his approval.

I looked out of the window. From 200, 2,000 or 20,000 feet, the world looked wonderful. Green and peaceful, a few houses here, a meandering river there, and above: a burning sun in an azure sky of cloudless cover; a fragile atmosphere yet supporting 100 tons of shining metal hanging aloft in floating magic.

'Who are these that fly along like clouds, like doves to their nests?' (Isaiah 60:8) I was 'in the moment,' almost in a trance, quiet and content until a mechanical noise materialised inside my headphones. It was human, but without body, seemingly out of nowhere.

'Speedbird 911 Frankfurt, maintain flight level three five zero, squawk 4563, and call Brussels on 135.25, Guten Tag.'

Immediately I pushed the transmit button and repeated back the message. Then I was aware of another noise, human again but much closer. It was odd because although only feet away and clearly coming from the man with four bars on his epaulettes, there was no reference to power, EGTs, track, wind, radio, or autopilot.

He was talking about a crew hotel, a duty manager, and a complaint about the size of a bed. It didn't make sense. Here we were cruising at close to the speed of sound with the earth moving away beneath us in a patchwork of art, and all this man could talk about were some mundane details of his sad little life.

I was irritated. Flight was about escape from reality. The aeroplane was God's tool to make better communion between Him and his children. I was like a child, one with God's gift of making the aeroplane fly, free of the veneer of sophistication that some pilots liked to flaunt.

Like this captain. There were too many pilots like him, who spent too much time talking about their trips, their allowances, the cabin crew, and their drinking habits so that they didn't have enough energy left with which to marvel at the beauty of God's world.

I understood why some pilots liked three crew aeroplanes. It meant less flying and more opportunity for chat. For them, the job was all about socialising and partying. For me, it was about freedom, escape, and peace.

Time to leave those things; down, away from God. Calculations: distances, rates of descent, minimum safe altitudes - not as romantic as the majesty of the skies, but part of the inevitable tedium of returning to earth.

I preferred to be up in the light, not down in the dark. I didn't desire just a job, a paycheck and a drive home from the airport. I wanted to stay up in the air with God as His Perfect Pilot.

9

Breakdown

On the sunny Sunday morning of 15 February 1981, just before 11 a.m., I drove my car at high speed to Neil's church, stopping inches from taking out the wall. A week after I'd passed my six-monthly competency check in the catacomb of the Trident simulator, I was ready to start my new job of being the Perfect Pilot. My mission: to help believers find their true path and herald the rapture of spirits skywards. Hallelujah!

Beaming in my old captain's uniform, I marched into the middle of the morning service feeling pleased with myself. Surprisingly, those present looked more concerned than pleased, which I thought was rather mean-spirited towards someone going to show them *The Way*.

As I advanced down the aisle, I saw a bear-like hand land on my shoulder, belonging to a member of the congregation who I knew to be a policeman. Off duty, but clearly concerned about my erratic behaviour, his six-feet-eight frame told me I wasn't going to heaven or anywhere else without his say-so.

Meanwhile, someone had called the on-duty police, who quickly arrived and put me into their patrol car. Minutes later, they were driving me around the roundabout at Junction 13 of the M4 to see if I knew where I was. Disorientated by the blur of motorway traffic, I must have failed this test because I ended up handcuffed in Reading Police Station.

Stumbling in with my burly escorts, I felt weak and was finding standing up difficult. A crimson veil of blood was forming inside my eyes as I imagined my brain collapsing and that I might be dying. What was supposed to be the start of a fulfilling new life with the Lord wasn't working out, and a red mist was enveloping me - I believed it was the scarlet cloak of the Devil. Frightened, I tried to fight it but was too tired, exhausted from six months of extreme mental activity. The police guided me to a room with a table, which I climbed onto and curled up on, grateful for somewhere to rest.

Soon after, they put me in a cell with bare walls, a hard bed, and a lattice-patterned skylight of thick glass. I didn't understand – I hadn't done anything wrong; in fact, I had planned to do so much right. Having examined the lock and dismissed the possibility of forcing open the door, I repeatedly called the officers to let me out, but they ignored me.

Anxious and helpless, I paced in circles, realising that the only way out was via the bell and the cooperation of the police officers. Using the remnants of my willpower, I shouted and yelled at them louder still, feeling trapped and alone.

So, I hit the door. It was a full-blown, straight-on punch with all my weight behind it onto a solid, metal-jacketed surface that would have needed a canon shell to penetrate it. I only did it once because, within seconds, my hand had become useless. The third and fourth knuckles of my right hand - my best hand - were forced back towards my wrist so that the bones compressed together.

The hand began to swell like a balloon. It hurt, a shouting, growing, throbbing pain telling me it was only going to get worse. Awareness was growing within me that things were not going well. God had not made me the Messiah and didn't seem to be showing much interest in me.

An officer called Don White was called away from his Sunday lunch who I gathered had dealt with types like me before. He interviewed me sympathetically and efficiently but was probably missing his roast. He couldn't have met too many airline pilots who had gone off the rails, but it was down to him to decide whether I was up for any criminal charges or whether to call the duty doctor. He chose to call the doctor, who didn't look too pleased with having his Sunday disturbed either when he arrived.

Saying nothing, the doctor looked me up and down, then at my pilot's licence, which I had pulled out of my jacket as ID. I worried about the implications of this and did some fast talking to explain what had happened as if trying to demolish the side of a church was normal behaviour. The doc wasn't impressed, and the sinking feeling in my heart told me things were getting serious. Desperately I tried to tell him that I was fine, but I was constantly afraid that he would report me to the CAA. Reaching inside his battered leather bag, he gave me a tranquilising injection before sending me to Reading Hospital to have my hand checked.

Part of me refused to believe what was happening, while the other part said I was crossing the line into a dark place from which there was no return. The physical effects of the tranquiliser were unpleasant, giving me the feeling of wanting to go somewhere but being unable to. Where I *was* going was Wallingford Psychiatric Hospital, a giant, redbrick NHS prison that would be my home for the foreseeable future. In the back of the ambulance, I asked why wasn't God sorting this out? Where was Lynn? What was I doing there?

I had been booked to start a course to learn about flying the Trident 3 the next day. The image of being in the classroom with other pilots was turning into the reality of a journey in an ambulance filled with medical equipment. As this registered on my weakened mind, I started crying, asking why me? Was it a test that I had to go through for something even better at the end of it? Who could I blame? My parents? Lynn? It didn't do any good - it was all my fault, and I would suffer the consequences. I was in a living nightmare, knowing that I could never wake up from it.

To go from working on the flight deck of a 700-mph jet to an isolation room in a secure hospital in the space of a few days was unusual. To my knowledge, no one from the outside world had seen my breakdown coming, so few people knew about me. My parents weren't too happy, and neither was Lynn; her move from Northern Ireland wasn't turning out as expected. Therefore I didn't get many other visitors, but one who surprised me and made a difference was Peter Edmunds, the BAA (British Airports Authority) Senior Airport Duty Manager.

On shift, Peter was responsible for Heathrow's entire airport operations and had more stripes and stars on his uniform than a Japanese admiral. An ex-pilot in the Fleet Air Arm, then a Traffic Officer for British Airways in Rome, he had a healthy disregard for paper-pushers and commanded respect wherever he went. The fact that he turned up to see me was a major morale booster as he had no interest in doing so other than showing he cared. Otherwise, I was on my own.

Feeling sick because of the drugs and in between psychological tests, I shuffled around the locked ward in a state of numb desolation. To pass the time, I would occasionally play table tennis with one of the nurses, a sport I thought I was good at. Dark-skinned, he had some distinctive raised markings around his eyes, making me think he might be the Devil incarnate in my vulnerable state of mind. His appearance unsettled me, and he also beat me at table tennis.

After three and a half months in Wallingford, someone realised that I was covered for private health insurance under the terms of my pilot's contract with British Airways. In conjunction with Peter Edmunds and John Eagles (a pilot from the AAACF), Lynn arranged with Human Resources to have me transferred to the £1,000-a-week private St Andrews Hospital in Northampton.

There I was given an individual room with a colour TV, with squash courts, a gym, and a swimming pool within walking distance. After exercise, a choice of high-quality food was provided, with fresh flowers on the dinner table where I listened to the gossip about the rich and famous coming in for detox and therapy. It was another planet compared to Wallingford.

Dr Keith Comish was my consultant. A short, friendly-looking man, he had a habit of widening his eyes from time to time for no apparent reason. Putting his feet on his desk during consultations, he never lectured me, psychoanalysed me, or gave me any sort of psychospeak, and refused to put a label on me.

He saw my condition as a chemical imbalance and spent most of the time he allocated to me getting me stable on the right combination of drugs, in my case, lithium carbonate and carbamazepine. The lithium was to regulate my moods and reduce the chances of a relapse, but I didn't understand why I had to take the carbamazepine. I had to trust Dr Comish, take the pills, and follow the program.

This included as much strenuous exercise as I could manage, making wicker baskets in Occupational Therapy, and having monthly blood tests to check my serum levels. Swimming 50 lengths three or four times a week and playing squash with the sports coach took my attention away from the grim reality of my situation.

It also cleared my head to the point where I fell asleep in the relaxation classes while giving me some self-esteem about my increasingly fit body. Sitting around the hospital talking to the other patients, I felt they were all in a far worse state than I was. Some of them told me I had the face to become a film star.

More worryingly, I started hearing talk amongst the nurses about giving me ECT (Electro-Convulsive Therapy) where electrodes would be attached to my head. An electric current would then be passed through my brain to sort out my synapses, hopefully without turning me into a vegetable. I didn't like the sound of it at all, and thankfully Lynn refused to give her permission for this under any circumstances, which was probably the best thing she ever did for me.

She did visit me, which I appreciated, even though we both knew things would never be the same. She'd been giving some thought to her future, probably without me as a husband. It wasn't a great surprise when Dr Comish received a letter from her solicitors about divorce proceedings, but it was another devastating blow to my morale. The hospital staff were sympathetic, but I felt rejected and unloved. If I didn't have Lynn, who was going to support me?

My parents voiced their concerns but didn't know what to do. God had turned out to be a massive disappointment. With an almost constant anxiety gnawing at my stomach that I would never fly aeroplanes again, I felt I'd lost everything, including my job. This gave me the additional worry about what I would do when I was no longer a British Airways employee, and therefore not entitled to private health insurance. To avoid going back to an NHS Hospital, I would have to sort myself out.

Three things helped me to get well enough to leave St Andrews: medication, exercise, and looking at the golf course from a window. Every weekend, local golfers would turn up in their smart cars and comfortable clothes to play their nine holes. So easy, so relaxed, and so normal; I envied them. Why couldn't I be like them?

Well, I could - if I did normal things, got a normal job, and thought normal thoughts. Brought up being different, I craved acceptance by other men. I wanted to be a regular guy, the kind respected and liked by other men just for being a decent bloke. Being looked up to for being a pilot was looking increasingly unlikely. Dr Comish would be talking to the CAA consultant about my case, who would ultimately decide to reinstate my pilot's licence or not. It didn't look good.

However, Dr Comish did approve my driving licence with the DVLA, which was a significant boost to my confidence. At the same time, I wrote to the British Airways

Executive Aircraft Service (EAS) for a job, the private aircraft handling service that I had used when I was an air-taxi pilot. After six weeks at St Andrew's, I was discharged.

Lynn was still living in our house but was in the process of divorcing me. We were civilised about our break-up, and she went back to her parents in Ireland as often as she could using my airline concessions, until one day she never returned. I considered emigrating but had nowhere to go. Instead, there were meetings with the Citizen's Advice Bureau, my new solicitor Mr Darbyshire, and my parents - after they had returned from a month's holiday in St Lunaire, presumably to keep their sanity.

As far as I knew, they didn't understand anything about mental health issues or at least didn't talk about them. I didn't feel much empathy from them, just the slight feeling in the back of my mind that they thought it brought shame on the family and reflected poorly on them. So, when they told me that my brother John had been admitted to hospital with more or less the same diagnosis as mine, I wondered what kind of a family I was a part of. Certainly, it was artistic; my father a musician, my godmother Denise a painter, and John, a dancer.

Then I was asked to make an appointment at the Harley Street office of Air Vice-Marshal Dr Patrick O'Connor, consultant in neurology and psychiatry, to the CAA and British Airways. As I trudged the streets of London, I hung on to the tiniest glimmer of hope that Dr Comish had convinced him that I had recovered. I knew what had happened looked bad, yet still held out hope that the telephone call between the two doctors would produce a miracle.

Instead, they had agreed on a diagnosis of hypomania, a milder form of mania - it was the best they could do. I asked myself how and why my life's ambition had been destroyed. From A1 fit School House Captain to an RAF Flying Scholarship and selection for airline pilot training, I had everything going for me.

All those memories of flying to and from White Waltham, Liverpool, Newtownards, the Isle of Man, Stansted, and Heathrow were reduced to entries in my logbooks. All for nothing, pointless and irrelevant. A captain on Piper and Cessna twins, a co-pilot with one of the world's leading airlines about to become unemployed and possibly unemployable.

As I sat in front of Dr O'Connor, I could feel my fire and ambition being extinguished. He confirmed that my condition meant a permanent bar to holding a commercial pilot's licence. I had expected it, but it still hurt. Feeling battered emotionally and alone, I set off for home.

Instead of checking in as a working pilot, my next visit to Heathrow was to hand in my headset, pilot's uniform, ID card and flying manuals. Then I wrote to anyone I could think of for a job, initially freight and shipping agents at the airport. That was when I realised that telling the truth about my medical history would cause me problems getting decent employment.

Against all my principles, I considered lying but dismissed the idea, knowing I would get found out. I gave up on God helping me out, given that He'd fucked everything else up for me, and instead decided to rely on my excellent eyesight and hand-eye coordination and two years of pilot training to get work - as a window cleaner.

Having bought a ladder, I knocked on doors offering my services, hoping I would meet a rich widow wanting other services too. Instead of being kept warm, I got cold and wet before being approached by a whistling, geezer-type man with the swaggering gait of an Ulster piper, who explained to me the facts of life about window cleaning rounds in the area and how I was on his patch.

Demoralised, I thought all my problems would be solved by doing the Reader's Digest Prize Draw and by moving to Valerie's spare room in Burnham. Valerie was a

British Airways stewardess dating an oil company engineer who was away most of the time. She would talk to me about her relationship and told me I had depth that surprised and pleased me, although it was probably more to do with the fact that I never made a pass at her.

The truth was that I was trying to find a new identity for myself as a non-pilot, starting from nowhere. Household bills were piling up, and Christmas was looming - which I was dreading as pretending to be jolly wasn't in my plans - so I rang Lynn in Newtownards to plead poverty and asked that she cover some of them. She refused, so Mr Darbyshire told me to sell everything.

Given that I wouldn't have to lie about my medical condition within British Airways, I applied for internal jobs: Air Safety Investigator, Flight Crew Administrator, Assistant Manager Training Standards, Cabin Crew Superintendent, Terminal Coordinator. Without the skills for dealing with myself, let alone others, I didn't have a chance.

Desperate to avoid being unemployed and alone with my thoughts, I filled out forms to join other airlines as cabin crew, dispatcher, operations planning officer, and even pilot, hoping that I wouldn't have to complete a medical questionnaire. The lithium was doing its job in keeping my emotions in check, but if I admitted taking it, I would have to face people to explain why I had stopped flying and expose myself as weak and vulnerable. I was running out of options.

Then British Airways offered me some temporary work in the windowless Flight Crew Briefing Centre in the Queen's Building at Heathrow, handing out weather and briefing information to departing flight crew. The job was likely to have been the one I had turned my nose up at while working for Woodgate's in the Isle of Man.

There were staff who worked there full-time, men and women with families, and I found a few microseconds to think about their lives instead of my own for a change. It was winter, and I'd arrive before it got light and leave after it got dark, but I was grateful for the work.

After a few weeks, the news came through that I'd got the job with EAS. I was pleased that I'd been given a lifeline, yet apprehensive that something would go wrong, and it would be taken away from me, as everything else had been.

Until British Airways confirmed my contract as a Station Officer in Ground Operations London, which came with staff travel and a uniform. After freefalling from the manic heights of the 'Perfect Pilot,' I had finally landed on my feet – broken, but with a parachute – as permanent ground staff.

10

Grounded

When I flew the kidney from Belfast to Heathrow in Woodgate's Aztec six years earlier, the man who had met me was David Oldfield. A 40-year-old total aviation enthusiast, he had been ready to provide me with all the services I needed at Heathrow at two in the morning, as well as a friendly chat. It was to David I had written to for a job when I was in St Andrews Hospital.

Now he and I would be colleagues as Executive Aircraft Service (EAS) Officers for British Airways, providing handling services for non-scheduled aircraft, from Aztecs to The Sultan of Brunei's private 747 airliner. It was supposed to be one of the best ground jobs at the airport, exciting and varied with lots of people contact. 'Ground' wasn't my favourite word, but I was going to have to get used to it.

Dr Comish must have said the right thing to British Airways for them to allow me to work with passengers and near aeroplanes at the world's biggest international airport. Taking my pills was part of the arrangement under the supervision of the British Airways Medical Centre. They would monitor my lithium levels through regular blood tests to make sure I didn't go off the rails again.

My new uniform had the four thin rings of a Station Officer. Even hotel porters' uniforms had thicker rings, like those on my captain's uniform, the four gold ones I had worn with pride. Lynn had liked me being a pilot and would slip her fingers under the epaulettes in my shirt before sending me off to work. Wearing a pilot's uniform had defined me; it had told the world I was fit, competent, and to be admired. Now I was ground staff, which was one level up from a holiday camp rep as far as I was concerned.

To drive airside on the airport roads beyond the security gates, I had to pass a driving test which I approached as if it was a simulator detail, even if it was in a Ford Transit van with an examiner who looked slightly embarrassed at having to check out a trained pilot. Another test in speaking French earned me an extra £100 a month on top of my ground staff pay.

At least I had some money coming in to supplement an ill-health pension of £26 a month, my last remaining connection with flight crew admin. There was one more test where I could demonstrate my skills: the jetty test, driving a passenger airbridge away from the terminal and stopping the wheels in a rectangular box. I passed.

When I entered the EAS office on my first day, I felt that everything I knew about aviation was sucked out of me. For me, flying was about being above the clouds, not being in a cramped and grimy office under a walkway off Terminal 2 at Heathrow. Half-opened Venetian blinds and dozens of aviation-related stickers squandered most of the daylight, with calendars, delicatessen menus and aircraft photos making a valiant attempt to brighten up the dirty cream walls.

Noise insulation provided reasonable respite from the din of the ramp, giving way to the mechanical clatter of two telex machines competing with three telephones, pilots speaking on the VHF radio, and EAS officers talking into walkie-talkies discussing shift times, flight plans, and meeting points.

A toy parrot bounced from the ceiling on a spring, a pair of uniform epaulettes arranged on its wings to look like captain's stripes. A few feet along, a life-sized plastic arm was hanging down between two ceiling tiles, as if there was a body in the roof space. Boxes of aircraft spare parts lay on the floor, next to old armchairs where visiting crew might sit to observe the atmosphere of organised chaos around them.

In the form of an altimeter, the office clock sat above the flight movements board, a whiteboard that dominated one wall. Details of aircraft, parking stands, ETAs and ETDs were written in a combination of neat print and scribbled alterations in black, blue, and red marker pens, telling the story of the shift in progress. My kidney flight would have been on that board.

The room would be my home as an EAS Officer, with a designated radio callsign of X-Ray 10, the X standing for Executive. The other X-Rays were a group of experienced ground staff who made me feel accepted, respected, inadequate and pitied in more or less equal measures. One said I had the management ethic, which I wasn't sure was a compliment or an insult. I had the feeling that while they were all generally sympathetic to my situation, they expected me to do the job professionally, like everyone else.

Part of me thought I was superior to the others because I had been a pilot. That didn't last long, particularly when referred to by other ground staff as a 'Nigel' - their slang for a pilot - which meant a bit of a knob without much savvy about the real world. The other part of me wanted to fit in, to be part of the banter.

Tony Hamilton-Hunt, X-ray 5, was allocated to train me. Ex public school, 15 of his 20 years in the airline, had been handling private aircraft and their crews, so he wasn't impressed by my flying experience. If a crew member or passenger needed a service, he would find a way to get it, even if it meant breaking rules, especially if told it was not possible, preferably by a manager.

With a background in following procedures and flight manuals, I had to adjust to Tony's way - there no compromise. After the regulated environment of flight operations, it all seemed like anarchy.

Tony didn't just teach me how to switch on a Ground Power Unit and transfer VIPs onto Concorde; he showed me that getting a job done was more about *how* I talked to people rather than what I said to them. One difference between us was that Tony spoke to everyone the same way, while I felt I had to talk to air traffic controllers in a more upmarket way than to baggage loaders, a symptom of my wanting to fit in and belong.

His training programme included showing me how to switch off the ignition in our minibus and restart it with his foot flat down, creating a massive bang that would almost blow the exhaust off. The tunnels were favourite for this activity as there was a better echo. I didn't understand how this improved customer service and met these performances with stony silence.

As a pilot, chocks, steps, ground power units, passenger and crew transport, fuel, toilet wagons, catering, and tractors simply arrived when I asked for them. Now I was in a place where I would have to source them, with the pressure to meet departure times while accommodating the peaks and troughs of irregular demand. I had to build relationships with personnel from other airlines, chauffer-drive, fuel, cleaning, and catering companies, and the BAA.

I learnt which catering managers would bring round the best trays of free sandwiches, which ODMs (Operations Duty Managers) to be overly polite to when requesting slot times, and which marshallers would shop me if I went over the wrong white line.

Some of the clients were billionaires, so I also learnt which customer reps would give the biggest 'thank yous.' These took the form of a few banknotes discretely transferred with a deft handshake or in a plain envelope. As British Airways employees, EAS staff weren't supposed to accept tips from passengers, and I wrestled with the moral dilemma of doing so until I was told that there was a team code that needed to be followed. There was also the likelihood of offending people from certain cultures who liked to express their appreciation of good service tangibly.

A highly efficient self-management system within the Section had evolved to provide the best service to the most generous clients, resulting in a little extra cash finding its way into our pockets from time to time. At Christmas, bottles of wine, hampers, and cakes arrived too, and I was given the responsibility of fairly distributing the loot, feeling trusted and useful for a change.

The variety of types of individuals I met opened my eyes to a world I never knew existed, except in newspaper articles. They were some of the most influential people on the planet: royalty, politicians, spies, industry leaders, sports champions, pop stars and arms dealers, who I would shake hands with on a daily basis, arriving and departing with their bodyguards on aircraft types from military helicopters, executive jets, to custom-built airliners.

Part of Tony's training was to show me how to interact with the clients without allowing myself to be treated like a doormat. In return, some of them would speak to me as a trusted confidante, occasionally revealing secrets of international events and of a personal nature the press would have paid well for. By respecting the cultural differences I observed across nationalities, I learnt to tactfully adjust my responses to avoid giving offence while taking the opportunity to interact with interesting people.

There was the smiling, enigmatic Tiny Rowland, the respected and dashing Dr Tony O'Reilly, and the imposing Aga Khan; the on-edge John McEnroe, the imperious Robert Maxwell, and the cheek-patting Julio Iglesias. I felt sorry for the Onassis family with their history of early death, drug overdose, divorces, and mistrust, and stayed silent for Jonas Savimbi and members of the Bin Laden family while escorting them through the controls. In contrast, I did my best to make the 15-year-old Mariah Carey feel welcome on her first trip to the UK and reminisced about the Isle of Man with Nigel Mansell as I made him a sandwich for his lunch on the day he received his OBE.

The communications aspects of language and culture in these brief but memorable meetings fascinated me and were more intrinsically rewarding than receiving tips, not always on offer anyway. They also motivated me to learn a few Greek words in preparation for my attendance at a Greek Royal Wedding hosted by John Latsis at Spencer House in St James's, central London.

Mr Latsis had been a fisherman before becoming a billionaire with five private jets, which we handled at Heathrow. As a result, the whole EAS team was invited to His Majesty King Constantine's 50th birthday party, which - according to The Daily Mail - made us some of the world's 700 richest people.

Glittering ballgowns and gold-plated décor aside, Their Majesties, Their Royal Highnesses and their friends treated *us* like royalty and looked pleased to have some 'real' people to talk to. I thought I was getting on well enough with one of the princesses to wonder what it would be like to marry into The Greek Royal family. I rehearsed my chat-up line:

'I am ground staff at the airport. I used to be a pilot, then had a breakdown, after which my wife left me. I have a two-bedroom flat near the airport and a ten-year-old Hillman Avenger that's done 80,000 miles.'

Unsurprisingly I stayed single but was finding out that even the super-rich were human beings too, including 'the Arabs.' Organising the loading of anything from sawdust for their horses, dead sheep, or £100 million worth of gold for them, I would term anyone from anywhere in the Middle East 'Arabs,' until I was invited to a party thrown by an embassy of one of the Gulf states.

The main event was in a palatial room on one side of a corridor in one of London's top hotels set out with container amounts of food and drink, ice sculptures, and hundreds of guests trying not to look as if they were hoovering it all up. Recognising me, the security guard jerked his thumb towards a smaller, more discreet room with subdued lighting. He directed me towards a nervous-looking individual who looked like he would be more comfortable in a charity shop.

It turned out that was where he spent most of his time. I made small talk with him then moved on to other invitees. They would present me with their card and wait to speak to one of the hosts. They were asking for money. Some had travelled from all over the country, and I was there to make them feel at home. I felt humbled to be in the presence of those whose mission in life was to do good works and found a new respect for the 'Arabs' handing out their wealth.

Organising private jet charters for clients was part of my function, sometimes having to handle substantial amounts of cash in the process. Perhaps because I didn't keep one payment of £5,500 for myself, Mahmoud, the local Saudi Embassy rep, invited me to play squash at the Intermet in Richmond, where he had arranged for us to meet two young women.

So, there was a man from the Saudi Embassy, Claudia from Rio de Janeiro, Ludmilla from Russia, and Philip from Bounds Green. Refined, sophisticated conversation took place where I pretended I knew the difference between a Lamborghini Countach LP400S and the 500S until it was time to retire to my rusting Avenger. In contrast, Mahmoud took the girls away in his Merc. He beat me at squash too.

My second television appearance after *Crackerjack* came about after Paul McCartney had been convicted for a drugs offence in the Caribbean, and he and his family were returning home on a British Airways flight from Barbados. I was responsible for organising their transfer to a chartered jet which would take them to Lydd Airport, near their home. They had to clear customs at Heathrow, but I kept them away from the waiting press and TV by driving them around airside for 20 minutes until their bags arrived in the terminal. Once he'd given me his views on drugs and the law, Paul started singing; to have a music superstar singing in the back seat of my car was a special moment.

Having successfully negotiated the mass of pushing, shoving photographers in Terminal Three Arrivals without injury, and had my few seconds of fame on the BBC and ITV news channels with the McCartney's, it was time to drive the family to their waiting jet.

En route, Linda told me she'd left a small Louis Vuitton handbag in the baggage hall. I didn't want her to have face the press again, so I said I would get it. While carrying bags hadn't been my chosen career, I didn't think it was the best time to throw it away by evading Customs, so having found the item, I headed straight for the Red Channel and the friendliest looking Customs Officer I could find.

He searched the bag and found 3.19 grams of cannabis in an empty film canister. He said that if it were up to him personally, he would let it go, but in view of the previous offence in Antigua, he would have to check with his boss. The communication chain went right up to The Head Customs deity in London and eventually back down the line. The answer came back:

'Bring 'em in,' said the Customs Officer, 'and all the bags.'

It was all very agreeable. Paul and Linda were interviewed in the Customs Custody Suite, and 14 large suitcases were searched over an eight-hour period. One of the Customs Officers produced a cartoon of the McCartneys in the interview room with Paul singing 'Yesterday, all my troubles seemed so far away...' Linda McCartney was subsequently fined £80 for possessing cannabis.

My characteristic of wanting to please helped me to adjust to a job that revolved around serving others. Doing something for someone else made me feel good, such as providing a reference for an old College friend to get a pilot's job in the Middle East.

In return, he let me fly an HS125 executive jet from Gatwick to Heathrow and land it as a thank you. He managed to act as if he just happened to be a pilot, so I wasn't envious of him. I knew he felt sorry for me but didn't show it. He repaid me with something worth more than money, giving me a boost to my confidence and the hope that I might fly again.

Far removed from the god-like apparitions I'd encountered on my first flight, I began to see pilots as human beings, to the point where I wondered if I might be one, i.e. a human being, not a pilot. Occasionally I made friends with some of the visiting pilots, but I was there to provide them with a service, as David Oldfield had done with me. Most were quite different from the British Airways pilots I was used to.

The Lonrho crew was Bill the captain with a US Marine crew cut who reputedly carried a loaded pistol into nightclubs under his leather jacket when overseas, and his co-pilot, a giant German known as Baldrick[7]. I enjoyed watching them forcing themselves to be polite to me, knowing that if I made a mistake on their overflight clearances through Africa, they could end up with a surface-to-air missile up their tailpipes.

I had more empathy towards Tommy Armstrong, the American captain of a private Boeing 727 airliner, for the paternal relationship he had with his co-pilot, Kenny. Tommy was an ex F-14 test pilot, brash with a loud, booming voice belying his kindness towards a man who had spent five years in a cage under the care of the North Vietnamese Army.

In charge of handling a Boeing 757 charter to Jeddah, I discovered that my old friend and best man from Northern Ireland, Nigel Crowe was the co-pilot. From being an instructor on Cessna 150's training aircraft at Newtownards

---

[7] As in Edmund Blackadder's servant and sidekick in the BBC TV historic comedy series, *Blackadder*.

to finally getting his commercial pilot's licence, he had achieved his goal, but without the benefit of being sponsored by an airline.

Pleased for him, I handed him his weather briefing and gave him his slot time. He flew off into the blue, and I went back to my ground job. The only thing we had in common was that we were both single, with Nigel recently divorced.

Reminding me that there were those much worse off, I helped arrange the last flight for Steven Moon, an 11-year-old lad with a terminal disease. The owner of a locally-based jet offered his aeroplane free of charge; fuel and catering were provided at no cost, and the BAA waived the landing fee.

To explain what was happening on the flight, I was given the honour of accompanying Steven. I'd never met anyone so young who was so obviously about to die. Moved by his quiet, resigned composure - as was everyone else connected with the flight - I explained the technical details, then left him to his thoughts to enjoy the experience in his own way as he looked out of the window. He died shortly afterwards.

Steven's death served to kick me out of my introspection for a while. I tried to put myself in his position as a young boy with the kind of dreams I'd had at his age but with no prospect of fulfilling them. He had a loving family and people rushing around trying to do their best for him, yet for him, it was not just the end of a flight or a career, but the end of everything, of his whole living, breathing existence. I realised I had nothing to complain about.

11

Escape

Watching the arriving and departing aircraft from the Heathrow Air Traffic Control tower made me want to escape again, or at least do something adventurous to distract me from my impending divorce hearing. The offer of a courtesy visit had given me the opportunity to see the world through a different type of window to an aeroplane's.

One of the controllers soon grabbed my attention with her diamond-clear blue eyes, and I surprised myself by quickly asking for her phone number and getting it. An invitation to her home soon followed, giving me a long-overdue boost to my self-esteem. Then she explained she was in a failing marriage and also seeing someone else. For a good, lapsed Catholic boy, this was far removed from my Disney-like expectations of a new relationship.

However, I persevered to the point where I introduced her to my parents, my first prospective partner after Lynn. Even without knowing all the details, my mother made clear her disapproval, but I didn't care; I was trying to move on in my life. Then Jennifer wanted more, and by more, she meant more sex, which was when she asked me to rape her.

Never having understood rape - how a man could get aroused with an unwilling woman or why a woman would ask for it – I refused. Even if it was a game for her and she *was* willing, I was strong and afraid I might hurt her. Telling Jennifer that I wanted to end our acquaintance there and then, I realised that my mother might have been right for once. But it was a start.

Next, having made friends with private jet stewardesses from Switzerland, Austria, the US, and Mexico, I prepared to visit them. After weekends away in Geneva and Graz, I ended up in the Park Lane Hilton in London, where Joanna, a private Boeing 727 flight attendant from Texas, was in bed with flu. She had a broad smile, a cheerleader's body, and an openness that made her the type of woman I'd want to marry. She liked me for not taking advantage of her while she was ill, and I actively - but briefly - considered moving to the United States on the basis that their Federal Aviation Administration might be more lenient about reinstating my pilot's licence, always at the back of my mind.

The thought of wholesome Christian American girls made me spend more happy-clappy fellowship weekends with the AAACF, not with the aim of finding the Lord again, but to target the single females who I thought might be kind and caring towards me. As soon as I mentioned being divorced or why I had to stop flying, the conversation soon turned away from romance.

Dr Comish had mentioned my medical condition was more likely to be passed on to boys if I had children, but the possibility that anyone would ever want to have them with me seemed remote. Instead, the women assured me that the Lord loved me, but I had comprehensively lost my faith in Him by then.

To try and make friends closer to where I lived, I became Secretary of the Residents Association for Greenacre Court in Englefield Green and organised a housewarming party for my new flat. I invited Lynn, but she didn't come; only about six people did, including Dave Lonsdale, my instructor colleague from Liverpool. I was so desperate, I even paid for his flight from Manchester.

If I had come from a broken home, been bullied by knife-wielding thugs from the local estate, and with only school dinners for food during the day, I might have had an excuse for driving people away, but having a good education and parents with old-fashioned views who liked classical music didn't get much sympathy from anyone. So, I decided I would jump out of an aeroplane.

The reason was a charity jump at the Joint Services Army Parachute Training Centre at Netheravon to which I had been invited, together with 38 mostly female cabin crew. Ellie, a stewardess with more personality than Billy Smart's Circus, asked me why I had stopped flying. Having learnt that giving out too much information was counter-productive, I said: 'medical.'

On a glacial November weekend, we jumped into space from an Islander at 2,500 feet. I couldn't get out of the noisy, freezing plane quickly enough and headed for the open door like a greyhound out of the traps. Ellie and I exchanged phone numbers and agreed to see each other again.

As I sat next to Ellie at her friend's dinner party a few weeks later, one half of me couldn't believe my luck. The other could sense another opportunity to fuck up, especially if the conversation turned to my work history. While I didn't have to reveal everything, I didn't want to lie or come across as having something to hide.

My story would be that I worked for a special unit within British Airways looking after off-radar flight movements coming into Heathrow, about which I couldn't give full details. But the subject of my health never came up - I had every opportunity to start a proper relationship with a popular and lovely girl.

Ellie invited me to her flat for a party soon after. I really liked her, and she seemed to like me, so there was a possibility that the real me was showing through at last, and it had nothing to do with having been a pilot, special flights, or my medical.

She welcomed me into her bed, where I was unable to express any kindness or good humour, let alone produce a physical response, almost certainly a side-effect of being on medication. With my confidence still in pieces less than two years after my breakdown, I ran away, going home at four in the morning.

Ellie might have been disappointed but was kind enough not to let it show. I made the matter worse by writing complicated letters of apology. She replied:

The fickleness of your character certainly seems inversely proportionate to that of your attitudes! 'How the hell then do you manage to radiate such complacency when all you do is twist your mind into knot and thoughts? I think you're making your life unnecessarily complicated without realising it – or was this perhaps, just a well-acted – well-rehearsed yarn to enable a quick exit? I also have a crisis of who am I on my hands!

She was right, of course. I was only interested in myself. So much for the real me. Feeling ashamed of myself, I found my first girlfriend Gail's address in Liverpool in an old diary and wrote to her hoping she might make me happy again. I had no expectations that this would happen, and I was right again.

She told me about the wonderful man she was very fond of and thanked me for my offer. Her rejection confirmed my perception of myself as the lowest form of animal life. In a bid to feel like a man, I went to a karate class. As I watched the instructor doing one-handed push-ups with all the effort of a man picking up a box of matches, my sense of worthlessness was complete as I wallowed in self-pity.

The final court hearing for my divorce was set for almost exactly five years from the date Lynn and I had been married. We met at the courthouse in Slough and exchanged pleasantries, with her telling me she was staying with John Corcoran while she was over from Northern Ireland.

She told me he had made a pass at her, but I didn't mind; I would have done the same in his place. I never really understood jealousy. Protecting a loved one from unwanted advances was fine, but I didn't think that threatening death and destruction to anyone who looked at 'my woman' was the way forward. I wondered if that made me soft.

I wanted to hug Lynn and make everything all right. But she had married a pilot with the promise of a bright future, something I could never be again. That had been my entire identity, and now I was something else, although I didn't know what. Turning 22 a week later, Lynn was ready to start her life again elsewhere, and I couldn't blame her. She wanted a man who would take care of her, not a thinker like me.

As our two respective solicitors went in to see the judge, I felt numb and apprehensive. The papers were in order, but the real surprise was that I had no financial obligations to Lynn. She had said she would take me to the cleaners, but she got nothing. From that perspective, it was a good result for me, but I felt like a man about to be hanged being given the rope rather than having to pay for it.

For a break, I went to St Lunaire to see my parents and get some decent food. Most of the guys from my old beach crowd were making lots of money running companies or doing something important-sounding, so I wasn't too keen to tell the story of my breakdown. I lied about it until I met a man called Jean-Yves at the tennis club, who was from an adjacent village.

A French government psychologist, he seemed both sympathetic to my story and interested from a professional standpoint. He asked if I would like to visit him and his family at their home, which I assumed was just down the road.

It turned out to be 10,000 kilometres away, on Reunion Island, a French territory in the South Indian Ocean; he was visiting his parents nearby. This was my chance to really get away from my situation, so I said: *avec plaisir* (with pleasure) and booked a staff discount flight with Air France for New Year's Eve 1982.

Ready for boarding at Paris Orly, there was a commotion with an awkward passenger. The crew from my flight were close by; at least I think there was a crew because I only had eyes for one of the girls, a classic French beauty with flawless, tanned skin, dancer's legs and soft brown eyes set in a perfectly symmetrical face, topped with shining raven-like hair. In her tight uniform skirt and white shirt, she looked fabulous. I immediately fell in love with her and saw an opportunity to impress.

Sauntering over in my white jacket, I flashed my ID, and in French, offered to help deal with the oaf. The police arrived, and I watched wistfully as Mademoiselle disappeared into the front cabin of the 747. But my performance as a sky marshal hadn't been in vain, as my dream stewardess had me upgraded, and I thought I was actually in heaven, sitting in Business Class with a glass of champagne in my hand. This was the me I wanted to be, a 'James Bond' type hero just doing my job.

Once airborne, the crew dressed in funny hats and invited me to make a routine cabin address in English. Obviously, as a secret agent, I declined, which was when my man-of-mystery persona started to crumble. My girl asked me lots of pointed questions about who I was and what I did. When I told her I was ground staff for British Airways, she quickly lost interest. However, acting the part had been fun, even if it hadn't felt like acting.

Stopping in Djibouti for fuel, my creative mind imagined it was the sort of place Biggles would have found himself in. Looking out from my window seat at the dry landscape full of rusting Russian Migs, it was like watching a film. I felt remote from the world and its inhabitants - a watcher, not a participant – snug in the intimacy of the Jumbo Jet cabin. Back at 33,000 feet, crossing the equator for the first time, I gazed out and lost myself in the view over Africa, loving the moment and looking forward to more champagne and dinner in the sky.

Jean-Yves, his wife Martine and their two young sons met me in the 30-degree heat, making me feel like a visiting dignitary. They drove me around the island with its lush greenery, an active volcano and secluded waterfall, where I swam in the cold, clear water feeling the cleansing of my soul after the nightmare of the previous few years.

At a Hindu fire-walking ceremony, I saw a young girl on a 22-day fast 'in the spirit,' just like I had been in my happy-clappy days with Neil Dove and The Whitley Wood Evangelical Church except she was walking on red-hot coals instead of a wooden floor. At night I marvelled at the stars and shooting stars in the Milky Way in the bright Southern Hemisphere sky, awe-struck and wishing I could be up there.

The path up the 2,631-metre climb to the crater of The Piton de la Fournaise (*The Peak of the Furnace*) was marked by whitewashed rocks, one step away from a freefall down to death in the dark. After a four-hour hike, Jean-Yves and I arrived at 3.30 am, with a heavy mist obscuring the view and a sound of rumbling like distant thunder. The volcano was simmering.

Then the mist cleared, and I watched a firework display of fiery embers climbing up from the glow of a small fissure within the main crater, primaeval nature at its most awesome. The next day we flew over the volcano, one kilometre across, in a single-engine Cessna to watch the billowing smoke emanating from its source: the centre of the earth.

Once I'd got over the fact that someone else was flying, I began to feel there was more to life than being at the controls of a plane. The trip to the volcano had the effect of heightening my senses, particularly fear, even with the medication taking the edge off my emotions.

With its danger never far away, I was feeling more alive but closer to death, including when Martine - without a driving licence – drove us home. Bottom-clenching as this was, it became worse when her father Luc, an alleged schizophrenic Freemason, took over with his habit of driving down the middle of all the island's roads. Much as I loved the company of Jean-Yves' family off-road, I decided it was time for a change of scene.

As a result, I booked myself a flight and a few days in Mauritius at a sandy beach hotel, where I tagged on to a French family with a teenage daughter I couldn't take my eyes off. Content simply to be in her presence, I felt like a starstruck teenager, although what I really wanted was to be part of her family, a normal one.

Back on Reunion Island, more opportunities to die presented themselves with the driving duties handed to Marc, an ex-French paratrooper friend of Luc's who had been wounded in a knife and grenade attack in Chad. Looking wild and deranged, he drove like a man who was looking for death as a long-lost brother.

While some aspects of my life might have been better, I didn't want to end it spread over a road 10,000 kilometres from home, so I reached forward and pulled on the handbrake. Once we'd stopped, I took out the keys and told Luc to drive us back to the house, although I was ready to do it myself.

Feeling my behaviour was reasonable in the circumstances, I was becoming accustomed to the craziness of some of the island's residents. I was sure they'd have locked me away if I'd done anything like that in the UK. Experiencing the disparity between the two cultures almost to their extremes helped me believe I might not be as odd as I had thought.

Before leaving for Métropole *(Mainland France,)* Jean-Yves and Martine invited me to become godfather to their youngest boy. It had been the best holiday of my life, and I'd felt normal, mesmerised by the sights and sounds of a tropical paradise. I would be eternally grateful to Jean-Yves and his family for their care and hospitality.

The Club Class Moët on the British Airways flight to Miami was equally as good as Air France's, as was the upgrade. I was making up for the feeling of being trapped in my ground job by taking another holiday, making the most of my travel concessions. Sitting comfortably, stable, and still, I only had one thought in my head, whether to have beef or fish for dinner. Would I have been as content in myself at home? Probably not, but I didn't care.

As I boarded the onward Aeromexico flight to Mexico, I was excited to be escaping again to somewhere exotic and unknown. As envisaged at school with my old friend Harold, I fancied myself as an international jet setter to be entertained by adoring women in a foreign country.

A few weeks earlier, Juanita Hernandez had arrived at Heathrow as the flight attendant on the Mexican President's private jet, and my Spanish had been good enough to get an invitation to Mexico City to stay with her. Dark-skinned with neat, cropped hair and short enough to stand comfortably in the cramped cabin of a Falcon 50 on a transatlantic flight, she had looked attractive in her tight uniform. Juanita met me at the airport, not looking quite as glamorous as she had on the presidential jet in London.

As we drove through the city past luxurious shopping centres and miserable-looking locals selling their fruit and trinkets on the pavements, I wondered if the reality of the adventure would match my preconception. On reaching her mother's small apartment, I was given a room while Juanita slept on the sofa.

The next day she took me to the tourist sites, as well as expensive bars and hotels, where it was clear that I would be paying for everything. Fair enough in return for a holiday in Mexico, but I was starting to feel uncomfortable with Juanita, with anxiety gnawing at my stomach, reminding me how it felt to be out of control.

As we watched 11-year-old cowboys tripping up bulls at a rodeo, Juanita turned to me.

'Hey, Feeleep,' she said, 'You like children?'

I shrugged.

'Yeah, sure I like children.'

'Well, Feeleep...' Juanita deftly opened her purse and thrust a picture of a Mexican boy in my face and carried on, 'This is my son, an' he is 14, an' my husband he beats me, an' he must not find me, an' I have no-one to look after me an' my son.'

Suddenly I understood why Juanita had invited me to Mexico. Vain enough to think she was there for my benefit, I hadn't considered her needs. However, taking on a violent Mexican husband 5,000 miles from the UK wasn't part of my plan.

Fortunately, there was no harm done, so I politely excused myself and made a break for it, to the other side of the arena, where I had spotted a family of four, made up of a portly, balding father, a slim, chic-looking mother, and two attractive young women in their twenties. As I approached, I could hear they were French tourists and started chatting to them.

The father turned out to be an Air Inter training captain, so we talked aviation for a while as I tried to impress him, his wife, and their daughters. In age between them, I was unsure how to navigate the generation gap, so I settled for being myself, a lonely opportunist trying to find somewhere to belong. Yet, I was still able to turn on the charm well enough to be invited to their home near Paris, to ski with them in Val Thorens, and to spend a week on their sailing yacht in the Mediterranean.

Pleased with myself for having made new friends, and after collecting my things from Juanita's flat without getting a knife in my back, I flew to Villahermosa en route to Cancún. The captain looked like a pantomime bandit, showing off a medallion on his hairy chest, which had me preparing to take over should it get caught in the controls. My escapist fantasy scenario was complete when I checked in to a hotel that looked as if it had come straight out of an old Humphrey

Bogart movie: rotating fan, greasy, unshaven guy behind the desk and cockroaches everywhere. I loved it.

I didn't feel so clever the next day when my hire car came off the road with a wheel over a concrete barrier in the middle of the jungle. Serious concern turned to fear when half a dozen men with machetes appeared in the distance. This was in an area where Spanish was the second language to a local Indian dialect, and I thought they were going to kill me. But with broad grins, the men sized up the situation and got me out of the ditch. Never was I more pleased to part with some Mexican pesos or more ashamed of my lack of faith in human nature.

The car wasn't damaged, and still feeling as if I was playing a part in a movie, I drove on to stumble upon an airport. Sitting forlornly on the edge of the overgrown runway was a Cessna 404 of the type I flew out of Luton with Executive Express. I could have flown this one if it had any engines, propellers, and tyre pressures above zero.

Even the shell of a wrecked aeroplane was enough to make me imagine I was in the left-hand seat flying it over the jungle as a rakish bush pilot. Having returned the car, I settled instead for a passenger seat on an Aeromexico DC-9 towards the hot, white beaches of Cancún.

At my hotel, also enjoying an airline discount, was Laura, a bright and pretty United Airlines check-in agent with short shorts and great legs. Taking her first break in years from looking after her invalid father, her situation made me feel caring and giving for a change, and I went out of my way to entertain her for the week we were together.

Laura and I were inseparable and happy, whether intertwined on our beds or checking out Mayan ruins. Feeling I belonged with her as part of the airline ground staff fraternity was surprisingly satisfying, and grateful to British Airways for my job and travel concessions.

After Laura went home to America, I flew to Cozumel, with Aerocaribe waiving their 16-dollar fare on the basis that

I was a pilot, which also gave the green light for the captain to demonstrate his macho flying skills. With no other passengers on board his Bandeirante, he took it down to 50 feet above the Caribbean waters while I nodded enthusiastically and called out: '*muy bien*' (very good.) I kept to myself that I could have flown *under* his aeroplane in my day.

However, I respected that Captain Bull's Balls had a pilot's licence, and I didn't. After a week alone watching honeymooning couples laughing and smooching, I returned to the UK, already dreaming of my next destination to run away to - Australia.

I'd met Rocky Donovan on an AAACF Fellowship Weekend, leading to an invitation to visit him in Cronulla, near Sydney. Rocky was a steward with Qantas who kept his religion to himself and concentrated on the business of being a good bloke.

'Come on over to Oz, mate.' he had said.

'That's great, thanks. Very kind - thanks.'

'So, when are ya comin'?'

'Er...well, I'd need to get a ticket and book the leave.'

'Right, so what, a week, coupla weeks?'

'Er, yes, great. Thanks.'

'Are you gay? You don't seem too keen, mate.'

'No, no, not at all.'

'Right, The Lord doesn't really go with all that, ya know.'

'I know.'

'Hey, I know what ya thinkin'. Cos I'm a steward; I must be gay. I know you've got a few in your airline, mate, but that's okay. A lot of regular guys join Quantas as it's got heaps of travel and the chance to meet a few gorgeous women. You'll find a few ex Australian Special Forces guys pushing trolleys too, and they're about as queer as a buck kangaroo. The story goes that when a new stewie joins the

747 fleet, one of the boys hides in the little cubby hole that the engineer uses when he's checking stuff under the floor. The bloke takes a crate of Foster's down with him so that when the next passenger calls for a beer, the rookie sees a hand appearing from under the floor with the tinnie, and there's a shout of 'Comin' up!'

Rocky made me feel as if I'd been living in a prison cell all my life. He seemed to be constantly laughing and joking with everyone, with a perpetual smile etched into his freckled face. His enthusiasm for fun was continuous, and I felt like a prophet of doom in comparison. I wondered why he had invited me. Perhaps he felt sorry for me.

In any case, I believed that God owed me one and decided that a trip to Sydney through the AAACF would be the payoff. Also, I had visions of fit, tanned Australian girls throwing themselves at me in a city where there was supposed to be a shortage of single, available men. I told Rocky I would get the tickets.

A year later, in November 1984, having arrived late at the airport to pick me up after my 24-hour flight, Rocky took me straight to Cronulla Beach to teach me body surfing and how to avoid rip tides.

This unexpected welcome was explained when we eventually arrived at his flat where Barry, the lodger, was still in situ, leaving me with nowhere to sleep. Rocky seemed so casual about everything – his guests, job, and *life* – in complete contrast to how I had been brought up. He reminded me of the children who occasionally came to our house to play with my brother and me and who would break the toys that we looked after so carefully.

Yet I wanted to be like Rocky, seemingly with popularity and lots of friends. Instead, I had the superior manner of an airline pilot, but without the health, assertiveness, and licence to be one. The medication appeared to have taken away not only my confidence but my spirit too.

Surrounded by Rocky and his happy-go-lucky attitude, I felt compelled to try to emulate him, to fit in, to conform. I needed someone to tell me what was right, wanting structure and a clear course of action.

On the other side of the world and feeling threatened by Rocky's relaxed way of living, all my fears of not belonging, being different and lacking social wherewithal overwhelmed me. The conflicts in my head made me panic, which I had never done in an aeroplane, even when faced with extreme danger. I called the police, who came and, having seen there was no likelihood of violence, quickly left, leaving me surprised I didn't get arrested for wasting their time.

Feeling like a pariah, I said goodbye to Rocky and set off for the Gold Coast, ironically looking for adventure and freedom. Joining an outback tour, I slept under the stars, saw kangaroos and a duck-billed platypus, and woke up in a tent with an Irish nurse. Then I disobeyed the hire car rules to cross the crocodile-infested Daintree River and swam naked with a girl in a youth hostel lagoon. On my own, and without any emotional attachment to anyone, I felt liberated.

Back in Sydney for a Christmas party with the Irish nurse and two of her friends, I called British Airways to check the flight status for my staff standby ticket. They told me to fly back to London on Christmas Day to be sure I was ready for work a week later.

Crestfallen and meekly reverting to my anxious, medicated self, I agreed and left the heat of an Australian summer for the cold of an English December, cursing myself for not taking the chance to stay on, and if necessary, paying the extra for a regular ticket. It was a lesson learned; to take risks and live life more to the full, like Rocky and his Quantas mates.

St Lunaire, France. Ronald and Simone Appleton, 1951-2021; Me, 1954ish

Piper Aztec D, Keenair, 1976

Front page, *Liverpool Echo* 24 March 1976.
Bottom left is the wingtip of the plane

Piper Navajo,
Geneva, 1979

Trident Base Training, British Airways, Prestwick, 1980

'X-ray 10', British Airways Executive Aircraft Service, 1982 - 1993

News at Ten, McCartneys,
17 January 1984

Godson Loïc and his brother,
Île de La Réunion, 1986

Daily Mail,
1 June 1990

Happy Days, Appleton 5

12

Role Models

Back at work, I was kidding myself that driving a car was like being in the cockpit of an aeroplane, even though there were a lot fewer dials and there was no going up. I was parked near the Heathrow General Aviation Terminal (GAT) airside, close enough to smell the kerosene of the departing aircraft. Secure in the warm, muffled peace of the comfortable car, it was a spot where I could sit alone with my thoughts, watching the planes take off and land.

A Pan Am 747 carefully nosed its way past the holding point and turned slowly right onto the white marks painted on the tarmac, heat haze from its four engines distorting the background view of the BA hangars. I looked at the cockpit windows, envy of the guys behind them twisting my stomach.

Thundering past, the aircraft accelerated to a distant rotation and a laboured climb until it became a gently turning silhouette against the winter sky. Heavy with fuel, it stayed low, seemingly too slow to fly. I watched it until it was out of sight.

Turning my eyes towards the landing runway, a mile away to the North, I saw three sets of shimmering landing lights in a ragged line crawling its way down final approach. The lights were supposed to frighten the birds away as well as other aeroplanes. Each aircraft disappeared silently in turn behind the red brick clutter of the central area, hiding the sea of humanity busy rushing around like ants in a colony.

There was probably some deep psychological meaning behind why people preferred take-offs or landings. I liked landings where the pilot did a perfect flare out of the sunset and kissed his aircraft on with a puff of burning rubber, but they weren't so romantic when all you could see was the dirty underbelly of an aeroplane with its bits dangling down.

Then came the noise and the shaking airframe when the cowlings rocked with reverse thrust and the handling pilot stood on the brakes to turn onto the closest taxiway. So, I preferred the take-offs – they were all about escaping.

The clock ticked on until, at one o'clock, I heard the high-pitched whine of the helicopter. It was on time; the Army flights always were. A small yellow BAA van, its yellow light flashing, raced into position, stopping alongside the protective blast fence between the runway and the helipad. The marshaller stepped out, waiting to guide the helicopter down by waving a pair of what looked like fluorescent table tennis bats. Leaning forward onto the car's steering wheel, I craned my neck upwards as I started the Granada's engine.

One hundred feet above me and approaching from the West, the Scout descended towards the white 'H' in the area that marked the Southside helicopter landing pad. I watched as the pilot checked its rate of descent just before a gentle touchdown, paper and light debris being whirled around by the sucking vortex. The whine began to die down almost immediately, so I pulled the gear lever to 'drive' and allowed the car to ease forward, my foot off the accelerator.

The Scout was painted in dark camouflage green and sat on skids. As the rotor blades unwound, the rotating beacon stopped flashing, and the marshaller drove off. The flimsy looking door cracked open, and a figure stepped out. From the back, I recognised a thinning patch of sandy hair, a worn camouflage jacket, an even more worn pair of jeans and some light training shoes, the informal uniform of the SAS.

By the time I had pulled up alongside the Scout, the SAS pilot had stepped down from the cockpit and begun to tie down the rotor blades. With the little machine secure, he picked up a slim briefcase from the back seat, locked the door, took a final look around and walked towards my car. Remembering that the SAS liked to keep as inconspicuous as possible, I resisted the temptation to get out of the car to open its door.

The SAS man opened the car's front door and installed himself, resting the briefcase on his knees and leaving his seat belt unfastened. I decided this must be normal for SAS men, something to do with being trained to leap out of moving vehicles or taking control of them. As I turned to look across at the man, my glance verged on becoming a stare as I checked the blue in his eyes to see if it was as icy as the last time we'd met.

He'd been through not only one of the most gruelling military selection programmes in the world but also passed helicopter flying training. I'd been fit enough to fly once so, for a moment, felt I was like him - but I hadn't been a soldier or even served in the regular military. He was both a pilot and a soldier, so he was better than me, as close to a real live hero as I would ever meet.

The SAS man's eyes were almost transparent in their clarity. Perhaps he had above-average eyesight. Maybe he could walk on water. He was probably one of those kids at school who was always quietly respected and never bullied. Because I was in his company, I felt I belonged with that type of person. I turned towards the roadway and drove off towards the British Airways Security offices.

I liked doing the SAS flights. The guys hardly ever spoke and would never complain. Even when there were three of them and their transport was late. They had climbed over a 12-foot-high fence to find their pick-up as if it had been a crack in the pavement, and they were so reasonable afterwards. Others had laughed politely when they had disembarked from their helicopter on the Royal Stand, and someone had asked them: 'Are you from the gas board?'

'How's it going then?' asked the SAS man.

I was pleased that it was him who had made conversation.

'Yeah...well, okay. You know, the usual; sometimes you sit around doing nothing all day, and other days your feet don't touch the ground. Thing is, those who can afford private aircraft don't like being told what to do. We had a Greek in last week who thought he could bring his departure time forward by buying the French air traffic control system.'

'Are they still giving you those cheap tickets?'

'Yeah, but it's not so easy to get on these days. Because we're into this 'customer first' stuff in a big way, you really need to want to go to Iceland in the middle of winter to be sure of getting on. Even 'firm' tickets aren't so firm anymore. I've even been bumped on duty travel.'

The SAS man was looking out of his window. Perhaps he was bored, or perhaps I was boring. I felt dull and boring whenever I opened my mouth because I had nothing funny or interesting to say. I drove us past a row of gleaming white executive jets through the GAT security checkpoint to landside and towards the Southern perimeter road.

'So, when do you reckon you'll get back to flying then?' asked the SAS man.

'Ask me a question on sport,' I replied, 'They've redeployed about 250 surplus Airways pilots, so I don't know really.'

'Do you miss the flying?'

'Sometimes. I miss the pure flying but not the airline stuff. I don't miss the night stops with crews who spend most of their time complaining about allowances or working conditions. When I was an air-taxi pilot, I had to pull the aircraft out of the hangar, clean out the ashtrays, load the bags and make the coffee, never mind the flying.'

'What about your present job, do you enjoy that?'

I shrugged.

'It's okay for what it is. Pays the bills.'

The SAS man turned away. We were into the stretch of the perimeter road that ran towards the staff car park northside. A Finnair DC-9 roared off into the sky, into 'finnair' as the joke went, away from the putrid atmosphere over the sewage works. At least I had a better job than the guys wading about in the shit over there.

I dropped the SAS man outside the two-story block that housed the Airways Security offices near the Cranebank Training Centre on the east side of the airport, parked up and waited in the car as a British Airways Boeing 757 hauled its ugly profile overhead. Perhaps I'd have been in the right-hand seat of that 757 if I'd still been flying. I'd be looking at an empty, clean runway instead of a gravelly car park and random vehicles spattered with the grey dirt of Hounslow road spray.

Being close to Cranebank brought it all back. Here, three years ago, I was learning the systems on the Trident, my first jet. Now I was wearing steel toe-capped, ramp workers safety shoes and hated myself for being who I was, ground staff rather than flight crew. I was unhappy because I was a pilot once and wanted to be one again. Maybe it was the medication that was making me feel uncomfortable. The sooner I came off it, the better.

I turned on *The World at One* and listened to a story about an IRA bombing. Having lived and worked in Northern Ireland, I followed events there with morbid interest. After Airde, Lynn and my apparent religious conversion, my perception of the province now centred on images of grim-faced Sinn Fein men and hooded IRA killers, the loud, intransigent voice of Ian Paisley and camouflaged troops patrolling the streets and countryside. Television coverage focused on blown-up buildings, sectarian conflict, and the sound of a grating accent that was as hard as nails.

A British Airways security man came out of the building and walked over. I wound the window down.

'You okay?' he said.

I didn't like people asking if I was okay – why wouldn't I be?

'Yeah, one of our guys stumbled on an exercise at Pier One last week. Plod were supposed to be acting as the defending forces. The boys[8] ran down the length of the pier and 'shot' them all in about 45 seconds.'

'Serves 'em right. See you around.'

As he walked over to his car, I wondered if he was checking me out. As a security officer, he was undoubtedly ex-military. He had that air of getting things done without a lot of fannying about and self-doubt.

Out of the 100 model aeroplane kits I made when I lived at home, it was always the military ones that excited me. If I'd have joined the RAF, I could have flown fast jets - a fighter pilot instead of a wimpy civil pilot, and perhaps even a helicopter pilot too, attached to the SAS.

Ten minutes later, the SAS man came out for me to take him back to the Scout. Setting off along the Eastern perimeter road towards the site of the new Terminal 4, I continued my chat.

'Did you ever see that Clint Eastwood film where he goes on to the flight deck disguised as a pilot?'

'No.'

I had guessed that the SAS man was some kind of sky marshal. Having been in the school shooting team – once scoring 101 out of 100[9] - I saw myself doing the same. Sitting for hours in an aircraft cabin watching passengers and crew, assessing and analysing their actions would have suited me, and ready for instant action if the situation demanded it.

Back at the GAT, the helicopter looked out of place among the gleaming white Falcons and Gulfstreams in the executive jet parking area. The compact little machine looked lifeless without its pilot, its rotors flexing gently in the breeze.

---

[8] An SAS team on training detachment.

[9] All ten shots were in the 'v-bull,' the dotted inner part of the bullseye.

'You'll have to come down to the Special Forces Club in London sometime - have a drink, for Christmas,' said the SAS man.

'Thanks, that would be great.'

'Right then, see you soon. I'm Rob.'

I shook his hand. It was a good feeling to be a mate of the SAS, to be one of the lads. As Rob walked to the helicopter, waiting like an insect at rest, I manoeuvred the car to get the best view of its departure. The sky was overcast, but the fresh westerly wind was helping to keep the visibility good.

Rob would have a long flight back to Hereford. Now once more, an anonymous pilot doing a technical job, he set about his pre-flight checks as I would have. Walking around the aircraft, checking for obvious damage, he removed the dust covers and tie-down lines, then strapped himself into the right-hand seat. I watched enviously, wishing I could be him, a man doing what he did best.

As Rob flicked some switches in the cockpit, he pulled out a map. Then he put on a heavy-looking helmet and adjusted the mouthpiece, mouthing some words as he called for start clearance. The red beacon lights flashed their warning message, I moved clear, and the starter motor whined into action, the igniters cracking life into the powerful single engine.

A minute later, the rotor blades were at maximum RPM, and the little machine had turned into a buzzing blur of whirring metal straining at the ground to release it. It lifted slowly off, causing my car to rock gently in the downwash. The helicopter dipped its nose and accelerated forwards and upwards into the cloudy bright. I felt emptiness and silence in my mind, wanting to be up in the sky.

Taking a final look at the disappearing Scout, I turned the car towards the GAT checkpoint and was waved through by the guard back towards the perimeter road. At the entrance to the cargo tunnel, I noticed flashing orange lights ahead, casting sweeping bright reflections on the tunnel walls, which meant there was a holdup. A marshaller was holding up the traffic in front.

Then I heard a muffled cheer from the drivers echoing down the tunnel bore. A mother duck was escorting her seven ducklings across the two lanes. I felt softness and admiration that movement at the world's busiest international airport could stop to allow a moment of kindness towards these little creatures going about their business. The marshaller checked that the ducks were clear of the road, then the two opposing convoys set off on their grinding journeys.

Exiting the cargo tunnel to the central area, I entered a world of constant movement, incessant noise, and activity everywhere. In contrast to the quiet calm of an aircraft cabin, there was no peace during the day. Containers crashed, sirens wailed, diesels chugged, men shouted, and that was without the aeroplanes. Closer and bigger, the jets screamed and whined 20 or 30 at a time, the racket only abating during the night or in the thickest fog. Passing the Hotel cul-de-sac, a Ghanaian DC-10 and a Bee Wee Tri-Star sat trapped, like painted dinosaurs.

Looking up to the edge of the terminal's multi-storey car park, I saw children's fingers hooked into the safety fencing. The airport car parks were a favourite launching point for desperate people to finish their unhappy life journeys. I wondered what it was like to commit suicide - to drive up to the top storey of the car park and climb over the fence or cut through it, feel the chill wind, and hear the noise all around.

Then look around for anyone who might interfere and wonder if wallet and other bits and pieces in pockets might fall out. Push off into space, see the impact point on the way down, and perhaps regret it and scream in terror. Not die but be seriously injured and end up paralysed but conscious. I didn't have the urge - it was just an idle thought.

Turning right up Pier 1, I heard the wail of bagpipes. A KLM Dutch airlines baggage assistant was practising, pacing the pavement outside his ramp office next to EAS. My spirits briefly lifted by the incongruous sound - a pleasant change from the sound of jet engines - I entered the security of my new workplace home.

Tony was the early shift allocator, marking his authority with a line of half-used cigarette ends on the windowsill. Rolling the next one, with his feet up on the desk, he glanced over to me as he was handing over to the afternoon shift.

'And here's the man on a NATO cosmic secret job. You off now?' he asked me. I wasn't sure if his question was a wish or a statement.

'If you don't need me,' I said.

'Nope, no-one to give you a lift, I'm afraid. I'm going to rule the world when I get out of here.'

For a moment, I suspected he was referring to the grandiosity sometimes exhibited by people with similar medical histories to my own. Tony might have appeared laidback, but he was always completely in tune with everything that was happening and must have been told about my medical condition before being assigned to train me. I pretended not to hear his comment and moved across to the ops board to draw a line through Army Air Corps Flight 341.

Seeing an obsolete navigation chart lying in a messy pile of papers on top of a locker, on impulse, I slipped it into my briefcase before heading for the door and the walk to the staff bus. As it graunched its way through the main tunnel and onto the perimeter road towards the northside car park, I noticed the Trident that the emergency services used for fire training parked on the remote Stand 157. It had steps and ground power, and the threshold of 09L was only 100 yards away. I wondered if it was airworthy and if I could get it airborne before anyone could stop me.

Back at my flat, I made tea and a sandwich and took them through to the living room. Rummaging in my belongings, I found my old topo (topographical map), pilot's licence, logbooks, and clipboard, still with an Air Continental navigation log on top, from my last Navajo flight as a freelance pilot.

Sitting down on the sofa, I pulled the airways map from my briefcase and spread the two charts out on the coffee table. Finding Heathrow and seeing the familiar names of the radio beacons that had guided me across the British Isles made me feel nostalgic - Bovingdon, Daventry, and Honiley near Birmingham, which always reminded me of the Puff the Magic Dragon song and the land called *Honahlee*.

In my mind's eye, I saw an instrument panel in front of me and remembered the feeling of belonging in the sky. I thought of the safe, comforting feeling of being pushed through clear air by two 350hp engines rumbling a few feet from my sides.

Whether on a rainy night over the Irish Sea or with the sun rising over the Alps at five in the morning, flying in command was my comfort zone. But I would never have that feeling again. In comparison, my life was empty. I needed to find something to do outside work, so I found a pad and started to write a book.

13

Relapse

In an attempt to improve my career prospects within the airline, I enrolled in a part-time DMS (Diploma in Management Studies.) But when I applied for management jobs, I was rejected. The feedback was that I was precise, analytical, and detailed but without any engagement with my audience.

Suitable for a fighter pilot, where audience engagement meant blowing the bad guys to smithereens, but not so good for relating to those I had to work with. I had the desire to achieve, to make a difference, but I didn't know how to go about it.

Wanting to show I was more than just a bag-carrying servant and VIP driver, I was constantly looking for ways to make the EAS working practices more efficient and for opportunities for promotion. I got myself heavily involved with the office move to a more spacious, central location, drawing up plans on graph paper and liaising with facilities managers and technical departments. Finding some unexpected enthusiasm for this project, I set about it with energy and focus. Perhaps, as a result, I ended up in the right-hand seat of a Navajo.

Topflight, one of our regular client air-taxi companies, had been chartered to fly a nervous passenger to the Isle of Man and asked me to fly as unofficial co-pilot. Although not legally required, it would give their passenger the impression there were two pilots on board the flight, and it would take me away from my ground job for a day.

It was a strange but enjoyable distraction watching someone else do what I'd done so many times before and to be transported to a place where I'd lived and worked in another life. Before returning to Heathrow, I called into Woodgate's office at the airport to see if anyone remembered me, but nobody did; further confirmation that Philip the pilot was dead.

Then a Belgian pilot I was escorting through Heathrow offered me a job as a Trident captain for Air Zaire, with a medical certificate and licence included as part of the deal, perhaps an omen. I considered flying around Africa in an aircraft maintained with Russian car parts for a few seconds, then politely declined. It reminded me that a world existed outside the cosy confines of Europe, where rules were different but where people still travelled and did business, families met, and life went on.

Yet, the trip in the Navajo had made me think about flying again. The medication was keeping any excessively fanciful thoughts at bay, but there was a part of my brain that was wondering if regaining my pilot's licence was a possibility. I wanted to be in a cockpit again, feeling drawn to them like bats to a cave and asked for some time in the Trident 2 simulator as part of research for my book.

Inspired by my contacts with the SAS, I was working on a story of a suicide mission to kill the high command of the IRA by flying a plane into Buckingham Palace with them on board. This was partly inspired by a flight that my old chief pilot at Keenair had undertaken to fly senior members of the IRA from Northern Ireland to a private landing strip near London to meet the prime minister at the time, Harold Wilson.

Surprised to be given a session, I wasn't sure whether the simulator staff felt they were providing therapy, checking out that I wouldn't go crazy on a real aircraft, or just felt sorry for me. As ever, I felt lonely and without purpose, throwing the machine around and aiming the imaginary Trident towards and over the various buildings depicted by points of light. After I'd finished and thanked the operators who had given up their time for me, I pondered what to do with my life. I had a job but was unfulfilled, and my personal life was a disaster, so I applied to join the Territorial Army (TA) SAS.

Rob had been as good as his word and invited me to the Special Forces Club in London for a Christmas drink. Having met other SAS members, including senior officers in my work at the airport, I saw him and his colleagues as exceptional human beings and role models. However, they were also just men with the same values as I had. Able to trek 45 miles across Wales in a day on a challenge walk, I thought I might be fit enough and have the right mindset.

It wasn't just about physical fitness. In his book *Who Dares Wins,* Tony Geraghty had written about intelligent misfits, one-offs: *The psychologists who test SAS recruits look for those who, on the tests, are: above average in intelligence; assertive; happy-go-lucky; self-sufficient; not extremely intro or extraverted. They do not want people who are emotionally stable; instead, they want forthright individuals who are hard to fool and not dependent on orders.*

Assessing my education and performance at an all-boys school, an all-men college, and in the male-dominated profession of flying, I felt I ticked most of those boxes with 'not emotionally stable' top of the list. I fell down on 'hard to fool' based on my immaturity but scored well on leadership. 'Happy-go-lucky' didn't apply to me, but I aspired to be an officer making the big decisions rather than a squaddie competing for the number of pints he could drink in an evening.

At school, I looked down on the Army as being made up of the more brutish, physical types than RAF personnel until the SAS captured my attention by rescuing the hostages at the Iranian Embassy siege in 1980. Watching the event on TV with Lynn in our house in Reading, I had realised how brave soldiers had to be to confront people face-to-face who were trying to kill them, but also clear-thinking and calculating.

Researching the 22 SAS Regiment's history, I found respect for their 'hearts and minds' approach to winning people over, with violence as a last resort. Some of them had suffered breakdowns and psychological issues, so I didn't think my history would necessarily be a bar to entry.

While always keen to avoid fights, I also felt that the aggression I had displayed in the past – almost always directed towards myself - might be useful to the Army, where it could be properly channelled and controlled rather than manifesting itself in outbursts of frustrated emotion. I knew I was capable of justifiable anger, trusting my self-restraint and sense of fairness only to use force if I had to.

My only real experience of violence at home was when my father smashed the cuckoo clock in a rage during a colossal row I was having with my parents about me not coming into the house quickly enough from somewhere. He usually would smack my brother and me on the back of the legs for transgressions, which he didn't enjoy, but the clock incident was more frightening for its unpredictability. As for killing people, I felt that it should only be done by trained professionals within the framework of the law.

So, after running around a track at the Duke of York's Headquarters within the allotted time, I came face to face with an officer for the interview for 21 SAS[10], which was when I knew I belonged there. I met his stare and was accepted for training. This was no fantasy. The only questions for me were around practicalities and passing the medical.

Logically, the physical aspects of the training could only improve my mental health, but I also wanted to contribute. Remembering how I could be when off medication, I believed my high-energy behaviour could be an asset to the SAS, as much as it was detrimental to everyday

---

[10] 21st Special Air Service Regiment (Artists Rifles)

life. So, I would come off it and be a real man like Rob, away from the influence of women, particularly my mother.

Soon it was clear that undertaking both the DMS and the TA while doing shift and weekend work was impossible. The TA SAS would be a significant commitment and not compatible with the regime of medication that I had to comply with to be employed by British Airways. Stretched to my limits physically, I might function better off lithium in some ways, but I had to earn a living, and it was all too much to ask of myself.

So, I continued taking my pills and studying for the DMS with its own challenges, such as staying awake during lectures on financial management, strategy, and statistics after a six a.m. start on an early shift. Completing projects such as one on the improvement of ground support services for large VIP aircraft, I felt my life was tedious and uninteresting.

That was until Army Air 442 appeared on the EAS movements board, scheduled to drop off passengers at Heathrow then fly on to Battersea Heliport for fuel on my day off. I decided I could fulfil my wish to be in the SAS after all, if only for a few hours and without running up mountains. I turned up at the GAT wearing brown cords, a green shirt and a tie and asked Rob if I could fly with him.

He looked me up and down very carefully, then agreed. One of my EAS colleagues drove us out to the helicopter, where Rob invited me to sit on a canvas bench behind the two pilot's seats. In the front was a bigger man, wearing jeans and a light, zipped jacket. He looked hard at me, then turned to face the front. There was no doubt in my mind he could handle any untoward behaviour on my part, on or off medication.

It was possible, even likely, that the two SAS men knew about my medical history from my EAS colleagues, but it didn't matter - I was thrilled and elated to be part of their military operation while ensuring I looked calm and impassive to the outside world. Rob took his seat, checked we were all strapped in and started the engine. We got airborne and headed South before turning East, staying low. Rob was sharp in avoiding birds and did an expert job controlling the light helicopter in the gusty conditions as we landed at Battersea.

But all of this was minor excitement compared to exiting the aircraft. Everyone at Battersea, from the air traffic controller to the fuelers and hangers-on, was watching our arrival. For those few minutes, I was an SAS soldier and played along with every fibre in my body, loving every second of the experience.

I didn't feel that I was *acting* like an SAS soldier; I *felt* that I was an SAS soldier. And not just a soldier, but an officer. As I sat in the back of a cab leaving the heliport, I thought of the SAS men I'd driven around Heathrow, hard and silent. I couldn't tell anyone what I'd been doing, but that was part of the mystery, the mystique – it was my moment.

Was I out of touch with reality? Possibly, but the feeling of being in the SAS for that moment was genuine. Actors pretended to be someone else all the time, so why couldn't I? I had been cast as a 'First Soldier' at primary school, and the SAS were definitely first when it came to soldiering, so maybe I wasn't crazy after all.

If I was an actor, I could play a pilot, a soldier, even an SAS officer. As a real person, perhaps I could be those too. There was the dichotomy: reality or fantasy? Mad, bad, or sad? That evening, I looked hard at the little white pills that had been part of my life for almost seven years. I hadn't needed them when I passed selection for the RAF and British Airways; I had been in the prime of my life then.

Turning to the bathroom mirror, I assessed my body. At five feet ten and three quarters, I could have done with another couple of inches, but I looked fit enough, on top at least. I wasn't so happy with my lower half; although my legs were strong, my feet turned out, and my backside was fat and white. I would need to do more exercise to get more muscle definition. The pills were slowing me down. They had turned me into a shadow of myself, a shell of the confident-looking guy in a captain's uniform standing outside his twin-engine plane on the tarmac at Geneva. I had failed in finding a girlfriend and had people feeling sorry for me instead of looking up to me.

Every time I broke the tinfoil on the tablets, I felt subjugated and enslaved. I wanted to be the leader, pathfinder, and decision-maker I had been before, standing up for myself instead of being a wimp and a coward. The pills were manipulating my very essence as a man, taking away my soul. I pushed them to one side and went to bed.

I felt my ground job was holding me back. It had prevented me from joining the SAS and the military brotherhood, where I should have been in the first place. So, when I heard the London and Washington Oman Association (LOWA) was looking for a co-pilot for their Saudi-registered HS125 business jet, I was sure the job was meant for me.

Also in charge of operating a luxury, customised Boeing 707 airliner, LOWA's Chief Pilot was Ray Hanna, an ex-RAF Red Arrows leader and one of the best pilots on the planet. Ray's flight and cabin crew seemed to be in favour of me joining their team. I'd served them faithfully every time they came into Heathrow, taking their rubbish away and making a special effort with their flight plans and slots. Now I would get my reward.

This was the job I'd been called for; working with EAS had been a test, preparing me to fly again. With my surname beginning with an A and my future boss being Doctor Omar Zawawi, Special Advisor to His Majesty Sultan Qaboos, it would be A to Z, the beginning to the end. Perfect.

The Saudi licensing authority was based on the US Federal Aviation Authority (FAA). I was sure the Americans would give me a second chance; with their 'can do' mentality, they couldn't be as fussy as the Brits. If I had to, I'd go over to Washington to see the FAA Chief Flight Surgeon to confirm I didn't need any medication. The FAA medical examiner in London was supposed to be a good guy, so I fixed up an appointment with him as a start.

There was even a message from the Americans themselves. The Space Shuttle was due to do a flypast at Heathrow on the back of a Jumbo Jet. I saw this as a sign I was going to get an FAA airman's licence.

There were other signs. A senior SAS officer left a list of top-secret phone numbers in my car - undoubtedly another test to see if I would return it, which of course I did without making a copy. Another time, the British Secretary of State for Defence Michael Heseltine arrived in a Gazelle helicopter to be met by security staff and his driver, escorted by me. The driver had been given the wrong address, so I took charge and told him to follow me.

It was obvious I was ready to retake command of an aircraft. I also received a call from the CAA to go to their Head Office to have an EEG and a CAT scan, which could only mean they were reconsidering my diagnosis. Surprisingly, they treated me rather abruptly, and they never gave me any feedback on the results either. Strange behaviour on their part, but their problem, not mine.

EAS work became less and less tedious as I looked forward to becoming a pilot again, an undercover pilot with special responsibility for security. Energised by my thoughts, I was ready to make my contribution to anti-terrorism.

Inviting myself to Paris to see the French family I'd met in Mexico, I looked forward to bonding with them again in their seven-bedroom house, perhaps sharing a room with Béatrice, their eldest daughter. Her parents would surely approve. I got down to business over dinner.

'So, last time you mentioned that you had a friend in the GIGN[11]?' I began.

'Yes, our neighbour.'

'We have the SAS; they probably trained your guy.'

'You mentioned the SAS last time we saw you.'

'Yes.'

'Are you in the SAS?'

'I work with them, part of a special unit at the airport.'

Neither the father, his wife or their two daughters looked impressed; it was as if they didn't believe me.

'You used to fly, though?'

'Yeah, 3,000 hours, 1, 2, 3, 4 engine aircraft. Pistons, turboprops, jets.'

'Remind us, why did you stop?'

'Just temporary, I'll be going back soon. So, Béatrice, how are you?'

'Very good, very happy. I'm getting married in June.'

'Oh, right. To whom?'

'Gunther, he's German.'

'And what does he do?'

'He's an accountant with the EEC in Brussels.'

I smiled.

'Oh dear.'

'He trained after leaving the Army.'

'The Army? Didn't think Germany had an army.'

The father was looking hard at me. He wasn't smiling; I couldn't understand why.

'He was with GSG9[12] for five years.'

I paused.

'Yeah, well maybe, but it's generally acknowledged in the SF world that the SAS are the best.'

---

[11] Groupe d'Intervention de la Gendarmerie Nationale, a special unit within the French National Gendarmerie, primarily for counter terrorism

[12] Grenzschutzgruppe 9, the elite Police Tactical Unit of the German Federal Police

The family looked as if they'd had enough of me. Well, in that case, I'd had enough of them too, and I'd be getting back to London as quickly as I could. Forgetting that they had welcomed me into their home twice, given me a week's skiing at a prime resort in the Alps, and allowed me to spend a week sailing with them, I left them to focus on my work back at Heathrow. I made a point of volunteering for the high-profile flights, so I could practice being anonymous but alert, as a good security man would.

I was sure the other EAS Officers were sensing there was something different about me, something special. I started refusing the backhanders from passengers and crew as it was against British Airways regulations. Not wanting to antagonise the others, I put anything I was given in the tips drawer but didn't take my share at the end of the day to avoid feeling compromised. With a knowing smile, I would say: 'It's fine, just count me out.'

But some things were happening around me which didn't fit in with my newfound special status. One day, I couldn't find the parking stand for Thierry's chartered jet. Thierry was a senior banker of The International Division of The Midland Bank. He liked me because I would speak to him in French. I made him wait for his plane on the stand while I drove back to the office.

The wrong aeroplane turned up, and he missed his meeting in Zurich, and one of the other EAS Officers told my manager. But by then, I believed it was part of the plan to show how unsuitable I was to work on the ground before going back to flying. Life would be easier for EAS with me out of the way, a win-win situation all around.

I wrote a letter to the British Airways doctor explaining how well I was and how I should be considered for flying again, detailing the disparity between my academic and educational qualifications and my current salary. Dr Smith was a helpful guy, and I was sure he would see it my way.

I applied to join the Territorial Army Intelligence Corps, which would prove that my brain was in full working order. My intake achieved the highest scores ever in the written tests, and I told the Army there was nothing wrong with me at the medical. I was all set to complete the Attestation Weekend in Kent.

This involved some running around, a big Army breakfast and weapons handling training. I fancied that I knew more about the safety drill than the instructor, having shot for the school and been the school armourer and all. I didn't like it that we were waving guns around – even unloaded - and decided that we should be pointing them at the ground.

So, I marched around telling my fellow recruits to point their weapons down, unloaded or not. The instructor didn't like this much, so I was driven back to London in an Army Land Rover.

I didn't understand why I wasn't being praised and complimented more. I was off the pills and starting to feel good about myself again as a super-secret Intelligence operative who would be working as a co-pilot while undercover at British Airways and covert ops for MI5, MI6 and probably the SAS. It had to be another test, like the helicopter ride. I was sure they were all checking me out.

That evening, strutting naked about my flat and believing myself to be Mr Alpha Male Jet Pilot SAS Captain James Bond American Astronaut Russian Colonel Hero, tiredness finally kicked in as my brain struggled to function rationally.

I started shouting at the world in general until someone called the police because of the noise. They took me to a cell until a doctor arrived and stuck a needle in me. In hospital, I was led through corridors as patients with gaunt expressions stared at me until the tranquilliser kicked in, heralding the reality of my life once again.

14

Family

When I woke up screaming with nightmares in Isla Muir's flat, I thought I should probably explain to her about my breakdown and hospital admissions. But I didn't know how. It was 1986, and I was making a fresh start, trying to look forward, not back. Isla was a communications manager with British Airways.

Attracted by her calm professionalism and demure manner, and having failed in so many previous relationships, I had been pleased when she had shown some interest in me during my short visits to her shared office as part of my studies for the DMS.

Isla had made me feel important enough to ask her out for a beer, followed by inviting her to the Trident Dinner Dance, where I found out that, while she believed that pilots had a certain intelligence, she didn't like their arrogance. Yet, Isla had always wanted to marry a Frenchman, from a nation not always known for its self-effacing nature. I told her that I'd stopped flying because of a chemical imbalance analogous to diabetes, which was technically accurate, but not the whole story.

Nevertheless, as I swapped the heat of Reunion Island for the bitter cold of a Scottish winter, our relationship moved forward. Sitting freezing in Mr Muir's debenture seats at Murrayfield, I politely applauded as Scotland beat both my teams, England, and France in the Five Nations Rugby. With their white peely-wally complexions, the Scots looked hard and unfriendly.

Having been to Haberdashers' and preferring rugby over football helped my case for asking Mr Muir for permission to take Isla's hand in marriage, which was thankfully given. Once we'd convinced the Church of Scotland minister that my lapsed Catholicism and previous divorce were acceptable, a grand wedding in Edinburgh was organised, with a reception in the magnificent Signet Library. My parents accepted their invitation to attend, and for the second time, my stag night was a beer with my future brother-in-law.

During the ceremony, I had the feeling that I was being swept along by forces I couldn't control, the same one I'd had in Newtownards when I married Lynn. University educated, hard-working, and organised, deferring to men was not in Isla's scheme of things, so she had 'to obey' removed from our marriage vows. For my part, I had been less than candid about my medical condition, and while that bothered me, I looked forward to a life of long-overdue stability, even happiness.

Despite her ambitions for a career, I convinced Isla that making babies was more rewarding than producing a pile of magazines for 6,000 ground staff. Soon she was pregnant and ready to leave British Airways, but not before I bought two staff tickets for the Concorde from New York. I sneaked a look in the cockpit on the way past, feeling my usual envy, then grinned as we swung onto the runway.

The four roaring engines kicked us skyward, then to Mach 2.0, only the cabin instrument indicating we'd gone supersonic. At 60,000 feet, the sky was black up above, even in daylight, and the transition from West to East, away from the sun, was rapid. Even as a passenger drinking champagne, the flight had been unique, exhilarating, and unforgettable. As we disembarked, I looked at the pilots again, wanting to be one of them but happy that we had our unborn child with us.

134

Having arrived at 02.17 in the morning, our eldest daughter had her first drink of champagne at the age of 30 minutes when I slipped her a tiny drop off my finger from the small bottle I'd asked the hospital to keep in their fridge. I had told the staff the champagne was to help Isla recover; she'd been given pethidine the day before as I stared in wonder at how she was putting up with the amount of pain involved.

With all the associated yelling and blood, being present at the birth brought home to me what a mindblowing event bringing another human being into the world was. It was momentous, and I didn't contribute much, except to hope it would finish quickly. I didn't understand how anyone could claim men and women were equal after watching such a miracle. We named our miracle Elizabeth.

Another Elizabeth arrived a few days later; the Queen was on a flight I was handling. If I'd been off the pills, I might have made a connection between the two. But for once, I felt calm and stable - I even wondered if I might be all right. Within four years, we produced two more daughters, had a social life, and a four-bedroom detached house in Englefield Green, Surrey.

Isla ran them all with unwavering efficiency, energy, and commitment, while I did my best to get a better job with more money and status. Having no experience of husbands who'd had a major breakdown, Isla couldn't understand why I didn't become a lawyer or a doctor. As well as doing most of the childcare, she worked from home as a freelance public relations consultant, with some temping at a local company.

We had both decided we wanted the girls to go to private school, but I couldn't see how we could afford it. It would have more manageable if I'd been on an airline pilot's salary, but I wasn't; I was ground staff. After ten years, working at EAS was losing its appeal, partly because my aspirations for promotion had come to nothing, but also because the shift work and lack of structure within the unit were becoming wearisome.

Isla thought I could do better – which intellectually I probably could – it was what was going on in the rest of my head that was the problem. British Airways had been good to me by giving me an operational job working with aeroplanes, but the idea of becoming a manager was becoming more fixed in my mind. I wanted to make my mark, stand out, and do something noteworthy that Isla and the children would be proud of me for.

So, I decided I could run a private jet handling agency. I'd put together some figures about projected aircraft movements and revenues and looked into how to set up a new company. The money would come from Mr Sharif, one of our long-standing clients, a quiet, self-effacing man with a bagful of passports. I always gave him good service, and he would chat to me as if I were an equal while guarding his privacy and security like any man with millions would.

Mr Sharif was driven around London in a converted taxi by Danny Powers, an ex-Special Branch Officer who lived near me. I told Danny of my plan to sell off EAS as a going concern, and he set up a meeting with Mr Sharif at the Dorchester Hotel. Mr Sharif was professionally late, allowing me to look at the opulence in the hotel lobby and wonder what I was doing there.

When he arrived, Mr Sharif was polite and listened to me intently. He told me he'd let me know, which was when I realised I was out of my depth. Mr Sharif was just humouring me, a kindness on his part for a man so busy with bona fide business deals. I was trying so hard to be somebody else that I had made a fool of myself. I couldn't do much worse, except that I could.

I wasn't getting anywhere with internal British Airways jobs, so I applied for and was offered the job of Operations Manager at London Business Aviation's (LBA) new private aircraft handling centre at Hatfield. It would be a fresh start, so I accepted, with just the mandatory medical test to get through, references to provide, and reliability and counter-terrorist checks to complete. Wanting to be at my best, I decided to stop taking my pills, allowing five days for the medication to get out of my system.

Three weeks later, the company rescinded their offer of employment because I had approached one of their customers during my familiarisation visit, who had complained about the way I had done so. In my mind, I had had a friendly chat with a couple of pilots before a test flight. LBA said that my behaviour amounted to gross misconduct and was entirely inconsistent with the position that was offered. Which was when I suspected that someone at EAS had let slip the details of my condition.

I was standing on the edge of the abyss. My attempt at getting a proper job had collapsed. I went back on my medication and apologised to LBA. They were unimpressed, so I started legal proceedings against them for defamation, refuting their gross misconduct allegation and demanding compensation for premature termination of employment.

That didn't work, so I tried to get back into British Airways. But because I'd resigned to take the LBA position, I'd lost my old job at EAS. They didn't even want me to work out my months' notice. Sir Colin Marshall, The Chairman of British Airways, sent me a goodwill message while I contemplated how my life was spinning out of control.

With the help of a British Airline Pilots Association solicitor, I made a last, desperate attempt to get back into the airline by taking them to an Industrial Tribunal for constructive dismissal. At the hearing, British Airways offered me some money which the solicitor advised me to take. It was the end of 20 years in aviation, from student pilot to airline pilot to unemployed ground staff. They even took my staff travel concessions away. And there was no one else to blame - it was Olympic class hara-kiri.

This time I had Isla and three young children to look after. Isla coped and supported me in every practical way possible. She demonstrated her best qualities without complaint, holding the five of us together through a challenging time.

With me soon well enough to function normally again, we prepared to move forward. Fortunately, our financial situation was reasonably secure, by the provision Isla's parents had made for their seven grandchildren's education and beyond, through careful investment, and restricting themselves to one large house in the Murrayfield area of Edinburgh.

To my shame, my parents made no financial contribution to their grandchildren's upbringing at all, taking the view that Isla's parents were 'rich and powerful' because Donald Muir was a senior solicitor in Edinburgh and could therefore pay. This was despite my parents owning up to six properties at any one time in France and the UK: the house in Natal Road; three tiny cottages joined together in Steeple Bumpstead; Magali, inherited; Bécherel a quiet hideaway, also in Brittany; and a small country house in Conches, Normandy bought from my godfather.

With no interest in being entrepreneurs or in business, my parents bought these properties on impulse and emotional grounds, never once letting any of them out for their peace of mind. Some of them were little more than storerooms for boxes of memorabilia and old Christmas cards my mother accumulated to satisfy her need for artefacts to keep her mind active with memories in her later years.

Preferring to keep themselves to themselves, my parents hardly ever took in guests other than family, partly because of my mother's fear of being laughed at for her sentimental attachment to the items she liked to have around her. For his part, my generally anti-social father had turned his back on his English roots and family in favour of a more French way of life, severing all contact with his parents in 1975 through a castigating letter to his mother.

My parents also fell out with Aubrey (my father's brother) about a tent, and Denise (my mother's sister) over my grandmother's inheritance, to the background of an accusation from my mother that Denise had pursued my father when he had been married to her.

I envied Isla's large, clannish family, where having four children was the norm, with their shared culture and unified approach to hating the English. At least my half-French blood gave me some acceptability with her relatives and friends; the Auld Alliance between Scotland and France giving me a conversation piece with the generally dour Scots.

Isla's parents were kind, generous and hospitable people who I respected and liked. They had a wide circle of friends, busy social lives, and interests in the community. They had standards too, which included reminding their daughter to 'Remember who you are,' whenever she went out, the concept of PLUs (People Like Us), and her father scrupulously observing the rules of golf. He honoured me by taking me to play at Muirfield, where he patiently explained that when one is offered a stroke on a hole where one risks getting a cricket score, one graciously accepts rather than rudely hacking away and slowing the play down.

For the Muirs, it was custom and practice to invite my parents to visit Edinburgh. However, my father allowed the working-class chip on his shoulder to override the hand of friendship and declined. According to him, Donald and Moira Muir were middle class and therefore 'snooty,' contrasting with his more unorthodox approach to social norms. My parents would wait to be asked to help out, in case they did anything 'wrong,' while at the Muirs, proactivity was expected and welcomed, provided it followed established rules.

It seemed to me that my father both envied and despised people who took charge and managed others, while he preferred to immerse himself in the minutiae of a task, completing it to the exacting standards that he set himself, as did his father. He refused to play the piano at the Muir's on the basis that he hadn't adequately warmed up and practised, thereby depriving himself of an opportunity to shine.

While my mother would have loved to have visited Scotland, she never did. Being caught between the two cultures caused me to turn against my parents in favour of my wife and children, compromising my already fragile sense of identity. My mother had the traditional French view that children and grandchildren were *expected* to visit the grandparents, which wasn't going to happen with the girls' upbringing in England.

When they were young, St Lunaire was an excellent option, safe, and with plenty of accommodation. However, as the years went by, the girls didn't appreciate my mother's insistence on having long lunches indoors, with a sunny beach five minutes' walk away, as well as the intense questioning sessions that my teacher parents liked to administer to educate them. It was done in good faith, but this was not what the girls expected from grandparents, particularly with their Scottish ones being so different.

A consequence of all of this was that we took holidays in Tunisia, Portugal, and Greece instead, our best times as a family. My parents didn't understand why, so my mother started blaming Isla for everything. She believed that the Muirs 'looked down on mere teachers as vulgar and common,' and that Isla, with an older sister and one who had been born profoundly deaf, had been neglected as a child, which had made her domineering. She complained that Isla was bossy and accused her of preventing me from speaking to the girls in French while growing up.

For my part, I understood and accepted why the girls favoured Isla's parents over mine and enjoyed seeing them happy with their Scottish family on our visits to Edinburgh, despite the frequent severe weather. I also appreciated the Muirs' organised and uncomplaining Britishness. My parents did take us all to Euro Disney once, the best thing they ever did for us.

15

Amateur Dramatics

After leaving British Airways and LBA, my first job was telesales at the Moat House Hotel in Shepperton, trying to sell discount dining cards over the phone. The location by the river was idyllic and picturesque but spoilt by a sales manager half my age shouting at me to make more calls because it was all about percentages.

He and his ilk taught me about the psychology of hard selling and how to have an answer for everything, with the result that I got excited when I made a sale and realised that I had some talent for speaking fluently and engagingly. The job also kept me out of the house, something which Isla appreciated. She wasn't so convinced about my career choice, even with the high rewards promised.

Next was a meeting in a training room that briefly reminded me of *Top Gun*, with guys looking around to see who would make it through selection. Except it was in Luton and for learning to sell an exterior wall covering rather than fly F-14 fighter jets.

The company taught successful applicants how to convince 'prospects' that their houses were falling down to such a degree that they needed the special coating to be applied to their homes. I had to buy an eight-inch cold chisel to poke at the walls to demonstrate how a layer of the glop would protect properties and make them look fresh.

The price was 'only £4,000 because we happen to be in the area'; otherwise, it would be £6,000 the following week. The product appeared to be effective; it was everything else that I didn't like, from the managers in their sharp suits to the saddos like me trying to make the sales calls. On my first solo, they sent me to visit a 90-year-old man who didn't know which month it was.

I was barely ten seconds into my sales pitch when I stopped, closed my book, and decided there had to be better ways of making a living. It wasn't good work anyway because they weren't going to pay me until I made a sale. So, I had a chat and a cup of tea with the old boy and told the sales manager where to put the chisel.

There weren't too many opportunities for ex-airline pilots without any other useful qualifications. So, despite my sales career showing all the promise of a fish in the fryer, I signed up with Encyclopaedia Britannica as a sales representative in desperation. They didn't ask any questions about my medical history, and I sold a set to an attractive single mother on my first night out. I was sure it was a set-up, as she cancelled within 14 days.

With my British Airways smile on full power, I learnt a lot about aardvarks as I showed Volume One to passers-by at *Bird World* and shopping centres. The genuine buyers would ring up Britannica Head Office, who would then send a manager round to complete the sale and pocket the commission. Isla was less than impressed with my ten-sales tie after a year part-time with Britannica, even with a Scottish thistle on the front of their books.

Following Isla's lead, I took part-time work inputting data and editing reports for a management consultancy in English and French alongside students half my age but twice as bright. Yet, data inputting was like a night out with Wonder Woman compared to technical translating.

Working for various agencies, I would sit at home in front of a computer for 12 hours a day, turning French documents on Tender Decision Criteria, car part inventories and medical equipment into English ones, and my brain into blancmange. I told myself I was doing it for my family, not for me.

More interesting, socially valuable, and lucrative was ad hoc interpreting for Customs, using my old contacts at the airport to have me registered as an official legal interpreter in French. Having made myself an identity card, I put myself on 24-hour call to the Harmondsworth Detention Centre.

Because I wore a jacket and tie, I'd get respect from the Custody Officers, the contract staff, the solicitors, and the detainees. During the confidential consultations, the detainees would talk to me as if I were their only friend in the world, which I probably was at that point in their lives. Their main interest was to know their likely sentence and how the judge could be bribed.

I sympathised with some of the detainees who came through; they'd been promised $1,000 in Mali, Togo, or Benin to bring drugs into the UK, then the chief bad man would report them to Customs so that the little guy would get caught and divert attention from the primary carrier with a suitcase full of the stuff.

The mule would be invited to defaecate in the specially-designed toilet while the staff looked for the drugs in the fallout, and I'd get £60 per hour waiting for that to happen. When it did, we would all head for the Magistrate's Courts, although there wasn't much defence against having cocaine in one's bowel movements, so the next stop was usually the Crown Court, followed by prison.

With Haberdashers' and French on my CV, I eventually got a proper job. It couldn't have been because of what I said at the interview because I hardly said a word. The Managing Director (MD) did all the talking while I nodded and looked keen. Being the Customer Service Manager of a firm selling technical standards only 15 minutes drive from home looked promising. I was supposed to deal with customer complaints in English and French, and manage 14 sales and dispatch staff, all women.

Early on, I wondered why I was referred to as the Sales Manager and the Office Manager. Until I found out I was also expected to contribute to the firm's strategic direction, sort out sales queries and mediate disputes between office cliques. There weren't enough hours in the day to accomplish all the tasks required of me. I needed the skills of a circus juggler, the skin of a rhino, and the aplomb of a diplomat, none of which I had. If I had shoved a broom up my backside, I could have swept the floor and then called myself the Office Cleaning Manager too.

With no training or experience in management or any real idea about how to run a business, I always ended up working late to clear the outstanding workload - I was out of my depth, again. The women either felt sorry for me or didn't like me at all. By the end of my time there, someone had pulled the distributor leads off my car, and I was respected as much as a dose of leprosy. When he fired me, the MD said he was surprised I'd stuck it out so long.

To take my mind off work and with Isla's encouragement, I took up golf in a bid to achieve the normality I had envisaged while looking out of a window at the St Andrews Hospital golf course. I had the build for the game and was competitive but soon realised that sociability and following unspoken rules of behaviour were more important than just striking a little white ball. Unused to the company of men, I felt uncomfortable and started looking for a different hobby.

Joining the St Jude's Players' amateur dramatics group gave me an excuse to mess about on a stage, meet up in the pub every week, and feel a part of something creative. As Vasaleno, King of all the Gypsies in the Christmas panto, I prepared my entrance from the back of the village hall looking swarthy and mean, while the dancers performed *Thriller* in luminescent skeleton outfits.

The lights faded to a complete blackout, then at least 100 girls from the local Brownies in the audience began screaming. I had never heard such an ear-piercing, glass-shattering sound, even from jet engines at the airport. The spotlight was turned onto me as a young lad came out without warning to stand in the aisle and face me.

'You don't frighten me, mister,' he said, 'and it's not a real knife anyway.'

The Brownies backed him up with another deafening cacophony of high-pitched squealing that would have sent a whole squadron of banshees back to their cave. I loved it.

The amateur dramatics was a lifesaver for social contact and gave me some much-needed confidence, but I still needed paid work. One of the players suggested I become an extra, a background artist, a walk-on in films and TV. I made an appointment to meet Ray Knight, the owner of one of the well-known extra agencies, found out his son went to Haberdashers' and convinced him that I was serious. I was in. All I had to do was be available and wait by the phone.

My first job was pretending to be a ballroom dancer in the BBC's *No Bananas* in 1995. At £60 a day basic, I was soon offered more work standing around street corners on cold winter nights waiting to be a passer-by or being an anonymous person sitting in a café miming a conversation without looking as if I was miming a conversation.

In the film and television industry, I was on the lowest rung of the food chain - moving wallpaper. Being new to the business, I found it easy to say nothing and do as I was told, to watch and learn that a redhead was a kind of lamp, sticks were the camera tripod, and that the director was God. There was a strict communication hierarchy from him or her downwards where no one spoke out of turn, and extras were only supposed to talk to the second assistant director. No one moved equipment except the crew for safety reasons.

The experienced extras would talk about how good it used to be when there was central casting and how bad it became when the film companies would let anyone off the street do background work, i.e. people like me. I didn't care; I was hungry to get into the business and get away from myself.

All the time I was working, I was telling myself I could do better. I had the education, motivation, and ambition to have become a pilot; therefore, I reasoned I could apply the same dedication to being an extra. I wanted to regain some of my status as a pilot, starting at the bottom rung of a ladder, not knowing where the top was but determined to get there.

An introvert by nature, I wasn't a natural performer, but as the job entailed mainly waiting around to be told what to do, that didn't seem to matter. I chatted and gossiped with the other extras: strippers, ex-policemen, moonlighting cabin crew, bouncers, and wannabes like me.

I learned about the performing arts business from retired actors and enjoyed the pretty girls' company while avoiding the loud and rowdy show-offs. The ageing queens would flirt with me and tell me I was going to be a star, and I would smile politely, as I did when a very attentive man from the wardrobe department complimented me about the size of my calves while fitting me for tight trousers for my role as a courtier in Kenneth Branagh's *Hamlet*.

Then one of the principal actors came over to talk to me. I thought this was unusual as the actors usually kept their distance from the extras until I realised he was hitting on me. I respected him because he could reel off pages of Shakespeare but felt uncomfortable at his advances, extricating myself as tactfully as possible.

The pinnacle of background work was to get a line. It meant more money and was wannabe heaven. On an episode of *Bramwell,* Jemma Redgrave would be sawing someone's leg off in a tunnel, and the First Assistant Director asked me if I could say: 'Right you are, sir' on cue.

Well, of course I could say that. I was sent to Hair and Make-up when I realised delivering dialogue wasn't as easy as it looked from an armchair at home. Running the line over and over in my head, it began to take on nightmarish proportions. I kept getting the words mixed up and felt the pressure growing.

Then came the calls for 'Quiet please,' 'Sound,' 'Camera,' and 'Action', and I managed to say the line in the right place. No one seemed to notice, the crew did things to the set, and the Director discussed lighting changes with the DOP (Director of Photography.) There was another take to be done and then another; I repeated the line, and again, and again, and suddenly it wasn't a novelty anymore; it was a job.

Three days before playing a Customs Officer on *The Knock*, I'd done an interpreting job for the real HM Customs. Therefore, I felt qualified to make some suggestions on the basis that they would rewrite the script and change the entire shooting schedule on my say-so.

They didn't, but I was given two lines and got them right, despite having to do them seven times, while the lead actor got increasingly stressed as he kept getting his lines wrong. He had a lot more than I did, but I'd already decided I was getting the hang of acting and had marked myself down as having a regular part in the show as an advisor.

That didn't happen either, but I got plenty of other work, queuing up to get signed-off by second assistant directors who were usually so young they looked as if they'd just come off a paper round.

At 42 and dressed in a Victorian costume with a moustache on *Wings of a Dove*, somebody pointed out that I resembled the disappeared Lord Lucan. I signed up with a lookalikes agency with a plan to get booked for a job as him and then not turn up.

147

16

Star Wars

According to some of the other patients at St Andrew's Hospital, I was going to be the next James Bond. Messrs Saltzman and Broccoli were going to take the multi-million-dollar risk on an ex-pilot with no acting experience on the opinions of the inmates of a real Cuckoo's Nest. I didn't think this was likely, not while I was on the pills anyway. Besides, Pierce Brosnan needed the work.

Yet when the camera swept past me at my workstation in the MI6 Operations Room at Frogmore Studios on *Tomorrow Never Dies*, I admitted to getting a thrill about being in a Bond film, even if Pierce never acknowledged my sacrifice. I watched him and Judy Dench doing their work, thinking I'd made it into the final cut. Disappointingly I hadn't, although I was paid £450 for three days work, and took away my prop MI5 identity card.

The money was welcome, but to be anything more than background in a major film looked out of my reach. To have the opportunity to play a leading role, I would have to rely on amateur dramatics. So, when the Staines Light Operatic Society (SLOS) saw me in a St Jude's Players' pantomime and offered me the co-lead in the light musical *Free as Air*, I agreed. It earned me a National Operatic and Dramatic Association review: *This was a good piece of acting, and on the vocal side, there is a pleasing voice waiting to be developed.*

On a higher rung of the showbusiness ladder was the BJ Agency belonging to an old-school, full-blown, homosexual theatrical agent who would invite men to undress for him in his flat to see if they warranted a place in his casting book. He didn't ask me, though; maybe he didn't fancy me or perhaps it was the glint in my eye that told him I wasn't going to play ball or anything else. He still took me on, and I prepared to put all my self-taught acting training to use - as an airline pilot.

A German travel agency wanted to film a stuffed bird going across the cockpit window of an airliner for a commercial directed by Tony Scott, Ridley's son. The two pilots were supposed to look suitably amazed. Since I was the only person at the casting in a uniform with four rings on it, I got the captain's job and was paid £272.96 for the day, more than a real pilot's pay in 1996.

I'd always liked the look of Sandra Bullock so, when she came over to speak to me during a break in filming *In Love and War*, my heart skipped a beat. She was friendly and chatty, and I didn't know what to say. I was just an extra, and it never occurred to me that she might actually have wanted to talk to me.

More ambitiously, having been standing around on a balcony as the Italian Adjutant for most of the day while Sandra and Chris O'Donnell did their scenes, I was bursting to say something in an Italian accent to get in on the action. But Sir Richard Attenborough was managing perfectly well to direct the film without my help. With no acting pedigree to speak of, I felt privileged to be occupying the same few square metres of Shepperton film set as him and the stars.

Sandra did have competition for my affections. On the feature film *The Saint*, another wholesome American actress, Elisabeth Shue, tried to chat with me. Aware of my lowly status and unaware of who *she* was, I politely dismissed her approach, which made her more interested. I was staring at loveliness in the face and pushing it away.

Less interested in me but equally professional was a young actress called Keeley Hawes playing my assistant in a promotional video for a New Zealand band called The Mutton Birds. Neither of us had any dialogue, but I made the mistake of trying to be paternal towards her on the utterly spurious basis that my role in the video was more senior to hers. The ambition and focus in Keeley's eyes put me in my place, telling me that the video was just a few more pounds in her pocket on her way to stardom and nothing else.

I could see that crossing the line from being an extra to an actor would need considerable mental adjustment to balance my lack of self-esteem against my arrogance and occasional sense of superiority.

Sure that I wanted to be an actor, I contacted Malone & Knight, a reputable theatrical agency with a small number of clients rather than the hundreds on the books of extras casting agencies. They weren't in the top tier of agents, but Malcolm and Jane, who ran the agency, were decent and honest and took me on, which meant I had an agent to my name.

Waiting expectantly for my first audition for a genuine part on a TV production, I was surprised the first job the agency booked me for was as an extra on *EastEnders* at Elstree Studios. While grateful for the work, I didn't like the rumoured connections with real East End gangsters, which some, including the actors, found alluring. It was unlikely I would get discovered as a Cockney geezer, so I carried on waiting for my big break.

In conversation, I'd joke that I had been to the Nike School of Drama – with its motto of 'Just Do It' – and made lists of actors who'd never been to drama school. Bob Hoskins and Ray Winston were in that group in the UK, but I was told they were different. Well, I was different too.

When I researched how many well-known US actors had begun their careers, I discovered that many of them hadn't been to drama school. James Dean, Clint Eastwood, Sylvester Stallone, Brad Pitt, Ben Affleck, Matt Damon, Bruce Willis had all started out as extras.

Neither being professionally trained nor a great storyteller at the time, I would have to rely on my science-based ability to analyse characters instead. The actor's refrain of 'what's my motivation?' summed up the process. Once all the layers of sophistication, culture, fashion had been stripped away from human beings, I saw the same core emotions: happiness, sadness, anger, hate, fear, jealousy, and the rest.

For me, it was the same for all people throughout history, with infinite and complex combinations thereof. How these emotions manifested themselves into behaviours and how those behaviours could indicate what emotions were being experienced fascinated me. It was both simple and complicated and interesting to learn about.

It was marketing-manager-turned-actor Geoff Cotton who showed me how I could play at psychoanalysis, act, and earn a decent living; through corporate acting. It began with Assessment Centres for Pearl Assurance, where candidates interviewed 'clients' played by actors as part of their selection process, all the time under observation.

The roleplays had to be as natural as possible, so the candidates thought they were in an actual meeting. It was 'small' acting, more like film acting than 'big' theatre acting. Afterwards, I'd give feedback on what the candidate said and *how* they said it, with reference to their tone of voice and body language.

Corporate work suited me, and I was good enough at it to work four to five days a week. It was almost like a proper job, going to work in a suit during regular hours in various industry sectors, with constantly changing scenarios and daily routines.

On the basis that there were lines to learn and a named character to play, corporate work was considered acting, although I'd never get a credit for it, just a reasonable fee, which went down well at home. I began to feel as if I was part of the human race.

Sometimes I didn't have to wear a suit, as when I was playing a stroppy Firearms Inspector for the Independent Police Complaints Commission or a difficult member of the public collecting his dog from a candidate RSPCA inspector. The latter's brief was that I'd left my dog in my locked car on a hot summer's day. The dog was supposed to have almost cooked, then been rescued by the police and taken to the candidate.

One was an ex-military policeman who had all the charm of a psychopathic crocodile. By the time the roleplay was over, I – in character - was threatening to smash his head through the roof. He failed. Five minutes later, I was almost in tears because of how the next candidate, a 22-year-old female student, had made me feel so guilty about how I'd treated my dog. She came out of the assessment room to find me calmly drinking a cup of coffee, waiting for the next candidate.

'How on earth do you do that?' she asked. I shrugged and smiled in reply.

'It's what I do.' I said.

Back in the non-corporate world of television, I had to crash my way into a house through sugar glass windows to open an episode of *Dangerfield* before my character was found dead in a car that he had driven into a river. The Director wanted the car pulled out with me still sitting in it, keeping me there as long as he could, in case they needed one more shot, which was pointless as I was shaking with cold; not very realistic if I was supposed to be dead.

Lying naked under a sheet in the morgue was warmer but equally tricky because of the need to keep completely still. Concentrating on keeping my eyelids from twitching was a challenge, but what I was angling for was a proper actor's contract for being heavily featured. The production company wouldn't give me one because I'd been booked through an extras' agency.

In the end, they compromised by giving me a character name which wasn't a credit but looked better on my CV. When the episode was eventually aired, Isla thought that whatever she was doing in the kitchen at the time was more important than watching my most prominent appearance on TV to date.

Around the time the first Star Wars trilogy was on release (1977,) I was flying the BOC Cessna from Leavesden Airfield near Watford. Twenty years on, I was back at Leavesden to work on *Star Wars Episode I: The Phantom Menace*, 'the biggest film of all time.' The location gave me another opportunity to attribute some deep, meaningful connection to events, but instead, I just turned up for the wardrobe fitting at the converted hangars as instructed.

Four crews of three Naboo Pilots were chosen from hundreds of extras. My crew were selected as the primary one for the film, which made me a Naboo Fighter Pilot and the co-pilot on Queen Amidala's Royal Starship. I suspected that someone, somewhere, knew that I'd been a real pilot once.

The early starts at the studio had the same calm serenity and beauty as when I pushed the Cessna out of its hangar at Stansted. Rabbits appeared out of the mist again, and I felt similarly purposeful, although this time as a pretend pilot instead of a real one.

The production team always got the extras to the location early in case one of them didn't show up, and they had to get a replacement, but that didn't happen very often as to be on a Star Wars film was considered the ultimate in extra work, even by me. Everything was locked down, and we weren't allowed to take anything offsite on pain of instant ex-communication, although I did smuggle out a call sheet with my name on it.

Walking to wardrobe past the models of pod racer engines for a Gungan race was surreal. Tridents were a thing of the past; now, it was all about Naboo and Tattouine. They dressed me in four layers of heavy wool, equipment belts and a helmet, not ideal for a sweltering summer day under studio lights. My uniform cooked me alive, even with the runners constantly topping us up with water as we waited to run across the hangar floor or watch Ewan McGregor making friends with everyone.

Then 'Darth Maul' came in through the big doors at the end of the set with his black and red make-up and swinging his double-handed light sabre. We all stared in awe, willingly sitting through rehearsal after rehearsal and take after take before the lunch break, which I took seated next to a silent R2D2 robot.

Queen Amidala's Royal Starship looked remarkably like one of my real hero aircraft, the SR71 Lockheed Blackbird. However, inside, it turned out to be a construction of plywood and plastic tubes, with control knobs that had been stuck on with glue and air-conditioning made up from old vacuum cleaner parts. There was space for four crew, and some of the warning lights worked, but the thing was never going to fly very well with a 35mm film camera poking in from where the windshield should have been.

I turned up for the shoot and was introduced to the actor playing the Starship's commander, Ralph Brown of *Withnail and I* fame. As he, Liam Neeson, Hugh Quarshie and Ewan did their work, I set about being as unobtrusive as possible. I'd been chosen to be there but as part of the set. This was the high point of my career as an extra, an ex-airline pilot sitting in a wooden cockpit on a disused airfield.

Then came the biggest 'if only' moment of my life. George Lucas came over to me on set to chat. A quiet, shy man who didn't seem to get excited about anything, George was also a busy man and didn't talk to anyone without a reason. Fans would have sold their homes to have been where I was. And there he was, standing next to me, listening and available. All I had to do was say something intelligent.

Perhaps a little delusion would have been helpful for once. Harrison Ford had been an extra before playing Han Solo for George and then became a superstar. But rather than talking to the film legend about how I would love to work with him on his next project, I spoke about being an ex-pilot. I could sense his interest seeping away like melting butter. Maybe he was just being sociable - I'll never know.

George surrounded himself by the best in the business to make his vision happen. The producer, Rick McCallum, was a relaxed guy. Shortage of money was not his primary concern in a Star Wars film. One lunchtime, I sat down to eat, only to be joined by Rick and half a dozen Americans who talked about dollars, hundreds of millions of them. I felt even more insignificant than usual as I dug into my mashed potato.

I was fine on the surface: punctual, polite, attentive, and obedient as all extras should be, but with a chip still firmly attached to my shoulder about losing my pilot's licence. I still hadn't got into the habit of being nice to people, which seemed to be the key to getting on in the business. One beautiful, dark-haired girl did have this skill and was always ready to chat with me on set. She was 16 and playing one of the Queen's handmaidens. Her name was Keira Knightley.

17

Actor

The legal definition of insanity was an inability to distinguish fantasy from reality, so there were those, particularly my wife, who thought that acting wasn't the best thing for me. However, since being someone else was compulsory for being an actor, it looked like an attractive proposition as being myself hadn't been a resounding success to date. In any case, I couldn't think of what else to do.

One of the benefits of my Anglo-French parentage was the ability it had given me to change personas quickly. When I switched between English and French, my personality changed, as well as my body language and tone of voice. Similarly, I would talk to professionals in my usual voice and drop aitches when talking to the man in the garage. It was fun, but sometimes I wasn't sure what my authentic self was.

I wondered if the medication was stifling my creativity and acting ability and would be better if I came off it. But it was too much of a risk. I knew what happened when I was off the pills; it was better to stay on them and pretend to be an actor.

What I needed was the all-important Equity Card from the actor's union[13]. But it wasn't easy to qualify for one in 2002; evidence of paid work was required with written contracts and sponsorship by a member. I had my lines in *Bramwell* and *The Knock*; the dead Ben Stratton in

---

[13] Equity: the UK trade union that represents performers and creative practitioners working across the entertainment industry.

Dangerfield; The Mutton Birds video; the stuffed bird commercial; some walk-ons as a thief on *Crimewatch* and my appearance in *In Love and War*. My experience doing corporate roleplay and a voiceover as a Frenchman and a Scotsman would probably count, and I included *Free as Air* on the strength of the favourable review. I also had an agent and a friend who would vouch for me in writing – I just needed a new name.

Having been granted French citizenship and a national identity card earlier in the year, I decided that being French might give me something to differentiate me from the thousands of other actors looking for work. So, I set about finding myself a French-sounding name. 'De' in French names made them sound upmarket, and even as an extra I was usually cast as educated, professional types, so I went for 'Philip Delancy' after Delancey Street in Camden, where my brother lived. Delancy also worked well enough in English, as I needed to get work speaking English too.

When the Equity Card came through, I felt like an actor, even without having gone to drama school. With my perception of acting as an arty, liberal, weave-your-own-sandals type of activity, the acting profession was unexpectedly conservative, so I remained concerned that I'd blown my chances of getting recognised acting parts by having worked as an extra.

I had the idea that to be a 'proper' actor; you had to be able to talk theatre with your cigarette held at just the right angle and know or sleep with someone who liked you; getting on in the business appeared to be about hard networking rather than talent.

At least my Equity Card gave me credibility with my mother-in-law. Under my new name, I'd go to auditions as the actor Philip Delancy and wait for the eyes of the receptionist to dissolve into pools of love and devotion at the sound of my English with a French accent.

'If you could fill in the form please, then I'll take a photo.'

'Off coss. I feel ze passion. Eet ees not jus' a spak, but a flemm, a beeg roring flemm. I feel it now, burning, burning.'

'Take a seat over there. Can you speak English?'

'Sure, I can give you Northern, Cockney, Aussie or American.'

Even those who had worked in the business for more than five minutes would register some surprise at this sudden transformation in my character - I felt like a performer and enjoyed it. My Equity name was ready to be used for my first authentic acting credit through Malone and Knight, while under my real name, the extra work was still helping to pay the bills.

I signed up to more agencies, continuing to be singled out for special jobs such as playing a French Fire Commander, speaking French in a documentary about a fire in the Eurotunnel. I helped with the script and charged about in the smoke for two days delivering lines, frustrated that I was doing an actor's work with a special skill, for £150 a day.

On location, I watched and learned how actors went about their business, their hand movements, the way they walked, dressed and spoke. I wanted to be on their side of the line, to be a working actor. Standing around dressed as a British Airways pilot in *Parent Trap* was the point at which I decided actually to do something about it.

With an eye on my CV and to start building a showreel, I auditioned for a part in a student final year project at Bournemouth University, on one of the most sought-after film and media courses in Britain. It was a *Dr Who* trailer with some special effects and a night shoot.

There were over 20 applicants for the unpaid part, as there was always the possibility that the director would turn out to be the next Steven Spielberg. I got the part and dressed up in a black roll-neck pullover and looked mean. The

158

students treated me like an actor, not an extra. It was a good feeling, although Isla didn't appreciate the distinction when it came to the absence of a fee.

Productions, where the characters had names like Natalia Nickersoff and Madame Sexy Farquar, weren't going to be up for any Oscars, but they did count as stage work, something I thought I should try. I saw the ad for murder mystery evenings on a tube train and applied to work with them as Ménage à Trois, the smooth French womaniser. There was a loose plot, but the real entertainment was the interaction and improvisation with up to 300 guests at the Connaught Hotel for their Christmas night out.

After being propositioned a few times, I realised I was there to entertain the clients, not the other way around. We were sent home by Americans for being too lewd and had food thrown at us by Brits for not being lewd enough.

The hotel would run two events on separate floors on the same night, which was handy when one of the actors didn't turn up, and I had to run between the two shows to play the same character twice. It wasn't Shakespeare, but it was professional acting with written contracts giving me £45 at the end of the night.

Most of the other actors I worked with had been to drama school for two years and had done repertory theatre, musical theatre, and Variety. I'd hear about the gigs they performed, the casting directors, and the digs they lived in while doing fringe theatre on little money, their agents going bankrupt, and running off with their wages.

Because they were actors, they told their stories well. I heard about Catherine Zeta-Jones when she was growing up in Wales, Colin Firth at drama school, while I chipped in with tales about flying, claiming a working-class background when it suited me.

I admired those who wrote their own material and performed it in pubs to empty houses. There were ex-barristers, vets, doctors, investment bankers and psychologists who had become actors, as well as those who cheated and lied on their CVs and associated with villains. Some had done prison time. Some actors were friendly and relaxed with everyone, and others were full of themselves. Yet, I learnt to like them as human beings even if they took drugs and read *The Guardian*.

Actors seemed better attuned to picking up changes of mood and feelings than most other folks. Generally, they were sensitive and intuitive and would express their emotions freely and openly. Within five minutes of being in a green room, I'd know everyone's life stories and they about mine. They were often impressed that I had been a pilot and sympathetic about my breakdown.

The more I talked with actors, the less I worried about being found out and stigmatised as having been diagnosed with a mental illness. Many had had issues of their own, perhaps a consequence of artistic and creative personalities. Coming from a family where these characteristics were prevalent made me feel increasingly accepted and comfortable about who I was.

We were happy to hear about each other's good news and felt comfortable talking about our own. I would fancy one pretty girl after another until I realised there was no end to the stream of attractive women in the profession and learned to treat them as colleagues. In any case, they were usually more interested in the producers and directors. There was hugging, laughs, therapy sessions, running lines and ambition. It was exciting and made me feel alive again.

Even the journey to the audition or set was interesting, to see how people reacted to me according to what I was wearing. If I wore a suit, I'd get more respect than if I wore actor's clothes, usually as dark as possible with a t-shirt, loose jumper, and a backpack. If I were on my way to a class at the Actor's Centre, I would ensure that any papers I was carrying were well-creased and that anything I might need would take half an hour to reach under my laptop, waterproof and water bottle on a crowded underground train.

I couldn't possibly be seen with a briefcase, as only directors and producers used them. Scripts were fine to carry, but nothing too pristine, and always with lots of notes attached. I wouldn't have numbers on show, like credit card statements or other trappings of capitalist wealth. Keeping my copy of *The Times* hidden, I would buy a copy of the *Big Issue* when travelling to big auditions, where some extra karma might be helpful.

The Nike School of Drama and the Murder Mysteries weren't going to qualify me for a career in professional theatre. I understood why people did theatre acting, but serious literature and plays bored me, and besides, they didn't pay very well. Musical theatre needed skills way out of my league: singing, dancing, acting and sometimes doing all three simultaneously.

No, it was going to be film, TV and corporate for me. I loved the visuals in cinema, the close-ups, and the music. I liked that a film could be made perfect with enough takes and without unnecessary arm waving and exaggerated diction. There was a visual record too, which suited my keeper mentality.

On holiday with Isla's family in an insect-ridden part of Southern France with stifling heat and humidity and dogs nearby that barked all the time, the Star Wars production team asked me to come back to Leavesden for some continuity shots. I was off like the Millennium Falcon with its tail on fire. Returning to the massive sound stages at Leavesden was like returning home, or at least to a place where I felt I belonged.

The unit photographer took photos of me as the official but unnamed[14] Star Wars Naboo Pilot, which appeared in The

---

[14] Unofficially in '*Wookiepeedia,*' a Star Wars fan site, I was *Lutin Hollis.*

Star Wars Episode I Visual Dictionary, the Young Jedi collectable card game, and turned me into a ten-centimetre-high plastic model. As the subject of one of the world's smallest fan club, I was invited to Star Wars conventions where I felt privileged to have been in the film at all, even as an extra.

However, none of this was going to get my name on any credits. Four weeks on *Star Wars* was the highlight of my work as a background artist. From then on, it could only go downhill, and it did. When the set of *Shakespeare in Love* suddenly split into two beneath my feet four floors up of the Globe Theatre mock-up at Shepperton Studios, I was inches from falling to my death or being seriously injured. The action was intentional, but no one had bothered to tell me, least of all the Assistant Director, who was completely unmoved. From his perspective, there was no blood, and no one had died, so filming would continue.

There was lots of blood, albeit fake, on a TV production called *The Dark Room*, as the script called for me to have my face smashed in with an axe by Dirvla Kirwan. They built me up with a rubber mask, and I crawled around the floor in fake agony until it was time to wrap.

But the make-up artist used the wrong kind of glue for the mask, and it wouldn't come off. I wondered why it hurt so much when she tried but didn't complain because it was late and everyone wanted to go home, including me. The harder she pulled, the more it hurt, with bits of my skin sticking to the mask. Glad of my membership, Equity helped me to claim compensation to cover loss of earnings and some wear and tear on my face. Fortunately, it healed up.

Incidents like these were making extra work lose all its appeal, and in any case, there were easier ways of making money. 'Just look sexy,' said one agent before she sent me for a casting. I'd just come back from holiday and had a good tan, so wearing a white shirt and black trousers, I went for an audition at the studios in Camden Town and waited around listening to someone talking about a wig and dancing.

Which was when I realised I must have been in the wrong place, as I couldn't dance. A succession of long-haired rock idol types came in and out, all pally-pally, calm, and casual with the Casting Director, dressed in just the right clothes and without giving me a second glance. I stayed out of the way and fumed at the agency for wasting my time. Then someone gave me a black, long-haired wig and a red silk shirt to put on - a chance to strip off and show off my tan!

They played *Stayin' Alive,* and I was told to dance to it. The music went on for a while, and I noticed that a few onlookers had gathered to watch me make a fool of myself. Angry at everyone present, as soon as the ordeal was over, I grunted something, headed for the exit and called the agent. As I vented my frustration, she made soothing noises and got me off the line. I hated that side of the business, the vacuous modelling rather than the acting. At least with acting, I had to use my brain.

The thing was, I got the job, and it turned out to be the best paying job I'd ever had, earning £6,000 for a morning's work, plus usage fees, which was more than my first annual salary as a British Airways pilot. It was June 1998, and Microsoft's Hotmail had been created under the slogan 'Be who you want to be,' featuring a series of wacky-looking characters, including mine, the 'lurve_god.' For him, they wanted someone who looked like a prat; as far as I was concerned, they got the real thing.

Then I got my first television role as a full Equity-contracted actor, in an episode of *999* about the true story of an accident where a Whirlwind helicopter crashed into the sea off Lundy. It was for BBC Bristol, and I played the senior RAF officer on the board of enquiry. The script had my rank of Wing Commander as below the Squadron Leader of one of the other actors, so I explained the RAF rank system to the Director.

I didn't do this just for his benefit; I'd checked the script to see which part had the most dialogue. I was learning the business, taking opportunities whenever they presented themselves. When they asked me to make up a name for my character, I chose Wing Commander Appleton, then put my name down as Philip Delancy for the credits.

With a family, I was after the better-paid work, which meant in commercials. I wasn't going to get any of the really big paying ones, like the car or supermarket ads, as I didn't have a growth of beard or a 'guy in the pub' face. So I settled for being a square-jawed team leader in a cigarette commercial for Pakistan, the Golfer in the risqué *For Wayward Swingers*, and a doctor giving parents bad news in a Cerebral Palsy publicity film. These also counted as acting for my *Spotlight*[15] CV.

Being a professional actor seemed to include complaining about employers, agents, low pay, long hours, and poor working conditions. Instead of joining in, I signed up for an eight-week course in basic acting at the Actor's Centre. Attendance was Monday evenings, but the tutor worked the 16 of us participants hard, with homework on Shakespeare, improvisation, monologues, duologues – all new to me.

I loved it and wanted more, even taking additional private lessons to improve my skills. All I needed was a challenging role for me to practice on; something different, something out of my comfort zone – as a private jet handling agent!

It was to play a part in a documentary-style film called *Hard News, Soft Money*, 'mixing real-life incidents and media personalities with actors where fact and fiction are inextricably intertwined,' according to the writer and director Tim Purcell.

He had interviewed me for what I thought was a roleplay job months earlier, but I had heard nothing until he

---

[15] The main British professional actors' casting directory

called me to see if I was interested in this new project. There was no script; it was all improvised with no rehearsals; I would only know what I needed to know and wouldn't know what was real and what wasn't.

There were real individuals involved: an ex-Mossad driver, David Shayler (a former member of MI6,) Cynthia Payne, Max Clifford, Howard Marks, and 'Max Hansen' the main character, a shadowy figure from the world of international finance setting up a satellite broadcasting platform for free speech. Tim wanted me to play the fixer guy who organises a helicopter and a private jet to take Max Hansen to Paris.

'Of course,' I said. 'So, I'm real and not real?'

'Exactly,' replied Tim.

The plan was to fly Max from Liscombe Park to Luton in a helicopter, then in a jet to Paris, Le Bourget. I rang Tim a few days later with a quote for the charter, proposing to use Heathrow instead of Luton due to maintenance work at Luton during the planned shoot dates and my familiarity with the procedures at Heathrow.

I told him I could arrange the filming permits and the handling through EAS and need some upfront payment for the charter company. In reality, I thought the whole idea was pie in the sky - so to speak - but that a new career flying all over the world as an aviation consultant to the film industry might be beckoning.

I also wondered if I might be going 'high' and fantasising until a cheque landed on my doormat for £2,970 payable to the charter company, including a 7.5% commission for me. I set everything up, still unsure if I was an aviation person or an actor.

After turning up as a VIP passenger at Heathrow and checking in at the EAS desk where I'd spent many hours waiting for passengers of my own, I was taken to the tarmac to wait for the helicopter with Max on board, still with the niggling feeling that I was out of my mind.

Already seated on the Citation jet was a cameraman with a handheld mini DV camera and Valentine, who was supposed to be an MI5 Officer. I didn't know any different; in the same way, he didn't know I wasn't an aviation consultant, although I was. Max turned up in the helicopter, and we departed for Paris, still not knowing who or what was real and what wasn't.

Valentine and I played along, staying in our characters, with no one saying a word during the entire trip. I'd fixed up handling at Le Bourget, and the plot was for Max to do something shadowy and financial in Paris while the aircraft waited.

I was still half-convinced I was going mad, although I was sure I was taking my pills. The final confirmation of my insanity came when I met the handling agent on duty at Paris Le Bourget. Her name was Magali, the name of our family house in Brittany. I'd never heard of any other woman called Magali, yet there she was with it written on her badge. I began thinking that the whole trip to Paris was all about me.

Magali was exceptionally beautiful, and because she was providing a service to someone who had just stepped off a private jet, she was also very friendly and welcoming. Typically, I thought this was because she fancied me, so I turned on the charm. She was keen to chat; I asked for her phone number and got it. I was unhappy at home and caught up in the heady excitement of flying to Paris; I wanted to run away with Magali.

Once we found out that Max had been 'shot' in Paris, all captured on tape, I flew back to Heathrow on the jet and went home. Max had either set the film up himself as a vanity project, or he wanted to make out that he'd been killed so he could disappear. I never found out the truth and never saw him again.

At the wrap party, I renewed my acquaintance with Valentine, who *was* an actor but was still making out that he was a spy, insisting on communicating using his cover name.

He and the rest of the cast and crew couldn't believe that I'd been a real handling agent and that I was an actor too. Watching the movie with the rest of the cast and crew, we were all baffled about the project, what was real and what was fiction.

It seemed Isla wasn't too sure about my understanding of the difference between real life and my imaginary world either. I'd sent Magali my credit card for her to arrange a trip somewhere for us which she returned to Isla, who didn't believe me when I said I'd only had one conversation with the French girl.

However, it *was* true, as was feeling a failure at not having a profession that was acceptable to Isla, despite playing a vital role in a challenging project combining management skills, acting ability, and financial negotiation. I'd felt valued, respected, and appreciated on a relatively glamorous job, while at home, I felt an outcast. Within a few weeks, I was readmitted to hospital with a diagnosis of hypomania.

Discharged 16 days later, I shut myself away in the study with my aircraft models, wondering how life would have turned out if I'd have joined the RAF. The Phantom looked sexier than ever; flying one would have fulfilled my dreams more than airliners. I'd have been in the Services family, in an environment where idealism was encouraged, and I'd have been looked after.

It would have been exhilarating to do 700 mph at low level while trying to make the world a better place. I was arrogant and confident enough to believe I would come out on top in combat with 20 tons of fighter plane strapped to my backside, and also crazy enough to have been prepared to sacrifice myself for my fellow man.

18

Mad, Bad, or Sad?

Naked, I switch the light on, pull back the warm quilt, and head for the bathroom. After a long, satisfying pee, I turn to the washbasin and look up to the mirror. I see a tanned, square face with slightly bloodshot green eyes and short, brown hair, unwashed and messy.

I stretch my arms above my head, lower them and flex my pecs, helped by an intake of breath. My biceps could do with some work, but I haven't time for that now; alert and energised, I'm going to fly. I have been on reduced medication for a week, and there's a sharpness and freedom in my head which tells me I am ready.

With its four gold rings, a pair of generic wings, and a still-ironed white shirt with epaulettes, I note my pilot's uniform is still in good condition as I try it for size - the trousers are a little tight last wore them, 20 years ago. I look like a pilot; I am a pilot. The sound of a car, a dog barking, and water in the pipes register in the back of my mind, but I am unmoved, concentrating on my task.

I go downstairs and detour into the kitchen to put the kettle on, then to the study where I find the aeronautical charts I need, on top of an unopened pack of cigarettes with a cheap lighter hidden from my wife and kept for times of stress. I don't need them tonight; I am calm and organised. I glance towards the Phantom, 747, and Concorde models on my bookcase, motivating me to get airborne.

Passing through the lounge, seeing some of the children's toys, I feel a brief pang of regret, then move on.

Isla has taken the girls to her mother's for a break; I guess they know that sometimes I need to be left alone. The house is quiet, but the start of rain announces the presence of the outside world again.

I make tea, then study my route from Heathrow to Newtownards via the Isle of Man. My finger moves North-North-West to Liverpool, and I think of Gail, the angelic, golden-haired nurse I knew there, and start to well up. Pushing on towards the 'BEL' - the Belfast VOR navigational beacon - I remember the sound of the laconic radio chatter that spoke of my arrivals into Northern Ireland; so technical, yet so evocative of the green, rolling hills.

'Call coasting in,' the controllers would say.

03.00 local time, time to go; Heathrow, the giant radar tower dominating the skyline, and the outline of a Boeing 707 being towed to a distant parking place by a squat tractor, lost in the vastness of the airport, empty and soulless at night. Sitting silently, hidden, and unloved in a corner by a blast fence, the six-seat Navajo looks so tiny in the enormity of Heathrow, waiting for me to bring it to life.

The washed-out night lighting gives the aircraft a furtive, shadowy aspect, while the white-painted metal, with its blue and red flashes, looks familiar and reassuring. G-TAXY, the registration is straddling the split-level door with its lower section housing integral steps and the top to be pushed up until it clicks into place.

Settling into and adjusting my seat, I slowly go through the pre-start checklist, scan the instrument panel, and immediately feel at home. I am out of practice but confident. Turning on the radio and instrument lights, I note the fuel needles are indicating three-quarters full. The engines run with a throaty purr as I bring animation to the dead metal and plastic, and in return, it gives me purpose and delight. Feeling secure and comfortable, I carry out the checks up to 'Ready for taxi,' put on my headset and set the Ground Movement frequency on the comms radio.

It's a while since I've flown, so I am careful to get the essentials right: first heading after take-off, switch on the rotating beacon and navigation lights and release the parking brake. Engine run-ups complete, I declare myself ready for departure, excited but composed.

'Golf Tango Alpha X-Ray Yankee, you are cleared for take-off 27 Left.'

I line up the aircraft just off-centre between the two converging rows of runway edge lights bordering Heathrow's two miles of tarmac to avoid the nosewheel banging on the centre lights. A final check of the engines and instruments, then I slowly increase the power. The edge lights flash past as the airspeed builds - the Navajo is telling me it wants to fly.

At 85 knots, I apply gentle backward pressure to the control column, and the aircraft eases into the night, wings level. Seeing a positive rate of climb on the vertical speed indicator (VSI), I raise the undercarriage and look ahead into the blackness.

At night, with no actual horizon, I must immediately refer to the artificial one to avoid getting disorientated. I don't feel tired at all - in fact; I could not be more awake. My eyes dance over the panel as I feel the power in my hands dominating all the switches, levers, and controls. I see the glowing red exhaust manifolds in the bulbous nacelles of the engines, their three-bladed propellers disking round behind the slight asymmetry of the vibrating spinner.

'Golf X-Ray Yankee, call London Information on 133.05. Good night.'

I can't be bothered with an advisory service, so I turn the radio volume down, climbing to 1,500 feet in and out of the scattered cloud. Heading West with a sprinkling of lights illuminating the void below, I soon pass over the grass airfield at White Waltham, where I learnt to fly. Wanting to find clear air, I increase power and pull back on the control stick. The airspeed needle falls upwards, and the aircraft breaks out above the cloud layer,

Levelling off at 4,000 feet, I may have infringed controlled airspace, but I don't care. There's hardly any air traffic around anyway other than the twinkling flashes moving high above me seemingly so slow, signalling a lone overflying aircraft. I engage the autopilot, sit back, and look up at the moon and stars immovable in their infinite black dome. I am staring at space and beyond, practically touching the heavens.

Droning on, with Birmingham illuminated by the golden glow of its streetlights, I drink tea as I pass Liverpool and the Isle of Man. In my mind, I see the Keenair hangar, Gail's garden, and the Woodgate office, empty and quiet. I look North and think of the children safe in Scotland, vibrant with health and spirit, clever and sociable.

They have what I never had: lots of friends and normality. I'm glad they are happy; their Scottish family will look after them, their mother will explain everything in her no-nonsense way. They will remember me and ask after me.

The groundspeed readout shows 160 knots as I descend towards Newtownards, select flap, level at 1,000 feet, and slow to 140 knots. At the end of the Lough, I turn right, constantly scanning the artificial horizon, outside, altimeter, airspeed indicator (ASI.) Looking left for the runway, I see only darkness where the clubhouse should be – I'm too high.

Nose down, power off, RPM falling. Gear down, level off at 700 feet. Runway in sight. Power on, 120 knots, three greens. I turn left and drop another notch of flap. Marginally low. Power on, full flap. The landing light has picked up the runway. Power off, flare, settle for a thumpy landing, clear left, and bring the aircraft to a stop.

As I stretch for a break from the confines of my seat, the sound of the rain falling provides respite from the oppressive, dark stillness of the night. The absence of other sounds allows my thoughts to wander from the narrow view of Newtownards Airfield before me and into the broader aspects of Northern Ireland and its history of violence. The news film of the two corporals who strayed into a Republican funeral then taken from their car and shot by the Provisional IRA[16] comes into my mind.

I can only imagine the terror they must have felt as they knew they were about to die. My secret story had me picking up Gerry Adams and three other men to take them to the mainland. I see Adams' beard and his henchmen with faces like granite as they climb aboard my aircraft and install themselves. I want to strike out at them.

Switching on the taxy light and releasing the parking brake, I move towards the runway threshold, opening the throttles fully as I line up; nothing will stop me now. Airborne, I set climb power and check the artificial horizon as I turn left to East, levelling at 3,000 feet where the air is smooth, and there's tranquillity.

I am in my cocoon, my comfort zone, going somewhere, this time with a mission. I feel affection for the Navajo and my intimate connection with it; we are as one. I switch over to the auxiliary tanks and look out of the window again, where a bright moonlight reflects greyness off a carpet of stratocumulus. Night-time above the clouds is utterly beautiful, surrealism in monochrome.

Showtime. I disengage the autopilot and ease the nose down slightly with a touch of power to increase speed. Then I make a gentle turn right, quickly reversing left and pulling up round for a barrel roll. Upside down at the top, I push forward to keep the nose above the horizon, carrying on through 360 degrees and wait for the wings to level and engage the autopilot again. Not bad. If I had joined the RAF – as I should have – I could have been a display pilot with the Red Arrows and then joined British Airways as a Concorde pilot.

I'm alert and the master of my world high above the rest of the earth, savouring the satisfaction of being in charge in readiness to do something special. I want to reconcile

---

[16] 19 March 1988

Protestants and Catholics for all time and regain what I had with Lynn. I didn't understand why anyone would wish to fight about a border that was just a line on a map. There weren't any paint lines in the fields drawn on the grass; farmers just milked their cows and went home to their families.

I wanted to face the hard men of the IRA to explain to them the difference between good and evil to make them, and their sort change their minds and follow the path of peace. Planting bombs everywhere hadn't helped their cause and certainly hadn't advanced that of religion. Life was too precious; I wanted to defend underdogs from bullies. If I had been an RAF pilot, I would have been a defender and protector, dispensing fairness and justice, 'speaking softly and carrying a big stick..,' as per the African proverb.

Suddenly aware of the reality of my surroundings - locked away in a box remote from the rest of the planet - I feel a wave of panic and anxiety as I think about my kids. They have always been there, constant, and reliable. I know that my wife has taken them away from me - I don't know why - I just want to call them, to hear their voices, and to make sure they're all right. But I can't, I have to finish my job. I focus on the windshield.

The Navajo is flying beautifully with all the instruments and gauges reading correctly. I'm not ready to descend into the murk of a winter night, down into a world of emptiness. I turn right onto a South-Easterly heading, maintaining 3,000 feet. I want to stay up where I belong, suspended from gravity and with the comforting power of two big engines around me.

Everything is still, but the ASI tells me we are travelling at 180 knots. I tune the Bovingdon beacon near Watford. The fuel quantity needles show less than one-quarter full on the main tanks - 45 minutes flying remaining, destination, London city. Lights through breaks in the cloud hint at the existence of other human beings; reluctantly, I will have to join them soon, blissful though it is to be alone.

Beyond, the rising sun paints a spreading water-colour landscape of English countryside, still and calm - nearly there. Staring forward, I start a slow descent, eyes unblinking. We have overflown Bovingdon, where a delicate mist shrouds the hills and radio masts as towns and villages stir into life. The slumbering metropolis is waking itself into action, its clutter moving towards me.

I'm aware of both the instrument panel and the outside view in a single scan. The combination of the slowly changing panorama and the drone of the engines is hypnotic and trancelike. Being airborne is such a privilege.

Looking outside, and now feeling detached from the machine, I aim for the BT Tower, over thousands of homes full of sleeping citizens, their lives, hopes and dreams oblivious to my solitary journey. I can see the silvery twists of the river now, reflecting the moon's fading glow off its water. As I turn sharply right, almost back on myself to head South-West, I see The Mall.

Fatigue is creeping up on me, but I feel serene now, soothed by the rumble of the engines, steady and strong at 200 miles per hour. I can see the occasional car head and taillights. It's only a matter of seconds before I reach Buckingham Palace. The Victoria Memorial is in sight. A gentle left bank will avoid it as I head for the dark outline of the windows. The Palace looms in front of me, a vast artificial monolith of sculptured stone.

I'm drained. It's time to sleep. I've 15 or 20 seconds to think about death, but there's nothing left in my mind, soul, or heart. I'm going to hit the Palace on the first floor, just to the left of the balcony. The scene is set, with my eyes, the only parts of my being that are functioning. I don't need a brain anymore, just an end. There's nothing else to do. I level the wings and apply full power. As the image on the screen disintegrates, I close the laptop's lid, put away my notes, and go back to bed.

19

Conflicts

While drafting a book about suicide by plane provided a catharsis for my darker thoughts, I kept these to the contents of my computer. I simply didn't have the desire to crash an aeroplane anywhere. However, the other ideas in my head that had destroyed my aviation career were still present and responsible for making me unhappy at home. They weren't just about my marriage to Isla; they went much deeper than that.

From the scholarship boy at Haberdashers' to becoming a captain on commercial aircraft, I had been at my best, making the most of all I had been blessed with at birth. A brief Catholic education had taught me to have a simple perspective on life: a Walt Disney world of strong men and beautiful women, doing good things while evil was to be fought. My mother kept telling me I was handsome, intelligent, and well-behaved, to the point where I believed it for a while. Until that gave way to feelings of inferiority, exclusion, and anti-social tendencies.

Through English schools, even though it was not a major part of the curriculum, I was influenced by the more liberal Protestant ethic, where variant standards of behaviour were tolerated and even encouraged under the banner of freedom for the individual. For me, the differences between my two native cultures were epitomised by the punk hairstyles and aggressive music in the UK, and the gentle 'rock' dancing in France, with most of the boys I knew there wearing the same kind of navy jumpers.

I formed the view that England was a masculine country, typified by sports, tribalism, and military skill, while France was more feminine, focusing on sophistication, cuisine, and art. Stiff upper lip versus the less inhibited expression of emotions. Both countries would fight to defend their respective national identities in their own style, the English preferring the terraces of a football ground, and the French the dinner table.

As a teenager with roots in both countries, I found it hard to resolve the resultant conflict between being myself and conforming. I wanted to be a pilot to be free in a romantic French way but ended up locked in a box and controlled by medication. Confirmed by the firm yet fair way the police had treated me at the time, the English law-abiding, consensus-seeking side of me wanted to defend the weak and fight injustice too.

Which was why the SAS soldier had made such an impression on me – he was both a pilot and a defender. If I had joined the military, I would have been more fulfilled in moral purpose than when flying an airliner for money. I could have used all the attributes I had - youthful energy, aggression towards bullies, and self-sacrifice where required - to be a fighter pilot like Biggles to further the cause of peace in the world before settling down to a life of writing and service to the community.

But I didn't, which was a shame for my relationship with Lynn; as with an Army father, she was ready to be a Service wife and would have gone anywhere with me. Had I allowed nature to take its course and followed the ideals I was brought up with, e.g. no contraception, Lynn and I might have produced a baby as beautiful as the one I had held in my arms during the fly-in at Kirkbride. Lynn would have been the mother she was ready to be, and our lives would have been quite different.

Two years after my first divorce and feeling better in myself, I had gone to see Lynn near where she was living in

Yarm, hoping to get back with her, but there was nothing left between us. As I departed on the late evening flight after our meeting, she became a distant memory as I entered the surreal calm of the cabin and became mesmerised by the blue lights of the taxiways. Climbing away, I finally lost her in the scattered dotted lights below, disappearing into the darkness - final confirmation of the destructive power of the warring thoughts in my brain[17].

Having seen for myself the range of differences between my generally Catholic beliefs and British Protestant ones in the sectarianism of Northern Ireland, I had wanted to resolve these conflicts, eliciting 'God's help in the process. But with my head in the clouds, my brain chemistry was unable to cope. Not only was it trying to work out the struggles between good and evil, but it also had to deal with perfectionist parents, isolationist upbringing, and rejection. Lynn had borne the brunt of these as my first wife; with Isla, it was my turn.

As a staff-grade airline handling officer escorting VIPs around an airport, carrying pilot's bags and offloading sacks of rubbish from private jets, I had married Isla, an intelligent and hard-working junior manager, which put her on a more senior status to me, certainly in the British Airways hierarchy. It would have been the other way around if I'd been one of their pilots, in which case I would probably have never met Isla but paired off with a female cabin crew member.

But it didn't happen that way, and it brought us, as two polar opposite people together in Edinburgh on 31 May 1986. With clear guidance from her parents on how to behave and support from a large family, Isla did her best to make a happy home and be a good mother to our children. She made most of the decisions about their upbringing – as my mother had done when I was a child – which I accepted in my more vulnerable state. However, much as I saw the upsides, my

---

[17] In 2007 my ex-sister-in-law called me to tell me that Lynn had died alone of alcoholism at age 47.

parents' idiosyncratic way of behaving was part of my life and kept asserting itself.

I had a Latin appreciation of nudity, sex, and the body beautiful, while Isla was more about hard work and a belief that men had it easier. Isla's views prevailed in our home because I was afraid to stand up to her, not even sure how to behave as a married man. She heavily influenced our daughters; my role seemingly relegated to a token male presence with no real say in the family dynamic.

Having completed my function as an egg fertilising machine, embarrassment about my medical history and slightly eccentric family background made me feel ashamed and excluded. These feelings increased in intensity over our nineteen years of marriage, suppressed up to a point by the medication.

Living with four strong and independent women, I felt emasculated, inadequate, and inferior to many of the men I saw around me. Isla earned as much as I did, if not more, and thanks to her parents, the children's education at an all-girls school and their material needs were assured.

My perception was that being half-French was an amusing irrelevancy, with that part of my identity disregarded, subjugated, and shunned. So, the girls were brought up partying the English way with the emphasis on drink, rather than being more 'girly' by wearing the flowery dresses, which I saw as a manifestation of femininity.

With an English education, I entered the world of Anglo-Saxon capitalism, but without the skills to cope with it. My French socialist side didn't understand the English way of life, which my father had turned his back on in favour of his wife's through love. For me, big family meals under the apple blossoms in Brittany gave way to trying to fit into a culture of English humour, materialism, and an all-boys school.

Recalling my feelings of uncertainty on the day of the wedding in Scotland, I realised I had been trying to work out who I was from the time of my breakdown, probably earlier. The lithium was doing its job in keeping my moods under control, but I also believed it prevented me from being my complete self.

This state of affairs brought to the fore all the conflicts in my life, thereby exacerbating the stress I was feeling. Each time I had stopped taking the medication, there had been disastrous consequences, yet I also felt it was dulling my emotions to a point where the positive aspects of my personality had been adversely affected.

My dilemma was in trying to do the best for Isla and the children while dealing with this. Occasionally I stood up for my family's coaching method of tutoring the girls, rather than adopting Isla's preferred 'helping' style, which I saw as spoiling them by doing everything for them. I was scared of her because I knew she could always go back to Scotland, where her family would look after her and the children.

Given that my condition wasn't anything she'd ever come across before, I couldn't blame Isla for her attitude towards me, and for her part, she did eventually concede that it wasn't my fault.

The only words I wanted to be associated with me were grounded, confident, active, wise, intelligent, kind, listening, caring, dreaming, thinking, loving, modest, friendly, happy, brave, strong, honest, loyal, determined, relaxed, charming, funny, resourceful, self-sufficient, sexy. I felt I failed Isla and the children in all these respects. Isla told me I was a wimp, lazy, and a lightweight.

As a result, I turned into a miserable, sulking shadow of my former self. I relied on a few good friends to make me feel worthy of existence, including a magistrate and co-assessor on the Duke of Edinburgh Award Scheme that I helped with at the girls' school. In an email to the group leader, four months before my divorce was finalised, he wrote:

Philip Appleton is a lot more charitable and generous than I am, and obviously has the patience of a saint, and saw the positive in everything. He was really good with the girls (good cop, bad cop thing.)

* * *

As a self-employed Actor, Interpreter, Aviation Consultant, Presenter, Model, work was going relatively well. I had set myself an earnings target of £100 per day before tax. In the tax year 1997/98, I had reached just over half that. Always on the lookout for new ventures, I started as a guest presenter on the QVC TV shopping channel, scratching music CDs with sandpaper and hoping I could repair them live on TV with a product from a bottle. From there, I moved on to exhibition work on an eight million-dollar stand at *Telecom 99* in Geneva, delivering 16 performances a day of a memorised 1500-word technical presentation.

The Japanese client had paid half the £5,000 fee upfront, and on completion of the job, had completed the remaining payment promptly to all the presenters' agents. Mine[18] made empty promises to me until an even more empty envelope arrived on my doormat. Highly stressed, I was worried that getting angry would be seen as a relapse with my medical history, and I would end up in hospital again.

I agonised, then decided that my anger was justified, so I went to the agent's office, banged on the tables, and shouted. Looking me in the eye, she said she wasn't going to pay me for no reason. I stormed round to the Equity offices, told them the story, and their legal officer had the money paid by the following day. It was a lesson in the harsh side of the business and reasonable behaviour on my part.

With RADA (Royal Academy of Dramatic Art) on my CV, thanks to a one-week course on Advanced Drama in Television, I was ready to turn my back on extra work

---

[18] This was not Malone and Knight, but an interim agent who went out of business shortly after.

completely. It had been good for me financially and to learn about the film industry, but I knew that I couldn't progress as an actor while continuing to be a background artist.

So, when I was offered an extra's role in *Gladiator*, where I would be featured but without dialogue, I turned it down. It was just another film at the time, and I didn't want to be 'crowd' anymore. There was the fear in my mind that someone would find out I had been an extra later on, but that was too bad.

Instead of flexing my muscles with Russell Crowe, I took on Sooty the glove puppet. Having been put up for the part by my agent, I auditioned with the Casting Director and was offered a drama contract as 'Rrrolf, The Dog Warden,' out to get Sooty's cousin Sweep for not wearing a dog collar.

I rehearsed at home with my kids' furry toys spread out all over the lounge, turned up on time at Granada Studios in Manchester, delivered my lines, and ended up getting squirted by Sooty as the villain of the piece. It was what I had been striving for: to follow the system as a 'proper' actor instead of an extra, and with a TV credit to my professional name.

Moving from children's TV to a high-stakes redundancy training program for one of the Big Four accountancy firms saw me playing a woman, on the basis that I looked the youngest of the all-male group of actors hired to play the actual partners who would be fired the next week. I was tasked to do the first roleplay of the session in front of all the actors and trainers to set the level of performance.

Focusing on how a woman might feel in a situation where her world had ended – something I could relate to - I sat down, put my knees together and cried. When we'd finished the session, it was the praise I received from my fellow actors which pleased me the most, all of whom were far more experienced than me.

As someone who didn't know Chekhov from a strawberry yoghurt, I looked up to actors who had studied plays and worked in major theatres, such as the National. So, when asked to play opposite Adrian McLoughlin, I was nervous, even if it was for a corporate event at a Heathrow hotel for a firm of actuaries. With 14 pages of script to learn, I wafted on to the stage in white robes as Ra, an Egyptian engineer trying to sell a prospect a pyramid he didn't want. I held my own and was pleased not just with the live applause but also with the £400 fee for the day, more than I'd have earned for most regular theatre productions in a week.

With the promise of more contacts and better prospects, I reluctantly left Malone & Knight for another agent. Sheila Bourne had been a decent actress in her time, and she liked the upmarket Bond-type image I was trying to project. My photos looked the part, and my CV was acceptable; it was when I opened my mouth at the interview that I could sense her disappointment.

As my inexperience and schoolboy desire to please came through, my gravitas diminished. With the niggling doubts I had about not being a proper actor, I felt unsettled, which I knew was coming across to Sheila. I was revealing myself as an embarrassing person who asked lots of questions and tried to be funny all the time. Fortunately, she took me on anyway.

My general lack of confidence lurked just below the surface, compounded by my ongoing insecurity at home. I was winging it all the time - acting being an actor - fearing to be found out as a real person, rather than inhabiting the characters I was supposed to be playing. I felt more comfortable being foreign, especially French.

Playing the flamboyant fashion designer Xavier Soyeux in two episodes of the TV series *GOAL* restored some of my father-figure credentials, as the set was full of young actors bursting with energy and ambition. Not quite so young, but equally sexy was Alison in wardrobe, who I'd met at the Liverpool Playhouse 27 years previously. We agreed that neither of us had changed, which was a boost to my sanity given that Alison had known me when I was a fully fit flying instructor.

My French persona landed me a role as the Maître d' serving Del Boy and Rodney curry in the 2002 Christmas special of *Only Fools and Horses*, in a scene with the two principals David Jason and Nick Lyndhurst. All I had to do was deliver my lines and plan how to rearrange my showreel to fit in a classic British TV comedy video clip.

After Christmas lunch at the Muirs, I settled down to watch the show with Isla, the girls, and various aunts, uncles, and cousins from across Scotland, hoping they would be pleased with the result of my efforts to make a living. The titles and the familiar music rolled, and we watched, and watched, and watched.

There was no Maître d'. My mother-in-law didn't understand. She wondered if I'd got a fleeting walk-on part, and we'd missed it. But no, I had a proper part with a BBC contract and the script and the call sheet to prove it. But I certainly wasn't on the screen. They'd cut it and never told me.

Too much material I found out afterwards, and no, David Jason doesn't allow any outtakes, so you can't have a copy of the footage. I was gutted - another disappointment. Again, worse for having it in my grasp. I got paid, with the repeat fees going on for years from all parts of the world and included it on my CV, but none of that made me feel any better.

Back to the grindstone, hosting 'James Bond' themed nights at the Regency Hotel, London delivering immortal lines, such as: 'Ladies, you're making this hard for me,' 'That's a nice dress you're nearly wearing,' and 'I'm French, I'm a Eurobond.' It was only a prop gun that I had in my waistband, but it did feel good. If I'd had it with me on Sutton High Street while selling cut-price televisions as a 'resting' job, I might have been tempted to use it.

With a microphone, amplifier and wearing my clean-cut face and jacket and tie, I was reeling off my sales patter when four youths approached. Bored and looking for trouble, they sauntered towards me, taking everything in and trying to make eye contact. I avoided theirs, still trying to focus on my work. They got closer, getting in my line of sight. I turned to them and said: 'Hey guys, just trying to do my job here.'

They got even closer until they were in my personal space, preventing me from selling any televisions. One of the lads put his foot out and began playing with the on-off switch on the amp - the moment where a harmless prank had become interference with my life.

With the pent up frustration of failing again – at being a successful actor - I matched the foot artist's stare, grabbed him by the lapels and slammed him onto the plate glass window. It was toughened, so it wasn't going to break, and I did it flat, so it wasn't going to hurt him too much. Then I said to him with all the venom I could muster,

'Look here, you little shit, You're in my space, so fuck off. Do you understand?'

As the colour drained from his cheeks, I revelled in my ability to change from a soft-touch, smile-a-minute salesman into a furious bigger-than-him guy shouting in his face. It confirmed what I had learned about truthful acting: 'Don't act, be.' I was angry and had behaved accordingly, authentically and acceptably.

As the police arrived to escort the teenagers away, I asked myself what new depths I had plumbed in my dive from being an airline pilot. I must have had some vestiges of self-respect because I packed up the equipment and went home. I thought about going back to doing extra work. Never - I had come too far for that.

The Haberdashers' Aske's Boys' School 30-year reunion in 2002 was memorable because I didn't feel like a prat. It was as if time had stopped. Doug Yeabsley, my old chemistry master, was our host and still teaching. Among the mainly accountants and bankers present, I felt different, but myself - the first from the school to be selected for British Airways sponsored pilot training and become a professional actor. Allowing myself a few minutes of satisfaction, I celebrated by making friends with the arty Deputy Editor of the Radio Times rather than the suits.

My perception was that Isla would have preferred me to be with the suits. She had complained when I announced that I intended to go to one of the girls' school concerts with a growth of beard, required for my role as French nobleman Hughes de Ponthieu in *Battlefield Britain*, a major BBC series of historical documentaries. Hughes had just got back from fighting the English, so he hadn't had time to shave. I kept the beard but was so fazed I couldn't get into character on the rehearsal day, and my part was cut. I blamed Isla's lack of understanding of my new profession, one that she didn't rate highly but myself more, for allowing it to affect me.

In a bid to gain some respect for my work and following the example I had seen in other actors of giving something back to the community, I volunteered to do interview skills training at my local school for some young adults who risked being excluded. I sent each pupil an application form for any job they wanted to do in the world, then roleplayed as their interviewer.

One lad wanted to join the Army, so I dressed up as a recruiting officer. He lived with his grandmother, never saw his father and had given up his karate class to see me. I gave him feedback and coaching on how to present himself. It was the most rewarding job I'd ever done.

From teaching hard skills as a flying instructor to coaching personal development, I felt I had something to offer. My gravitas was increasing, but not my sense of humour. I could deliver a joke, but I wasn't really a funny guy. Playing an Italian mobster in upmarket murder mysteries at venues such as Gleneagles in Scotland and The Celtic

Manor Resort in Wales, my employer said that I frightened the paying guests and wasn't comedic. He was right, so I contented myself by driving us all home as I was a better driver than he was.

Pretending to be the perfect dad in a furniture commercial while my marriage was falling apart made me feel like an even bigger fraud than when I was trying to be funny. The perfect mum in the ad was being played by Kathryn Evans, the stunningly beautiful wife of Welsh rugby captain Ieuan Evans. Kath and I had been made up and were looking our best, ready to rehearse some scenes of domestic bliss around a Christmas tree on the hero sofa.

For a moment, I was in a happy place. Then Ieuan turned up on set to see me bouncing his children on my knee. He had won 72 caps for Wales and been on three Lions tours. As a rugby fan myself, the contempt for me I saw in his eyes made me feel ashamed to call myself an actor.

Then an opportunity arose to combine real-life with acting. When Tania Meneguzzi cast me as the Chief Customs Officer in her feature film *The Run*, I was still working as an official Customs interpreter. A one-woman powerhouse with more drive than the Starship Enterprise, Tania had written a hard-hitting story about drug smuggling and assembled the cast to deliver it. It was low-budget, so the actors weren't getting paid, but we all wanted to make the film as good as it could be. It was Tania's energy and vision we were working for and the chance to create something worthwhile.

At the audition, Tania and I discussed the script. 'You can't have this in the interview scene,' I told her, 'it doesn't happen this way. Nobody bangs on desks in Customs interviews; it's all very calm and evidence-based. I've sat through enough of them to know.'

'I'm not going to rewrite the script,' said Tania.

'No, but I will,' I replied and did so. Not only did Tania love it, but she gave me credits under both my names: one for acting and one for writing.

Tania took the film to the US, where it was nominated for Best Feature at the Malibu Film Festival. As my primary contact in Hollywood, I waited in vain for her to arrange for me to be the successor to the famous French heartthrob Louis Jourdan. In the meantime, I was settling for a job hosting a series of Christmas parties at the Royal Aeronautical Society off Park Lane in Mayfair, London.

Granted membership with the support of two senior BA pilots after my loss of licence, the last time I had been on their premises, I'd attended one of their medical lectures as an Associate Member. This had temporarily given me some letters after my name and the largest certificate I'd ever seen, but that was about all.

The venue had been turned into an ice cave, bathed in soft, blue-white light on a snow and ice theme, where I welcomed the 120 dinner guests as the Russian 'Prince Vladimir.' Smiling broadly, I delivered a few Russian phrases as a warmup, walking quickly away when a genuine Russian speaker confronted me. I told my standard multi-cultural condom joke during dinner, wondering what I was doing there. Ah yes, the money. Thinking about getting paid and seeing if I could scrounge some food during the evening made me a proper, professional actor.

* * *

It had been a beautiful summer's day, with work finishing early and the birds tweeting their heads off until I found Isla's boyfriend's car outside the house. I'd seen films where this happened but had never thought it would happen to me. I'd previously confronted him at the swimming pool where he had met my wife and asked him if he was the one who was having an affair with her.

We had sat down, and he had told me that my marriage had fallen apart well before he came on the scene. He was probably right, but to find him in my house that day made me feel angry and impotent, on top of all the other feelings of failure and uselessness that had been piling up inside me at home.

I knew that I wasn't going to kill him as a hot-blooded Frenchman might have done, but I did know that I wasn't going to turn around and go away. Apprehensive but resolute, I marched into the house and told him to leave. He was a builder, big and strong with massive hands and didn't look scared of me. But in my house, I wasn't afraid of him either and had the benefit of rage growing inside me. I had no history of hurting others, only myself, but it had taken six nurses to hold me down in hospital, so it would have been messy if I'd gone for him. Thankfully, he left.

Pent up stress and frustration welled up inside me. I wanted to release it but didn't know how. Isla didn't look as if she cared. Feeling a tightness in my chest, I took in huge gulps of air making me think my heart would burst. I had a vague idea I was having a panic attack but didn't know what to do about it. I rang a police helpline and told them the story. They were sympathetic and helped me calm down, but I knew this was one of those things that was happening to me, not one I could control.

The divorce was going to happen whether I liked it or not. I didn't want it to because I had nowhere to go, yet felt I had to keep working for the family, which meant putting my whole body and soul into playing characters with everyday lives while in the middle of another nightmare. As my stomach churned, I worried about the situation while I was at work, compounded by being unable to sleep or eat properly. When I had lost everything in 1981, I believed it had been my fault, but this time I felt someone else was responsible, taking away not just my home but my children.

Wrapped up in my emotional turmoil, I had no comprehension of what they were going through and didn't know how to handle them. With ongoing exams, the eldest hated me, the youngest was bewildered, and the middle one was caught between the two, subsequently describing the trauma of the divorce as 'shit and horror' and 'the worst year of my life.' The upside was the support they gave to each other and the unbreakable bond this would form.

The divorce was when I found out what it was like to be weak and powerless without the excuse of a breakdown. When my brain produced the red mist, I just had to accept that I was experiencing a little bubble of hell that I had to live through. With the help of the medication, I'd got myself as well as I could. This time I was waking up every morning wondering if it was the last day I'd be able to go into my kitchen, study, or garden or worst of all, not see my bright, healthy, and vibrant children again, so full of their lives. And I had to keep working.

In our nineteen years as a family, we had many good times and made lifelong friends. I was devastated by the divorce, but with the proceeds, moved to a maisonette in Windsor while Isla and the girls moved into a bigger house near our old home with their new stepfather and his family - he being once referred to as 'Dad' by one of my daughters in one of the worst moments of my life.

Within three months of the decree absolute, the make-believe world of my work delivered the final verdict - it was time for me to die. 'Captain Appleton' and all his passengers were killed in a fictional collision between two airliners over Tunbridge Wells[19].

Playing the lead pilot role in the TV documentary, I kept myself together, as well as helping with the technical details, during the shoot in a simulator in Bournemouth. The guy who played the co-pilot was also in the middle of a divorce, so I didn't feel so alone; a member of a club for men going through a divorce. It wasn't a happy club. Whether I was an actor playing a pilot, or a pilot pretending to act, part of me was dead.

---

[19] *Midair Collision,* Granada Factual, released 11 January 2006

20

House of Windsor

Having moved to Windsor and never having been brought up in a pub culture, I thought it was time to broaden my horizons. Finding a pub on my road and one in the town centre, I was welcomed with friendliness and warmth, in both cases by women. They were my first introduction to regular English pub life.

Everyone poked gentle or not so gentle fun at themselves and others, which was easy in my case because I was French and couldn't drink as much beer as the other guys. Someone explained to me the protocol for buying rounds and that 'I'm not thirsty' was an unacceptable response in English when offered a beer.

Known as 'French Phil,' I didn't understand the British reliance on drink. and behaving like a wild animal to 'have a good time.' Another difference I noticed between French and English culture was in attitudes to money. In the UK, I would often hear the value of everything measured by its worth in monetary terms. So, a house or a car was often referred to by what it could be sold for and what deal had been done in securing it. The frequent talk I heard around me about the property market, investments, or the price of goods bored me.

The British use of language baffled me too, as in 'white lies,' and 'jokes.' In conversation, phrases such as 'That meal is way too healthy,' 'Our team were owed a win,' and 'Bad Boys' in an admiring way, were incomprehensible to my French ear. English people would say things like: 'Yeah, just scraped in with a double first, a bit of luck really,' whereas a

Frenchman (Erik Satie) did say: 'I am by far your superior, but my notorious modesty prevents me from saying so.' As far as lying was concerned, my sense was that the French would be more inclined to do so straight to someone's face.

Less subtle phrases such as: 'I hate the French,' delivered in all seriousness in the pub by one educated fellow patron brought home that racism was alive and well, going beyond him just 'winding me up.' To be fair, this was a one-off in the context of the more usual English habit of laughing at everything, which I didn't understand. Perhaps it was a way of fitting in, which I wasn't particularly good at, so I sometimes thought I didn't have a sense of humour. Yet, I could cry uncontrollably and repeatedly with laughter during films such as *Airplane*, *Naked Gun*, and *Spy*.

I was never sure how much of the real me was English or French, so was in my element when playing both. Travelling between London and Paris on Eurostar up to four times a week, I played French and English customers for a two-day course on customer service over a period of six months for staff on both sides of the Channel. The unofficial story was that the French team needed the training but that the Brits had to be included to avoid charges of discrimination.

With only 22 miles between France and the UK, I was again struck by how different the two cultures were and how much they were both part of me. I focused better on work in the Paris office, where the emphasis was on hierarchy and pride - which the Brits called arrogance – while the UK office had a more team-focused and relaxed way of operating.

When I asked them, the French staff confessed they preferred to work in London as it was more fun. They also said that the English were impossible to understand, as they never said what they meant and apologised for everything.

In the pub, I understood that however wealthy or poor, people were generally accepted for what they were by everyone else, with the main requirements being buying one's rounds, telling a good story, and being authentic. Coming from a family of thinkers and talkers, I didn't always make the grade, particularly in warming to those reticent about their business. I saw a surface bonhomie, with its 'larfs,' but also with an undercurrent of secrecy that required considerable time to establish trust. Once that had been achieved, the sourcing of drugs and protection was an acceptable topic of conversation.

Other than alcohol, the only time I took non-prescribed drugs was to smoke a cigarette on special occasions, for work, or under extreme stress. It would relax me, and the rush to my head would cause a slight wooziness, usually pleasurable. I was offered cocaine once by an actress who had been kind to me after my divorce but had politely declined. I didn't see how snorting a white powder up my nose could be any better than what we were doing in bed.

But it made me think about drugs in general and how the 'highs' that I experienced off lithium might be comparable with those enjoyed by addicts of recreational drugs, including alcohol. There were highs and lows of mood in those cases, but I wondered, given how complicated the brain was, if I was luckier than most people in having the brain that I did, after all.

Having tried to find out if brain chemistry caused behaviour or vice versa, it was clear that nobody had all the answers but that for some, taking hard drugs was an acceptable part of their lifestyle. Having nothing to hide, I told my new friends that I worked for Customs from time to time and chatted openly about where I lived, assuming that everyone else did the same.

One night I was sitting on a barstool when a fit-looking man, probably about 30 years of age, came up to me. He introduced himself as Gary, and we shook hands, with Gary complimenting me on the strength of my grip. We chatted, during which he told me he was a boxer and did some work for his father, who he admitted was a villain. 'That's just the way it is,' said Gary. He was very polite and shook my hand again as he said goodbye, but I wondered why he had told me about his father. I never saw him again.

Then I realised he was checking me out and could find me if he wanted to. Having been brought up believing that anyone who broke the law went to prison, I could see that real life wasn't like that. The rule was that what you heard in the pub stayed in the pub, something I wasn't about to try and change.

Apart from astronauts and SAS commanders, I discovered other types I wanted to emulate: bon viveurs, the life and soul of the party, happy-go-lucky people that everyone loved and wanted to be with, living life to the full. There would always be parties with these sort of people, not necessarily wild and drug-filled but family gatherings too, with hordes of children flocking around their dad, who always had something organised to do and funny to say. The adults would go to the races with him and swap stories and laughter.

Partly because of my insular background, I simply wasn't like that and often didn't know how to behave socially. I was polite and tried to contribute, yet not always able to have 'fun' with those around me. I tended to keep quiet because it was better to let people think I was a fool than speak up and remove all doubt. With my previous history of strange behaviour, I was careful with my every action in case it was construed as unstable, even if being stable meant that I was so dull that no one wanted to talk to me anyway.

There was only one man I went out of my way to avoid, a newcomer to the pub. I had struck up a welcoming conversation with him, and within minutes he was talking about guns and how he had taken on five Travellers outside a pub in Wraysbury. On a later occasion, I was at the bar, and he came up behind me and put his fingers around my neck. I froze, thinking that while it was very unusual behaviour, I was safe from attack but was likely to get barred if I responded physically.

I was pleased I had kept calm; the incident left me feeling uncomfortable and ready to defend myself if the man did something similar again. In my few brief contacts with him, I recognised the visceral impulses for violence that motivated men in some situations because I had felt it in myself. I had grown up a little more.

Work was plentiful, engaging, and providing me with adequate income. Calling myself a Communications Skills Coach and Consultant, I built up my own business advising clients on how best to use drama in corporate training programs, hiring actors, and running workshops on confidence-building, assertiveness training, and interpersonal skills development for investment bankers and sewage treatment operatives alike.

My experience as an actor taught me how to see other people's perspectives, and I was deriving great satisfaction from believing that I might be making a positive difference in people's lives. Working with trainers, psychologists, and other coaches, I was constantly picking up tips and techniques from them and they from me.

As I learnt about personality profiling, learning styles and communication theory, the work kept coming in. There were jobs for British Aerospace, RBS, Barclays, Deloitte, Severn Trent Water to the point where I had to register for VAT.

Some wealthy companies expected to be charged a high fee to show they were using the best suppliers. I was happy to co-operate with that arrangement, enabling me to pass on some of it to associates who might be running a community project in a deprived area. In return, I believed we enriched our clients' lives, particularly with our out-of-the-box thinking on the human factors' aspects of their business.

My dark hair may have helped me find work for another Eastern client[20] as the MC (Master of Ceremonies) and 'Voice of God' at the 2012 Doosan Global Business Conference at the Lowry Hotel in Manchester. Seventy of the top economists and brains on the planet had been invited to meet and talk about where the world was heading. The guest speaker was the former British Prime Minister Tony Blair, and I was on stage at the final dinner in Manchester Cathedral, ready to introduce him.

Everything had been planned to the nearest second, with the Korean hosts referring every decision up to their higher management as usual, and everything was on schedule. Having delivered my scripted lines without error, I noticed a flurry of activity up and down the Doosan hierarchy. Someone had realised that it would take a minute or two for glasses to be filled before everyone was ready to toast with Mr Blair and that the program hadn't allowed for it. The senior manager turned to me and whispered: 'Say something.'

I opened my mouth and trusted it to deliver something suitable. Unprepared, but knowing there was no way out, it was time to practice what I preached in my coaching sessions on presentation and impact skills.

'I'm not a politician like Mr Blair,' I said, indicating the former Prime Minister. 'I don't understand economics, but I would like to thank Doosan for arranging this forum. It enables human beings from all over the world to meet and communicate. Without communication, nothing will happen for good. Across continents and between different nations, such as we have here tonight. ...'

There was silence in the Cathedral as I continued, either because the guests wondered what I was doing or because I had struck a chord with some of them. When the wine waiters had finished their job, I brought my remarks to a close and got a round of applause. I invited Tony Blair to take the stage,

---

[20] All the presenters working for the Japanese client at *Telecom99* had dark hair (see chapter 19.)

he shook my hand and proposed a toast, then I introduced the evening's entertainment: opera singers flown in from Korea.

Perhaps because they could see I believed in what I had said about cross-cultural co-operation, Doosan asked me back for the next four years. One venue was the Signet Library in Edinburgh, where Isla and I had held our wedding reception 26 years earlier.

* * *

A year after our divorce, I found myself in a similar position to Isla's boyfriend when I met Annie. She was married, but once I'd found out her marriage had been falling apart before I turned up, I began to take an interest in this quiet but captivating blonde who spoke four and a half languages and who was devoted to her chocolate Labrador, Holly. She referred to me affectionately as Batman, which I hoped was the 1989 version because I wanted a real-life replay of the scene where Kim Basinger looked adoringly at Michael Keaton in the 'I am Batman' scene.

Annie would arrive on my doorstep on a Friday night with Holly, we would go for walks, and I would make her laugh by making faces and speaking in foreign accents. She would tell me about her issues with her mother, jobs, and speeding tickets. Knowing I wasn't perfect, I got over her lies about a previous relationship, we took holidays together, and I cried with her when we had Holly put down. I was sure we would spend the rest of our lives together.

With Annie working for the Royal Household, I made it into Buckingham Palace without flying an aeroplane through the front windows. Through her, I received invitations to three Garden Parties, the first on a perfect blue sky day, bathed in 22 degrees warmth. Driving through London and down the Mall in sunlight, and with a cool, pleasant breeze drifting through the car's windows, I was living in the moment, calm, content, and entirely at peace with the world. Ready to join Annie and 8,000 other guests for a unique experience, I felt overwhelmingly privileged and glad to be alive.

The cloudless sky reminded me of 9/11, and I thought of terrorists who would destroy everything -around me if they could, then looked at the hundreds of workers and tourists on the pavements - all unique human beings alive and feeling all the emotions that God or some evolutionary creature from a swamp had given them.

Trying to put myself in the mind of a man flying an aeroplane into a skyscraper full of people, I visualised a scenario where someone would kidnap my children to try and force me to fly into Buckingham Palace to save them, but I didn't think I could carry it out.

The three hijacker pilots must have had a compelling reason for doing what they did - I didn't judge them for that - only wished that better communication between nations would prevent such atrocities. The events of that day appalled me so much that I briefly believed they hadn't occurred, that the US government had faked them to control their view of world events.

I found it hard to believe that human beings would torture others to death or commit mass genocide. Yet when I examined my own potential actions in a situation where I might have to hurt someone to reveal the whereabouts of a captured daughter, I came back to reality and accepted evil in the world as a fact, not a theoretical concept.

With tourists looking on quizzically, the police waved me onto the parking area on the tree-lined path to the side of the Mall draped in Union Jacks. The police officers made me feel safe and secure, their good humour making me proud to be British. My family background and upbringing had made me more likely to be on their side than that of terrorists.

At school, I had been happy to let the loudmouths talk until someone had to speak up for an underdog when I was happy to intervene, wanting to protect the weakest. For a few seconds, I imagined being a protection officer or undercover SAS operative with a Glock or a Browning in my belt ready to protect the Queen, Annie, or anyone else.

Minutes later, I headed for the Palace amid the crowd of guests in summer dresses, morning suits, short skirts, Army, Navy, and Air Force uniforms; some in wheelchairs. I was sure everyone else was there on merit, with me just a hanger-on.

As I walked around the Victoria Memorial, I looked up to Annie's office, on the second floor next to where the Royal Family came out to wave – exactly where the Navajo would have struck the Palace in the darkest corners of my thoughts. I realised then how much I *didn't* want to fly an aeroplane into Buckingham Palace. The red mist had gone, never to come back.

Annie appeared on the other side of the railings, looking her best and in her element wearing a flowery dress and a borrowed hatinator, walking towards me with her Royal Household pass. She ushered me in, and we walked through the Quadrangle, out to the terrace into the sunshine and onto the massive lawn, hidden from the outside world. Quiet conversation, smiling faces, the royal couple a few feet away, sandwiches and tea perfectly served.

While loving Annie, there was a niggling secretiveness about her that I couldn't shake off. I had suspected for some time that she was seeing someone else, reinforced when she didn't thank or mention me during her speech at her 50th birthday party. When I eventually found the proof, I picked up the phone to her at work and said quietly: 'I've seen the emails, come and get your things.'

It was a shame, but instead of getting stressed or emotional, I was resigned about the whole matter. I kept in control while giving Annie the opportunity to defend herself. She didn't, so I helped her to load up her car with the few things she'd kept at mine and watched her leave.

With no residual hard feelings towards Annie after our nine years together, I was optimistic that I could start again and find someone who would make my heart skip again every time she walked through the door. Through blind dates, dating sites, supermarket aisles, work, and pubs, I met dozens of women: stewardesses, actresses, vegans, snobs, career girls, lawyers, doctors, entrepreneurs, dancers, a diagnosed nymphomaniac, and one who taught me how to hold my knife correctly.

There were French, American, Indian women; and those with dogs, horses, and personalised number plates. Acknowledging my hypocrisy, though with no regrets, I became close to a married woman on her failing third marriage. Her husband gained my lifelong respect when he called me to ask what he was doing wrong, thereby turning his wife from my lover to a friend.

I was getting plenty of dates, sometimes four or five a week while learning to look at women as different and unique in their own ways. The nice girls I wanted to marry while I left the self-styled princesses to the Lombards[21]. I knew I couldn't be a real villain, one of those men who were described as lovable rogues with a heart of gold, always nice to their mums, but wanting respect, which to me meant to be feared.

Sometimes I wished I was more of an endearing bad boy, perhaps a smooth fraudster type, always on the run, having a couple of dozen women on the go, manipulating and charming my way through life, and having more 'fun.'

Many of my approaches to women were clumsy and doomed to failure, 'How do you see the roles of men and women in society?'; 'Should we split future bills 50-50 or take it in turns?'; 'I practise the purest form of Tantric sex and will only let myself go with my equal,' these on the first date.

Slightly more effective was: 'I will meet you in a diamond chariot pulled by a team of wild unicorns, then we

---

[21] Lombard = Lots of money but a real dickhead

will sip from a shower of golden nectar delivered by a thousand singing bees, dancing on a carpet of rose petals. Birds of paradise will fly overhead as pods of somersaulting dolphins cavort down the Thames, as the curtain of night draws across to the sound of new stars and galaxies forming.'
I eventually settled for something closer to the truth:

'My French side says, "I have fallen in love with you, and I want to be with you forever." My English side says, "Shall we take tea and discuss our potential for a future long-term relationship?" With me, you get two for the price of one!'

Or in the case of shoes, two for the price of two. I don't remember how much Victoria paid to buy me a pair of Spanish-leather brogues, but I remember her attractive picture on a dating site when she was cabin crew. Our airline connections soon helped secure me an invitation to her ten-bedroom house in Surbiton, a temporary dwelling until she could get her divorce settlement from a pot with 50 million pounds in it.

The trouble was that the photo had been taken 15 years earlier, and Victoria had 'filled out' somewhat. However, she was very keen, so we flew to Spain to have me meet her friends with their Lamborghinis and Ferraris, where she took me shopping as I tried to work out how I was going to extricate myself from death by drowning in money. Our short association did confirm my almost complete lack of interest in having vast amounts of it.

With only half as many bedrooms was Natasha, a 'princess' of the type I had previously disdained, who I thought was a perfect match. Equivalent in looks, opinionated, and self-sufficient, she was an alpha female with whom I shared chemistry unlike any I had experienced before. Natasha had left school at 16 to set up businesses worldwide in her ruthless drive to make money.

Divorced after 30 years of marriage and living alone with few friends, but with 7,000 followers on social media, she seduced me with her expensive bikini shots taken in the Caribbean, to where she travelled first class from online shopping benefits. Contemptuous of kindness and mistrustful of almost everyone, Natasha was like a cat on a sofa, waiting to pounce on her prey; supremely confident, yet vulnerable too. She sought freedom and 'moments,' but without any commitment to anyone but herself and her children.

In her bed, within days of our first meeting through a dating site, we shared intimate secrets about our medical conditions, hopes and dreams, and she told me I was everything she wanted in a man. I brought her flowers, sent her poems, sang French songs to her, and felt more virile with her than with any woman I'd met previously. I told her I wanted to be with her for the rest of our lives.

But outside the bedroom, she pushed me away and kept on seeing other men. She wouldn't willingly meet my friends, who told me she was a sociopath, an attention seeker and stringing me along. Yet I was smitten and persisted and asked her to marry me. I promised I would love her in a wheelchair, old and wrinkled, would die for her, and give her my kidney. She laughed and pushed me away more.

My Disney-like ideals of love and romance had not allowed for women like Natasha. She was driving me mad with passion and pain. So, uncharacteristically I let her go, confessing my fear of rejection by her, and at the same time, telling her the truth about herself based on what she'd told me. The worm in me had turned, and I came out of the relationship unscathed and the better for it. 'Perfect' Natasha had given me the lesson I needed in how to confront women: be courageous and walk away[22]. Surprisingly, she was the first person ever to tell me I didn't have an ego.

Natasha helped me see women differently, challenging how I assessed them on their physical attributes and always aimed for the most attractive. I had eliminated so many kinder

---

[22] In an odd quirk of fate, it was almost certainly Natasha's father, as a BBC editor, who had cut me out of *Only Fools and Horses*.

and gentler women on that basis, leaving me resigned to being alone as the norm. She also tempered my optimism in seeing the best not only in women but in everyone most of the time.

This all meant that when I found yet another ideal woman, I could make a friend instead of an object of worship. The unattainable Yvonne was a fit and curvy natural blond, also wealthy and self-sufficient, with sparkling blue eyes and a smile that would light up my days in Windsor when I saw her by chance. Seemingly always happy, grounded, and relaxed, her poised demeanour made me feel strong, loving, kind, committed, romantic, brave, and shy towards her.

She made clear her lack of interest in a romantic relationship with me from the outset, which I found easy to accept because she never led me on. Instead, she helped motivate me to move on with my life, warm inside with the memory of a few seconds with her. Yet I hardly knew her at all; she was just a daydream, a real one nonetheless, a kind and pure presence to have with me when I needed it.

Finding a balance between my perceived ideal way of relating to women and reality gave me insights into my relationship with my mother, enabling me to see her as a woman too. I also understood why it had been so difficult for me to find the love of other women after Gail.

In Liverpool, I had found true happiness and contentment with Gail. Whenever I thought about her, it brought tears to my eyes. The other important women in my life: my mother, Lynn, and the mother of my children, gave me respect and love, but not in the same way. The rest have been good to know, interesting, and usually fun to be with.

My relationship with my daughters was remarkable; even it took years for me to understand them as both independent women and my children. As the Deputy Governor of the Bank of England, it was left to Rachel Lomax to say at my eldest daughter's awards ceremony in 2006: 'There is nothing more important you will ever do than have children.'

Having had them, I saw myself as being happy with or without a girlfriend. For a loyal companion to live with, I could get a dog. Having found ways to deal with my anxiety and being criticised and feeling rejected, I became the man I wanted to be, with or without women.

When my brother died from leukaemia in 2017 after eight months in hospital, I wasn't sure how I should be. Seeing him in intensive care, unshaven and gaunt with blotchy skin and long fingernails, I felt sad at what he had become. I remembered him full of energy, constantly fooling around, and ready to perform to an audience. When we were kids, we played well together, equally competitive and sharp, although I had to resort to punching him when he teased me because he was exceptionally good at it.

With the perfect dancer's physique, he was also better at anything that involved balance and leg coordination, e.g. tennis, while being taller and with more upper body strength, I was more suited to rugby. I had the academic brain but envied his carefree attitude and - with me at an all-boys school - his exploits with the lithe young ballerinas at the ballet school.

I never understood ballet, believing it to be effeminate, yet I could see that the men were extremely fit and athletic. It was years before I learned that ballet was about showing off the best male and female forms in choreographed courtship on stage. John loved to perform and express himself physically, frequently making comments about pretty girls and strong men. He confided in me about his wish to marry and have children in line with our family's beliefs; while love for one's fellow man was encouraged, sex was a special activity designed to take place between men and women.

Modelled on their images of themselves, my parents were always clear on how they perceived the differences between genders, both in their physical characteristics and roles, occasionally pointing out good-looking men with bodybuilder's physiques or a beautiful girl with dark looks and long hair. While my father would deal exclusively with the car, admin, and work on the houses, happily staying out of the kitchen and away from making any decisions about home furnishings, where my mother was in undisputed control.

Having chosen such contrasting professions, John and I were united in suffering breakdowns in our late twenties and losing our careers, yet also sharing a commonality with airborne things; John with birds, me with aeroplanes. Yet, in one respect, we were divergent. Extremely stubborn, and single-minded John refused to take medication, considering it an attack on his freedom.

He saw me take it and co-operate with the doctors, but he declined to do that; he simply said we were different. Yet even with virtually no friends to talk with, like our father, John would frequently surprise me with his valuable insights into human character and behaviour.

Eventually, I conceded that he might well have been content in his world, believing that God would heal his knee and make him dance again at 60, occasionally smashing up his flat in frustration. We all tried to change him; my parents would tell him what he should do, my sister was unfailingly kind to him, and I tried using a coaching approach, but ultimately we gave up.

When he was Sectioned for having made a scene with his neighbours or passers-by, I would visit him in hospital and his home where he lived alone, unable or unwilling to integrate into the community, sometimes referred to as eccentric. As I watched him die in peace and without pain, I did think he had found happiness after all.

A year later, I finally vented my frustration at my parents for the stress I had felt for years at the way they had behaved: their impulsive, illogical decision-making (made worse by my mother's constant regrets afterwards;) how they treated so many others as hostile and out to take advantage of them (to the point where they refused to allow me the use of the flat in St Lunaire when they weren't present;) their actions resulting in losing contact with their grandchildren.

For their part, my parents admitted they had been too hard on my brother and me, blaming Granny Jennie Appleton for being too strict on her sons. While I didn't *feel* particularly loved by them, they were my parents, so I resigned myself to the way they were and that I wouldn't have existed without them.

I wanted them to pass their last few years in peace, so I made moves to reconcile them with my daughters and made myself *listen* to them instead of arguing with them. With their combination of French dynamism and energy and English steadiness and calm, they set an example to me by presenting a united front, remaining inseparable after 66 years of marriage. I gave my mother a draft of my memoir for her 91st birthday, which she said made her cry.

21

Red Carpet

Thirty-four years after flying to Nice as the pilot of the BOC Cessna, I was heading there again, but this time as a passenger on a British Airways Airbus, as ever marvelling at the spectacular scenes of sky, clouds, and land. The Alps had the same snow-capped, immovable, and awesome majesty, eventually giving way to the view of a sparkling sea from a hotel room on the *Promenade des Anglais*.

The following day, a chauffeur-driven car took me to a trailer in Monaco Harbour, then to meet the Director, stars, and crew of the big-budget feature film *Grace of Monaco*. Just down the cast list from Nicole Kidman, Tim Roth, and Robert Lindsay was 'Philip Delancy,' my professional actor's name. I had one line to deliver, learnt and rehearsed a thousand times. It was to be the best acting job of my life, in a career that promised to be even better than flying.

I was sharing the trailer in Monte Carlo Harbour with two other French-speaking actors, Olivier Rabourdin, a Frenchman, and Yves Jacques, a Canadian. They were both much more experienced than me, but they knew I wasn't there to make the coffee, and we got on well, helped by blue skies and warm sun. Everyone was full of hope and promise.

Shooting began with the exterior evening scenes in the square in front of the Casino Monte-Carlo, which included my arrival by limousine as the powerful American Secretary of State for Defense, Robert McNamara. Olivier Dahan, the director of the Oscar-winning *La Vie en Rose,* told me to give

McNamara some gunslinger, even to the point where he wanted my arms slightly away from my sides. While we awaited the arrival of Nicole Kidman as Princess Grace, I chatted to my screen wife, a charming extra called Sabine who rode horses.

It was a long chilly night, working until four in the morning, with constant retakes and changes of camera angle. This was made tolerable by watching others at work and enjoying hot cups of tea brought to me from time to time by the runners. Initially empathising with the extras out in the cold, I remembered I'd done my time as background and stopped feeling guilty.

Even as an unknown in the acting world, meeting Nicole and the other actors confirmed my feeling of belonging with them while knowing that the world of the stars was out of my reach. When I was introduced to Nicole, she knew that I had been a pilot - it still counted for something.

It also helped me make friends with the American actor Milo Ventimiglia, who soon gave me advice with my accent. He had given up a girlfriend to further his career, and I admired his dedication and focus. Having dinner with Robert Lindsay also gave me some insight into the life of an 'A-Lister,' including an understandable wariness to open up to strangers, i.e. me.

The scene with my line would be shot in the Hôtel de Paris ballroom with 300 cast, crew, extras and two 35mm Panavision film cameras. I would head a table for ten 'American' guests, mainly French extras. The filming was delayed by a day which I was okay with until I forgot my line. I had said it so many times in so many ways that my brain overloaded; my speech and memory had gone blank.

It wasn't a long line, but it was important to the plot and had to be correct. Worried, I spoke with Olivier and Yves, and they said that happened to all actors at some point and to forget about it, literally. That meant going out with the French actors that evening to a Japanese restaurant with waiters throwing knives around and doing all the zoning out, chilling and meditating that I knew how. In the end, it was probably a couple of glasses of wine that did the trick.

The next day Nicole, Robert, Tim, and Milo were all on the top table, and I was at mine, feeling confident and relaxed as I sat next to 'Charles de Gaulle,' played by a kind and patient French actor called André Penvern. Cue the MC to announce the opening of the 'International Red Cross Ball' from the stage.

Faced with a sea of faces, he fluffed his lines understandable the first time, and then he did it again. Every time he restarted, it got worse, and there were mutterings around the room. Sensing that most of those in the room were unsympathetic, I went up to him and tried to empathise, but he was inconsolable. He'd said enough for the editor to be able to make something out of it, but it was an eggy moment.

And I was next! The two film cameras were moved to my table, I turned to André, and we did a couple of line runs. I felt nervous but calm. Not speaking much English, Olivier asked his First Assistant Director (AD) to call a rehearsal. The DOP did some framing and his assistant some focus pulling. Fifteen years in the business had come down to this moment. The First AD raised his voice.

'Quiet, please. Sound. Camera. Roll Sound. Roll Camera Mark it, and Action.'

I turned to 'Charles de Gaulle' and said my precious line: 'You're not really gonna drop a bomb on Princess Grace, are you, Charles?'

And that was that. Except it wasn't quite.

'Okay, let's do it again,' said the First AD.

This was normal. I knew there would be a few takes to enable the editor to pick the best one. There were different lenses to try, various backgrounds to organise. In French, Olivier asked me to put more humour into my delivery. Getting into my stride, I did so a dozen or more times with various intonations, nailing it every time.

I was feeling quite pleased with myself until I heard Nicole give her big speech about love. There was complete silence in the room as she did it three times, two pages of script each time. Which was why she was paid six million dollars. I didn't get six million dollars but gave myself a satisfaction rating of ten out of ten.

But the red carpet that I had walked on from my limousine up to the steps of the Hôtel de Paris wasn't real. Neither was I Robert Strange McNamara. It was real carpet, but part of a film set. A walk on a genuine red carpet as me came a year and a half later at the 2014 Cannes Film Festival. *Grace of Monaco* was the opening film, but I didn't have a specific invitation to the première.

Having booked accommodation through Airbnb, I organised myself a flight to Nice, turned up at the production company's office to ask for, and was given a ticket. I ran into a couple of actors that I knew, who were involved with other films, but otherwise, I was on my own, as usual. Lunching and drinking coffee on the promenade in the sunshine next to the *Palais des Festivals*, I soaked up the atmosphere, savouring my moment as an actor in a major feature film.

On the day of the screening, wearing my dinner jacket and black bow tie, I watched Olivier, Nicole and Tim arrive on the red carpet via the cinema screen in the *Grand Théâtre Lumière*. The auditorium was full of film professionals, the press, beautiful women, and me. While I was entitled to be there, I also felt an outsider for not being with anyone, but it didn't matter this time.

I was happy in my own company and settled down to watch the film. Shot on celluloid, it looked stunning in Mediterranean colours and with its glamorous settings. I waited for my appearance, with the niggling fear the storyline had been changed and that it had been cut. But no, there I was for a few seconds making my entrance and delivering my line.

Then it was all about Nicole and her character Princess Grace of Monaco.

Then followed a few days wandering around The Festival marketplace, acknowledging that the film industry was a business, as well as a way of bringing magic to an audience. My contribution was minuscule in the context of the event; a trade fair, not a Saturday night out at the 'pictures.' But that was okay - I wanted to be there, alone or not.

Walking past the booths collecting giveaways and looking for opportunities to hand out my business card, I was attracted to a pretty blonde woman with a broad smile and blue eyes. We connected, and I quickly discovered she was from the US, doing something in media, and an inveterate traveller. We accompanied each other to parties and walked on the beach, but no more.

Christine was friendly and sociable and an expert networker. I tagged along, giving her my best chat, and we ended up in a large room with members of Spandau Ballet and their entourage. From there, we were invited onto the *IONA,* a yacht moored in the harbour, which had been chartered by a movie studio.

The boat and its setting under the stars were exactly what I had hoped for. We sat around a table on the aft deck of the superyacht, served first-class food, and chatted with the other guests between mouthfuls of champagne. It was the perfect way to end my moment in the spotlight.

I found out afterwards that the FBI was investigating our host for fraud at the time, but I didn't care. Part of my growing up was to accept that illicit dealings were going on in all types of businesses, including the film industry, but I would be fine as long as I didn't get involved. So, when I was approached to play the lead bad guy in a sequel to the Bulgarian feature film *Rapid Reaction Force* I immediately assumed that gangsters were behind the deal.

On the plus side, the production values of the first film were high, the shoot was only for a week, and the worst that could happen would be that I would be held to ransom for my Ford Focus with 100,000 miles on the clock. However, I'd always wanted to play a villain in a suit, so I agreed, on the basis that it was about time I did something different and exciting.

Stanislav Donchev, the writer, producer, and director, found me through my website, spoke excellent English, and his company *Dynamic Arts* seemed well-organised and professional. I noticed I had a resemblance to the villain in the first film; perhaps I was replacing him, or maybe my fleeting appearance in Star Wars had made an impression.

In Bulgarian, the script duly arrived, although I didn't understand the explanations of the plot and my character profile, even in the English translation. The film was an action-comedy, but knowing that I wasn't a funny guy, I would leave the three lead Bulgarian actors to get the laughs, as they *were* funny.

Stanislav met me at the airport, and once I'd settled into my four-star hotel in the centre of Sofia, a car picked me up, and I was taken to a restaurant to meet his wife and friends. They looked at me as if I were a properly famous actor, while I concentrated on not saying anything stupid, which wasn't difficult as I couldn't speak a word of Bulgarian.

Everyone was polite, generous, and kind - I was determined to do my best for them. I asked how they wanted me to play the character, and they nodded. In Bulgaria, nodding yes means no and shaking the head no means yes. There were friendly faces everywhere, but I was none the wiser.

Worried I might be shot for being a bad actor, I thought Emil, who was assigned to look after me, might do the shooting. At six feet eight, he looked as if he would pull the arms off anyone who messed with him, me included. He turned out to be one of the kindest and gentlest family men, simply wanting to be part of a film shoot.

I was beginning to like Bulgaria but was never sure if they liked me or were just being respectful. I felt guilty for not getting wildly drunk, and smoking dope like Brits abroad were reputed to, but my worst fear was of being boring.

All the actors, crew and extras had considerable talent and were unfailingly helpful and friendly. The girls working on the film were stunning, with male friends who had many tattoos and large muscles. Occasionally the crew would go off into a heated discussion in Bulgarian, which allowed me to stand around trying to look like a film star, but in reality, I was worried they were talking about me.

We went off into the countryside to film the final scene at an airfield on a blisteringly hot day. There was an Aztec in the hangar, but I was more focused on making my character look authentic than the aeroplane. With guys dressed in black dropping from the rafters, I finally felt I'd nailed my performance by improvising an imaginary conversation with Vladimir Putin.

The Bulgarians had treated me like a VIP, far better than I had expected, but it didn't stop there. They invited Annie and me to the premiere in Sofia two years later, this time on the red carpet as one of the main actors. There were photos with the real stars and my face on billboards and boxes of popcorn. I shook hands with dignitaries, fans, and more beautiful women. I held someone's child for a photo with his mother, hugged the cast, crew, and extras, and signed autographs. There was clapping, lots of smiles, and a meeting with Les Weldon, a full-on Hollywood producer who was married to the female lead in our film.

Les was one of the producers of my next major feature film, *London Has Fallen,* of which my scenes were cast and shot in London, so there was no red carpet for me in Los Angeles. But there was a luxury barge with polished wood, fruit and a cut-glass decanter moored just downstream of the Houses of Parliament for me as Jacques Mainard, The French President.

At the audition, the director Babak Najafi had asked me to improvise some lines that a French President might say. In French, I went for 'They will have to wait for me. The French President waits for no one,' which was good enough for Babak. So, with newfound confidence, I turned up at Lambeth Pier on a grey, overcast January day in 2016 to start work.

It was another perfect day. Babak went into his huddle with the DOP, then came out and told me what he wanted. There were long shots, medium shots, and close-ups, sitting comfortably in my barge, then looking concerned as I looked towards the London Eye as if it were being destroyed.

Extras dressed as security men ran to the boat to evacuate me from danger, upon which they and I disintegrated into small pieces of French meat thanks to a bomb located on a passing barge. We shot the whole scene in not much more than half a day, and I absolutely loved it. My face appeared in the trailers, and I was occasionally recognised. It didn't get much better than that.

There were other enjoyable jobs, particularly where I could fulfil some of the aspirations of my other potential careers, e.g. policeman. These included playing 'soft cop' while interviewing an 83-year-old lady bank robber played by ex-Bond Girl Honor Blackman and 'hard cop' with Ke$ha, the 25-year-old American female pop superstar.

Ke$ha had decided she wanted to make a film of her being interrogated and coming out on top. It was called *Warrior Interrogation*, and it was filmed in an old police station, with only enough space for the director, the cameraman, Ke$ha and me in the interview room. Having been given some questions and told to improvise, I slurped my coffee and paused before beginning:

'I wanna know your full name.'

'Ke$ha, with a dollar sign.'
'What's your date of birth?'
'March first, 1987.'
'Is it true your mother was an alien?'
'How do you know that?'
'Just answer the question.'
'Yes.'
'What about your father? What was he? Alice Cooper?'
'Kind of.'
'Is it true that your song *Gold Trans Am* was about your Hoo Hah?'
This was serious stuff.
'Yes, that is true. I admit fully, that it is. Because my vagina is gold, glittery too. Smells like candy.'

My questions continued in the same vein, 'Do you eat glitter on a daily basis?'; 'When did you last speak to your cat?'; 'Do you speak dinosaur?'

'I do,' said Ke$ha, 'do you wanna hear it?'

Upon which she squealed in what I thought was a decent impression of a dinosaur. She was bright and funny and, after she had taken her long legs off the desk, pretended to smack me in the mouth and be the hero. The Director creased up with laughter in the corner of the room, and the cameraman could hardly hold his equipment steady.

On the other side of the law, my joke application to be a lookalike for the fugitive Lord Lucan finally paid off when I was booked to appear as him on The Rory Bremner Show, working with 'Mahatma Gandhi,' 'Elvis Presley,' and 'Marilyn Monroe.' These were the jobs that made up for selling cut-price televisions on Sutton High Street.

However, despite being cast by Ross Noble as his 'Theatre Code Man' - dressed in tights and a cape telling the audience what to do before his show - I was usually offered serious roles, ultimately Obergruppenführer Fritz Sauckel, one of the most ruthless men in the Third Reich, for a National Geographic documentary.

Playing distinctly different roles was fun: a spoof newsreader for *Jackie Chan Adventures*; a Lawyer 4 U ('We are *real* lawyers',) and holding the Claret Jug aloft for Stella Artois, shot from behind as I didn't actually win The Open Golf Championship.

With my ability to produce foreign accents nurtured from my performance at flying college, I combined the two by playing the American pilot Captain David Cronin of United Airlines flight 811 for the BBC2 documentary on *The History of the 747*, followed by the womanising French chef 'Henri' as a guest actor in an episode of BBC's *Father Brown*.

There, my fortitude was tested to its limits on my arrival when the Director asked me to sing a song in French in front of the distinguished cast. After stumbling through a few verses, I realised that their deathly silence was their way of welcoming me. Talking to them and other successful actors, I also discovered that getting 'found out,' i.e. Impostor Syndrome was a common fear in the profession, even in those at the top[23].

At the other end of the artistic scale were the student graduation films, which I occasionally worked on if I liked the script. They usually paid nothing unless the writer, producer, and director's mother happened to be the Manager of The Rolling Stones. In addition to renting a house, paying for chaperones for two child actors, an owl trainer and expenses, the £1,000 fee for each of four professional actors seemed too good to be true. And it was.

Johnny, the film school student, was trying to make a feature film with only a camera operator and a soundman to do everything else. He knew what he wanted but was unable to communicate it to me - important as I was playing the lead character, a troubled war veteran. We took a trip to a Welsh farm for me to learn how to wrestle sheep for a scene in the film. Under the farmer's tuition, I had to grab the sheep by its

---

[23] E.g. Jodie Foster, Tom Hanks, Robert Pattinson, Kate Winslet

wool and throw it to the floor before realising how heavy and strong these animals were. I had to do it a few times as Johnny wanted everything filmed in one shot. The sheep were fine, but I was exhausted. At 60 years of age, I was feeling old.

When there were bad days, they were enough to make me want to give up the profession. Asked to self-tape for the co-pilot role in a British-French TV drama production, I was also requested to provide details of my flying experience, which was odd, as I was applying for the job as an actor, not a pilot. However, as I knew of no other bilingual actors who had been genuine airline pilots, I thought I had a good chance of getting the part. The script had all kinds of technical inaccuracies, but I improvised around them in my casting video.

This must have gone down well as I was invited to a face-to-face meeting with the CD (Casting Director) but this time to play the captain. Via my agent, the CD called me on the morning of the audition with the details of the appointment and to tell me she wanted to 'have a little chat about flying a plane,' both of which were unusual. However, I agreed and rushed into the studio in London to be on time, read the lines, and offered the CD a page of script changes the production team might wish to consider to make the flying scenes appear more authentic.

A week later a note arrived from the CD: *In the end (and it was very last minute) they went for an actor who the Director has worked with before and was always a favourite of his.* I was furious. I had spent hours trying to add value to the project; then, the Director had given the part to his mate, something I was sure he had intended to do from the outset. He had built up my hopes, milked me for my expertise and then dropped me. I never saw the program but remembered the name of the director.

With the corporate work being the mainstay of my work, the few TV and film jobs I did were the icing on the cake. The challenge of delivering a script well, chatting with other professionals, and bringing enjoyment to an audience made acting a worthwhile occupation. I survived in the highly competitive world of the business by sticking to what I could do well and working at it.

In return, the profession helped me to recover from my breakdown by giving me the ability to express my feelings and emotions while teaching me more about human nature. It taught me self-awareness, truthfulness, and being in the moment and gave me a thicker skin from the many rejections. And despite those, I had been a pretend pilot too. Perhaps I could be a real one again.

As 'Big Chief Thundercloud,' St Jude's Players, 1994

As a 'British Airways pilot,' in '*Parent Trap,*' 1997

As a 'Naboo Pilot,' in *Star Wars,* Episode 1, 1997

Bilingual technical presenter, Canon Medical, Monaco, 1998

The Dark Room, 1998

As the 'lurve_god,' for the launch of Microsoft's *Hotmail* campaign, 1998

As Lord Lucan, at *The Compleat Angler*, Marlow, 6 May 2012

As Robert McNamara, in *Grace of Monaco*, October 2012

As 'President of France,' in *London Has Fallen,* 24 Nov 2014

Red Carpet, Bulgaria, in *KBR2*, February 2016

221

22

Recovery

Forty years after recovering from the spin in the Cherokee over the Isle of Wight, I was sitting behind my youngest daughter in one of its descendants, contemplating a different type of recovery, that of my mental health. Having completed the most dangerous part of the day - driving to White Waltham - I watched the instructor taking her through the checks for her first flight in a light aeroplane from the same airfield where I had learnt to fly, confident I could have done his job equally well. I would have been immensely proud to have flown my daughter on her birthday instead of taking photos. No one would have taken greater care of her.

Clearly, there had been times in my life when I wasn't fit to push a wheelbarrow, and the increase in attention around pilots' mental health, particularly after Andreas Lubitz's suicide by plane, wasn't going to help me either.[24] Yet I had a letter from my GP stating I had been in full remission for at least 23 years, and to fly again as a pilot would be fun and official confirmation of my recovery from the 'Illness' that had caused the CAA to assess me as being 'temporarily unfit to exercise the privileges of my pilot's licence' in 1981.

So, with nothing to lose except £130 plus VAT, I attended an Aeromedical Centre that issued aircrew medical

---

[24] Andreas Lubitz was the co-pilot of a Germanwings Airbus who deliberately crashed into a mountainside on 24 March 2015, killing all 150 passengers and crew. He had previously been treated for suicidal tendencies and declared "unfit to work" by his doctor.

certificates for the Light Aircraft Pilot's Licence. Filling in the form outlining my medical history, I answered all the questions truthfully and included details of the medication I was taking.

Having passed the motor skills, hearing, and eye tests, the doctor who examined me told me I would need an assessment by a consultant psychiatrist approved by the CAA. So, a week later, I drove myself to the Priory Hospital in Woking for an appointment with Dr Timothy Dale.

'I am the doctor' wasn't the introduction I was expecting from Dr Dale. He didn't shake my hand either. Having worked in the interpersonal skills industry for 20 years, I would have behaved differently. 'The doctor' led me to his office and invited me to sit across from him at the corner of his desk. Taking copious notes, Dr Dale asked a lot of questions about my breakdown, but none about how I had dealt with it. Having mentioned that Dr Comish had refused to label me, I soon formed the impression that Dr Dale was a dyed-in-the-wool labels man.

In 2006 as part of an acting job for a pharmaceutical company, I had sat in a roomful of psychiatrists and listened to a guest speaker give a talk with the cliché introduction: 'My name is Chris, and I'm bipolar.' At the time, I had thought to myself; this guy is fucked because he is living a label instead of being himself.

While I could see that diagnostic terminology was useful to the medical profession, as a layman, I considered the term 'breakdown' perfectly adequate for what had happened to me. If a label defined me, I ran the risk of being subject to the prejudices, lack of knowledge, and fears of unqualified people. With some cursory knowledge of my condition, well-meaning neighbours would gaze piercingly into my eyes and ask: 'How *are* you?' as if they could fathom the depths of my soul in one glance.

Undoubtedly most cared, but others had probably read too many newspaper articles in a bid to make themselves feel more comfortable about anyone who didn't behave the way they did. I could hear the lids of the various boxes labelled 'manic-depressive psychosis,' 'bipolar affective disorder,' and 'hypomania' creaking open as people got ready to put me into them and keep me there.

It was time for Dr Dale's assessment on my fitness to meet the requirements for a private pilot's licence. The regulations stated that I wasn't fit to fly while on psychotropic medication. Even if my Mental Health Review six years previously had indicated that I was 'completely stable and well on present medication,' I had to accept that. It seemed that taking the medication was the obstacle to flying rather than the means that would enable me to do it safely.

I asked Dr Dale if he had known what medication I was taking before we began the meeting. Yes, the Aeromedical Centre had told him, so he knew I was going to fail before we started. Knowing my fate before entering the room, Dr Dale could have run the session as a consultation from the outset and talked about my future rather than dwelling on the past in return for his £250 hourly fee.

While I accepted that Dr Dale and the CAA doctors had a regulatory role, I was frustrated that they, and possibly 'the system', seemed to focus more on categorising people - and treating symptoms rather than causes - rather than promoting an integrated approach to getting well. The meeting with Dr Dale had been a charade, making me angry after everything I'd been through. As I looked at him, I was sure he was thinking I would lose my temper and that he would have to Section me or stick a needle in me.

But that wasn't going to happen because I had changed from an unhappy, immature child to a self-aware man, comfortable in my skin. I quietly explained why I was disappointed with how he had carried out the assessment, after which he changed tack. He promised to halve his fee and suggested that if I came off all medication, was stable for five years, the CAA might consider me for a licence. This sounded like a way forward for the long-term. Two years later, I wrote to my GP requesting a further mental health review, suggesting that I might be ready to come off all psychotropic drugs under medical supervision, on the basis that after 38 years, they might be ineffective anyway[25].

He immediately referred me to the community consultant psychiatrist for a consultation. Coincidentally the same week, I met another GP socially who advised me how best to come off medication. Taking the latter's advice and being aware of the risks involved, I gradually reduced my lithium dose to below the therapeutic level. Still, I was ready to take extra if needed. As recommended, I recorded details of my moods and feelings in a written diary.

While grateful for some of the help I had received in the past, I also felt it was up to me to take responsibility for my health, including taking medication. For me, the trick was to work *with* doctors and not fight them – as my brother had done - or come across as a victim and insinuate that I needed special treatment, and certainly never to volunteer any information about my medical history to non-professionals.

My daughters were vital as arbiters of my mental health, too, on the basis that they cared more about me than anyone else. They wouldn't allow me to drive them, let alone fly, if they didn't feel safe with me.

The combination of reducing the medication and three separate stressful events occurring within two weeks of each other at the end of 2019 could easily have led to a relapse and the undoing of all the progress I had made since the previous one, 20 years earlier. Instead, they were the means for me to demonstrate my control over them.

The first was a drunken afternoon at a pub Beaujolais lunch, including frequent visits to the toilet in case I was sick.

---

[25] Information gleaned from an episode of *Homeland* in September 2018, where the lead character works for the CIA while being 'bipolar.'

Dr Comish had warned me about drinking too much during my time at St Andrews. After a fitful night's sleep, I wandered around town the following morning before taking a lonely breakfast reading the *Times,* believing that some of the stories specifically applied to me, a characteristic of going 'high' that I was aware of.

My refuge was in taking on the persona of an SAS commander on the basis that such a man would be able to deal with the situation resolutely and unemotionally. This comforting presence stayed with me as I returned home, detouring on a whim to renew my phone contract for a better handset – another potential sign of elevated mood, given it was hardly outrageous behaviour.

Conscious of feelings of anxiety and guilt creeping up on me during the morning, my first action upon reaching my flat was to take my medication which soon took effect, helping me to react calmly to an unsuccessful attempt to speak to Natasha. Next, I called my youngest daughter, who introduced me to the concept of 'beer fear' – which I'd never previously heard of – and how it was usual to feel down after drinking lots of alcohol. She began to reassure me that perhaps I was normal after all, at least for someone unused to getting extremely drunk.

The second, more stressful event was driving my parents back from France four days later with my mother complaining about everything. It was the night of the London Bridge terror stabbing less than two miles away from their home in Pimlico. This caused my thoughts to switch once more into security mode, i.e. thinking how I would defend my parents and myself against an actual terrorism threat while aware of possible accusations of paranoia.

The third and final unhappiness of the recent weeks was Natasha's confirmation that we weren't together and that she was taking her Christmas holiday in the Caribbean with a girlfriend rather than with me.

Given that I was on a low dose of lithium, my reaction to these disappointments pleased me. Indeed, I had been sensitive and intense, but I hadn't said or done anything really bizarre. I had got drunk, been frustrated with my elderly parents, and felt upset at the breakup of my relationship with a woman I had asked to marry me. These were normal life occurrences that happened to lots of people.

Instead of getting more stressed and demoralised, I arranged to stay a week in St Lucia with my long-time friend Jerry. Ex British Airways, and with his wife having recently died, we would be mates for a much-needed break.

But my mini 'high' wasn't over. Indulging in a minor spending spree at Gatwick on the outbound journey relieved me of £800 for a new laptop and a set of top-of-the-range headphones before checking out my fellow passengers as an imaginary onboard sky marshal.

Arriving Bondesque in the tropical heat, I met up with Jerry, who drove me to the Marigot Bay Resort, where he had a first-class hotel room and a bed ready for me. He knew about my medical condition and quickly noticed the grandiosity that I exhibited 'as if I owned the place.'

However, looking up at the stars from Jerry's jacuzzi at three in the morning in what seemed like paradise on earth, it did seem normal to feel exceptionally good about life, and there were new worlds to conquer too, starting with a screenplay for a Hollywood blockbuster.

As my only viable contact in Los Angeles, Tania[26] would write, produce, and direct a feature film based on my idea around a fictional suicide by plane. Having contacted a dark-haired fitness actress called Catherine Holland to co-star, I went off on my own to have a body wax and to arrange interviews with some female guests as part of the project in a suite at the neighbouring resort – all legitimate and legal.

Jerry left me to it but contacted my children to express his concern about my behaviour. They, in turn, contacted the

---

[26] Tania Meneguzzi, the director of *The Run* (see chapter 19.)

NHS 111 helpline to find out who my doctor was in case they needed to contact him to start the process of having me Sectioned and obtain medical power of attorney.

Oblivious to this, I had taken some of my pills to deal with my anxiety around the film project, centred on losing confidence in my ability to carry it through. Tania had shown some interest, and when I looked at it again, the treatment appeared coherent, although I didn't have the skills required to turn it into a screenplay. While I did wonder if I would have been so creative had I been on a higher dose of lithium, more importantly, I had sought out the pills when I needed them - as I might take paracetamol for a toothache - instead of taking them out of habit.

Back home, when I eventually discussed the holiday with my daughters, I understood how much my behaviour had impacted them over the years since their teens. They frequently worried that I would be considered 'mad, aggressive, angry, sad, hysterical, delusional, embarrassing, strange, weird, perhaps even scary.' Sometimes they believed I sounded lonely and miserable when I called, not knowing whether I was happy or sad, and other times that I was deliriously joyful, speaking too quickly, or doing strange things. They didn't know what was happening with me, just that they loved me as their dad.

As a 65-year-old man, communicating with 30-year-old women presented its challenges. With some residual fear of being criticised by them and their mother still present, I couldn't be dispassionate and rational all the time, so the girls found it particularly hard when I tried to offload my feelings onto them. This was the most powerful motivator to agree to their request for me to see a therapist.

Meeting with a highly qualified, accredited BACP Counsellor locally, I warmed to her assertiveness and insight. I told her everything I could in the one-hour session, from my relationship issues with my children to my desire to take off my clothes, but not in front of her!

She announced that writing my book was my therapy, confirming that while the revelations within it were a lot for my children to take in, they could be addressed through effective communication. Loving and respecting them would make putting in the effort easy, but I would still have to work hard before I could claim I had allayed their concerns. Stopping blaming myself for the divorce helped, given that Isla had come out of it pretty well.

Following the visit to the therapist, I was able to identify my preoccupation with the body beautiful as the reason for my exhibitionist tendencies, but more importantly, the guilt I had about them. For some time, this had been exercising my brain in the context of my parents' long-standing fixation on looks, particularly my mother's whimsically stated wish to see me marry my sister.

By joining reputable sites, I became an official 'nudist' to try and make myself see people for what they were, whatever their shape, colour, and size. Forcing myself to ignore the look of the bodies on display, I tried hard to make friends with like-minded men and women from all over the world, irrespective of their physical attractiveness.

However, I wasn't particularly successful, which only served to confirm the importance of tribalism in my world, and therefore probably everyone else's. I was drawn to people – initially at least - who looked like me because that made me feel safe and secure, having more in common with French, Italian, and Greek types than with the average Briton's whiter, more hirsute look.

Then, as I got to know those closest to me, i.e. family, neighbours, and friends, my circle of acceptance widened until it included virtually everyone I came into contact with.

By looking at the animal kingdom, I rationalised male or female nudity in the context of mating and reproduction, sometimes depicted as art. The male peacock was a good example, with his human equivalent showing off on the sports field, boardroom, or stage. For breeding purposes, I also understood man would choose an equally attractive woman and vice versa. With seven billion people on the planet, there had to be a match for everyone.

My mind told me which people I would rather spend time with intellectually - there was just the connection to the rest of my body left to fix.

In May 2020, I had a two-hour consultation with the NHS consultant psychiatrist, who confirmed a phased reduction in my medication to zero by October 2022, together with a strong recommendation to reduce or eliminate my alcohol intake.

Surprisingly, she also told me that the medication was unlikely to be a physiological cause of the erectile dysfunction (ED) that had been troubling me for years. Being on lithium had reduced my confidence, while excess confidence had been the reason it had been prescribed for me, a chicken and egg situation which had decreased in intensity over time.

Feelings of failure and inadequacy after my breakdown – constantly reaffirmed every time I took a pill – had led to a reduction in my ability to become aroused, which seemed to be psychological rather than physical. Other medical professionals I had consulted confirmed this. Reducing medication wasn't the only reason for my erections to become harder and more frequent; it was by dealing with my anxieties effectively, in parallel.

I had blamed the medication for a string of failed relationships, even though it was only contributing a few milligrams of chemicals. Further evidence against this misapprehension was the second part of my holiday in Australia, where escape, freedom, and skinny dipping had rapidly restored my libido.

The resurgence in my potency had the additional effect of increasing my emotional and moral confidence too, enabling me to be more assertive in pursuing my old Catholic ideals, i.e. no sex before marriage and only with women.

Instead of trying too hard to perform sexually based on looks, I focused on the other features in a woman that attracted me: kindness, empathy, and a hint of vulnerability. Perhaps I had been spending too long in pubs and on dating sites looking for instant attraction and chemistry in environments where women were doing the same. Love was an elusive commodity, but at least I felt I was getting to the right starting place by loving myself.

Self-coaching, I worked out that the pilot Gail had loved was still in me: unflappable, solution-focused, and good at making practical decisions. I had highs and lows like everyone else – perhaps more accentuated because of my French ancestry – but which had reduced in amplitude over the years. The guilt, anxiety, intensity, and sensitivities had all been in my head. They just needed to be managed. I didn't have to change anything radically - just let go, accept who I was and what I was feeling, and enjoy that.

On a practical level, making myself go for long walks, recording the resultant thoughts had been vital to reset my brain and help prioritise my actions. Walking outside with a notebook and hearing the crunching of my trainers on the road, feeling the wind on my face and the air in my lungs immediately reduced or removed any stress.

Jotting down notes had become a habit ever since I had taken up writing the year after the breakdown. Typewritten text cut and pasted with scissors and glue had given way to entering characters onto a screen, but both helped clarify the issues that had caused my erratic behaviours and need for medication.

Passing one of my favourite pubs, I called in to speak to the landlord who I had known since I had moved to

Windsor 14 years earlier to ask him what he would say about me for my book.

'I don't know Phil,' he said, 'I don't know you very well. You come in here, have a few drinks, and that's it. I know you've done a bit of acting and had a girlfriend, but that's all.'

Perfect – not even a mention of being an ex-pilot – a grey man. No drama, just one customer among thousands of others, normal at last. I was living a new, quiet life with a fresh identity that I had constructed for myself - as an actor would - except this time, it was for real. I had kept a low profile, generally behaving unremarkably and certainly differently to the way that had previously got me carted off to hospital in public view.

There were people I had known and worked with for years who didn't even know I'd had a breakdown. I'm not sure my story of being a pilot *and* an actor was always believed, but I settled for occasionally being described as a nice guy, even a gentleman but definitely *different*, or perhaps 'neurodiverse[27].'

On the morning of 1 August 2020, after two years of easing off medication, I believed that I had fully recovered my mental health. Twenty-four hours previously, on my parents 67th wedding anniversary, I had offered to drive them down to the promenade in St Lunaire to enjoy a moment in the town where they had spent some of their happiest times before my flight home that afternoon.

Too tired to move, they preferred to stay in the flat a few hundred yards away, settled in the knowledge that my grandmother and brother were buried nearby and that they were prepared for joining them.

By listening to their stories instead of trying to change them, I'd got closer to my parents, warming to them more

---

[27] The idea of neurodiversity was first established in the 1990's by the Australian sociologist Judy Singer.

than ever before. This was even when I found out that they were against my brother and me playing with toy guns, which may have influenced my decision not to join the military.

Happy they were safe, I left them to their bed and their memories and took a luxurious swim out into a smooth, cool sea virtually alone before a blissful 8 a.m. coffee and a croissant at the beach bar. Totally content with life, I asked myself why I was returning to England. Unable to think of a good reason, I connected to the airline to postpone my return home by a week. Their website told me there were no flights available, so I set off for the airport as originally planned.

Back home, when I discovered I could have changed the departure by asking at the airport customer service desk, my despondency was as intense as my happiness had been in St Lunaire. Allowing my feelings to be, I called a girlfriend, ate French sandwiches for dinner, and installed some new blinds, which had arrived while I was away.

Up at 7 a.m. the following day after sleeping well, I felt down again because I didn't have the sea and the beach bar to look forward to. Anxiety was present in my bedroom, like a malevolent spirit ready to engulf me and take me away, screaming.

My head told me clearly what I had to do: get up and go for a walk, which I knew was effective to order my thoughts and turn my frame of mind from negative to positive. The alternative was to go back to bed and indulge in the self-absorption that I might have described to others as 'depression.' It was a key moment in making a conscious decision to 'do the right thing,' which didn't make it any easier but left me with only one option: to get out of bed and put some clothes on.

Out in the street, I traipsed sluggishly and without enthusiasm towards the corner shop where they baked fresh croissants, actually better than those from the *boulangerie* in St Lunaire. Damn, there were no chocolate ones left, only a plain. These minor details rankled when I was fed up. Never mind, it would have to do – I would get my own back on karma by taking a longer route home, just to be awkward. It wasn't the most enjoyable start to a walk I had ever made, but the time passed quickly enough, and I was soon eating the croissant from my usual spot at the foot of the Copper Horse statue of King George III.

Taking in the view across Berkshire, I heard a woman nearby talking to her companion about a roundabout on the M4. For a few seconds, I connected her comment with the drive in the police car around a similar roundabout 39 years earlier before being taken to Reading Police Station. It was a logical link, making me realise how easy it was to think everything was happening for my benefit.

But now, there was a better way of looking at events: that they and I were in harmony with the world. Heading off down the Long Walk with its long, straight path to the castle, surrounded by trees and well-kept grass, the concluding words to my book came into my head without any conscious effort on my part. Suddenly I wanted to get home and write them down, so I started running - life was good again.

From the swim to the walk, I had experienced a full range of mood from total and sublime contentment to disappointment and regret, and I was in control the entire time without the stabilising effect of lithium. The past was the past, and over. My life was in my head, and it was up to me to be the person to enjoy it wherever I was. It didn't matter whether I was in St Lunaire, Windsor, or the Caribbean.

Writing this closing chapter, I questioned if I'd ever had a mental illness; mental health condition might have been a better description. I'd been a pilot, been unemployed, married and divorced twice, had three children, had and lost girlfriends, been happy, sad, and content, become an actor, paid my bills, travelled to five continents, had an idea for a screenplay, written a book, and had friends I could count on. That was it, my life - no big deal.

Intolerance of anyone – male or female - who fell below my own and my parents' standards had made me oblivious to other's weaknesses and insecurities and ignorant of how to show empathy, compromise and accept opinions and views at variance with mine.

Over time, my breakdown helped me see other people as fallible – as I was -, to like them for what they were and to work with them on the basis there was a multitude of ways of accomplishing a task.

Being different made me the same as everyone else, eventually seeing human beings, including myself, as multi-faceted: good and bad, complicated and simple, and capable of experiencing the full range of emotions.

At 66, I'd finally found and adopted the traits and behaviours that I admired in both men and women: quiet calmness, modesty, assertiveness without aggression, protectiveness towards the vulnerable, kindness to all, with violence in self-defence as a last resort.

I had nothing to prove, with bravery, friendships, and good humour to be developed. I was able to say to myself: 'I am what I am,' with no regrets and feeling free; to fly, act, and occasionally take my clothes off!

Two follow-up consultations with psychiatrists – one with my middle daughter present - confirmed that I wasn't relapsing due to coming off lithium, indeed that I should continue taking only the carbamazepine on a reducing dose, as previously agreed. The consultant explained how lithium didn't act as an anti-psychotic and could numb creativity while suppressing emotion and intensity.

Telling her about my improved erections off it was both liberating and sobering, as I realised how controlling the drug had been in my life to the likely detriment of my relationships with women. She also repeated her previous recommendation that I should stop drinking, which I had effectively done anyway.

After 39 years on lithium therapy, inevitably, there were some residual thoughts about spies, benign conspiracy theories, and my film idea to come out, which they did, but categorised in my mind under 'imagination,' rather than paranoia. Similarly, 'Hope,' 'Dreams,' and 'Recovery' may have been delusions, but to me, they were as real as the peace, comfort, and contentment that I felt on my morning swims or walks.

Perhaps I was mentally ill once by being out of touch with reality, but I had co-operated with others by taking medication while having come to terms with the psychological and physical downsides of being on it. The recovery process had been challenging but given me the insight and tools to face the future.

As I write these final words, I note that it is 40 years to the day since I last flew as a pilot. Feeling warmth towards all the people I know, I think of my father's last words to me about peace-making as he lay dying with my mother by his side and his piano music playing in the background. They saw me as a good boy before the need to take a mind-controlling drug. I am that person again, the best of both of them, and with a personality I can now live with.

The blue sky I saw from my bedroom window in Natal Road is the same as the one I see over Windsor. The journey through it has taken me across the green fields of White Waltham and Hamble, into a red mist, then out of it to a hospital golf course and the lawns of Buckingham Palace.

Enriched by the myriad colours and personalities of the human beings it has been my privilege to meet, I now feel I am in the best time of my life; knowing that when I look up at the sunshine in that blue sky or the stars at night, even if it rains, somewhere there will be a rainbow.

Afterword

I hope you enjoyed reading this book. If so, then I achieved my main objective. There were other reasons I wanted to write it.

First, to show that mental health issues can affect anyone.

Second, to promote writing as therapy, a creative, fun, and portable occupation, and an attractive option for retirement from 'work.' With exercise, it has been the most effective way of improving my mental health.

Third, to encourage people to tell their full stories, whether to loved ones, friends, or acquaintances. I believe too many people live constrained by secrets that prevent them from enjoying full relationships, as happened between my parents and me.

Fourth, to use it as a springboard to speak about what I've learnt on my journey, potentially to help others through coaching and self-coaching, i.e.

1. To LOVE ourselves for what we are – to be truthful, realistic, and ambitious.

2. To be KIND to others. To love them for what THEY are and COMMUNICATE empathetically with them: assertively, non-judgmentally, and open-mindedly, and to LISTEN to people. Everyone has a story.

3. To DO things rather than just think about them.

4. To DEAL with issues head-on to reduce stress.

5. To MAKE ourselves do exercise, and to manage our own health.

6. To CARE for our body and mind, in respect of their needs.

7. To KNOW where our centre is, i.e. be comfortable, relaxed, and content in our own skin.

8. To have a VISION of where we are going in life.

9. To be prepared to CHANGE our behaviours – we can't change our character.

10. To PLAN, but to be ready to act on impulse.

11. To PROACTIVELY CHOOSE between necessary and unnecessary material things.

12. To ENJOY moments and LIVE for today, ready to die tomorrow.

Life is what it is, with a choice between pain or gain.

There are haves and have nots.

There are always two sides to an argument.

Using acting techniques, we can be who we want to be.

There are no problems, only situations and solutions.

10 February 2021

Appendix:

During the 1970s Decade Zoom Reunion organised by the Haberdashers' Aske's Boys' School on 8 March 2021, Flight Lieutenant Paul Hayler RAF VRT said I was the best senior cadet Warrant Officer he had seen in his 30 years in charge of the Combined Cadet Force.

Glossary (Aviation)

Airway	Corridor of controlled airspace
Altimeter setting	Calibration according to local pressure variations
Altitude	Distance from an aeroplane to sea level
Apron	Area of an airport where aircraft are parked, loaded, and unloaded, refuelled and boarded
Artificial horizon	A master instrument showing an aircraft's attitude in relation to the horizon enabling flight in cloud
ATC	Air Traffic Control
Attitude	The orientation of an aircraft with respect to the horizon
ATPL	Airline Transport Pilots Licence
Avgas	Aviation gasoline 100LL (Low Lead) petrol
AVM	Air Vice-Marshal
Aztec C, D, E	Six-seat, low-wing, twin piston-engine aeroplane
B-52	Long-range, eight jet-engine bomber used from the 1950s
BA	British Airways
BAA	British Airports Authority
Banking	Manoeuvre when one wing goes down, the other up
Barrel roll	A manoeuvre where an aircraft flies as if round the inside of a barrel, theoretically pulling 1g all the way round
BEA	British European Airways
Beechcraft Baron	Six-seat, low-wing, twin piston-engine aeroplane
BOC	British Oxygen Company
C of A	Certificate of Airworthiness
CAA	Civil Aviation Authority

CAT scan	Computerised Axial Tomography – X-ray scans that produce cross-sectional images of the body
Caravelle	French twin jet-engine airliner (90 passengers)
Carbamazepine	A drug used to prevent epilepsy sometimes used in conjunction with lithium
Cessna 150	Two-seat, high-wing, single piston-engine aeroplane
Cessna 401A	Seven-seat, low-wing, twin piston-engine aeroplane
Cessna 421	Eight-seat, low-wing, twin piston-engine aeroplane
Cherokee (Piper)	Four-seat, low-wing, single piston-engine aeroplane
Chocks	Rubber wedges to stop an aircraft moving on the ground
Clipper	Pan American Airways radio callsign
Comms	Communications
Concorde	Supersonic, delta-wing, four jet-engine airliner (100 passengers)
Control column	Used to control aircraft in pitch and roll
Controlled airspace	Areas providing ATC service for separation purposes
Cumulus clouds	The 'cotton wool' fair-weather clouds
Danger Area	Military area for live firing exercises
DME	Distance Measuring Equipment
EAS	British Airways Executive Aircraft Service
EEG	Electroencephalogram. Medical equipment used to find problems related to electrical activity of the brain
EGT	Exhaust Gas Temperature
Epaulettes	Gold or silver shoulder rank bars fitted to uniform shirts
F-14	High-performance, twin jet-engine fighter (US Navy)
F-15	High-performance, twin jet-engine fighter (US Air Force)

F27 (Fokker 27)	High-wing, twin turboprop-engine airliner (44 passengers)
Flaps	Devices on the trailing edge of a wing to increase lift and drag
Flare, Flaring	Final nose-up manoeuvre just before touchdown
Flight level	Measure of altitude based on a standard pressure setting of 1013 millibars
Freezing level	Altitude above which the temperature is below zero
Fuselage	The main body of an aircraft containing the cabin
G	Gravity, where 1g is one unit
GAT	General Aviation Terminal
Gauges	Instruments, usually for the engine parameters
Gear	Undercarriage (US terminology)
General Aviation (GA)	Non-scheduled aircraft; private and training aircraft
Grounded	Unable to fly for medical or technical reasons
Hamble	Location of the British Airways Flying Training School (closed in 1983)
Handling Agent	An organisation providing ground support services to aircraft operators
Heading	The compass direction towards which an aircraft is pointing
Heading bug	Cursor on directional indicator instrument
Height	Distance from an aeroplane to ground
Instrument Rating	Pilot qualification enabling flight in controlled airspace and cloud
IRA	Irish Republican Army
Knot (kt)	Unit of speed used in aviation = one nautical mile per hour.
Landing 'T'	Marker to indicate landing direction
Leading edge	Front part of the wing
Lightning	British supersonic, twin jet-engine interceptor (1954 – 1988)
Lithium	A metal administered as lithium carbonate used to control moods

Mach	Measure of speed relative to the speed of sound. Mach 1 = 760mph at sea level
Manifolds	Exhaust pipes
Nacelle	A streamlined housing for an engine
Nautical mile (nm)	1852 metres. A knot is one nautical mile per hour
Navajo (Piper)	Eight-seat, low-wing, twin piston-engine aeroplane
Nostradamus	16th century French apothecary and reputed seer
'O' Levels	National exams equivalent to GCSEs
Pattern	The rectangular circuit made by aircraft preparing to land
Piper	Piper Aircraft, Inc – manufacturer of light aircraft, e.g. Cherokee, Aztec
Pitch	Nose up and down movement
Pressurised	Purified engine air forced into an aircraft cabin to ensure the provision of oxygen above 10,000 feet
RAF	Royal Air Force
Red Arrows	RAF Aerobatic Display Team
Rotation; rotate	Transition from horizontal travel down the runway to the initial climb
RPM	Revolutions per minute
Rudder	Control surface on the tail controlling yaw
SAS	Special Air Service (British Army elite soldiers)
SF	Special Forces, e.g. SAS
Scout	Four-seat, single-engine military helicopter
Speedbird	The British Airways radio callsign
Speke	The old name for Liverpool Airport, now Liverpool John Lennon Airport
Spin	A sycamore-leaf type descent where aircraft wings are stalled
Spinner	The streamlined part of a propeller shaft in front of the propellers
Squawk	Transponder code enabling an aircraft's callsign, altitude and speed information to appear on an air traffic controller's radar screen via radio signals

Stall (aerodynamic)	Where the lift over a wing breaks down
Stratocumulus	A continuous layer of cumulus-type clouds
Synchronising (engines)	Equalising the rpms of multi-engine aircraft engines to prevent unwanted noises caused by harmonics
Taxiway	The ground 'roads' on an airfield aircraft use to reach the runway
Three greens	Undercarriage lights showing gear down and locked
Threshold	The first part of a runway, usually with the designator numbers on it, e.g. 27L
Tornado	High-performance, twin jet-engine, fighter-bomber used in the Iraq War
Track	The path an aircraft is making over the ground
Trident 1, 2, 3	British three jet-engine, airliner (up to 180 passengers)
Trimming	Adjusting auxiliary control surfaces enabling an aircraft to be flown hands-off
Type rating	An endorsement on a pilot's licence for a specific type of aircraft, after passing a flying test
Unpressurised	Reduced cabin pressure and therefore less oxygen for breathing. Oxygen is required above 10,000 feet cabin pressure
Vanguard	Four-engine, turboprop airliner (130 passengers)
Viscount	Four-engine, turboprop airliner (75 passengers)
VHF	Very High Frequency
Volmet	Continuous inflight weather information radio broadcast
VOR	VHF omnidirectional radio range
Warrant Officer	The most senior non-commissioned officer in the British Armed Forces
Windsock	Wind-driven tube indicating wind direction on an airfield
Yaw	Left/right movement of an aircraft without banking

Glossary (Acting)

AD	Assistant Director
DOP	Director of Photography
Equity Card	The actor's union (Equity) membership card.
Extra	Non-featured background artist in a film production
Featured (extra)	Standing out from the crowd (may have dialogue)
Forum theatre	A technique for gaining audience participation in training scenarios using actors
IPCC	Independent Police Complaints Commission
Le Bourget	Specialist General Aviation airfield near Paris
MC	Master of Ceremonies
MI5	UK Security Service (Military Intelligence 5)
MI6	UK Secret Intelligence Service (Military Intelligence 6)
Mossad	National intelligence agency of Israel
NEC	Nippon Electric Company (Japanese Technology Company)
RSPCA	Royal Society for the Prevention of Cruelty to Animals
Walk-on	Non-featured background artist